D1131230

CREATING BEAUTY FROM THE ABYSS

THE AMAZING STORY OF SAM HERCIGER,
AUSCHWITZ SURVIVOR AND ARTIST

LESLEY ANN RICHARDSON

ap

ISBN: 9789493276116 (ebook)

ISBN: 9789493276109 (paperback)

ISBN: 9789493276123 (hardcover)

Publisher: Amsterdam Publishers, The Netherlands

info@amsterdampublishers.com

Creating Beauty from the Abyss is part of the series

Holocaust Survivor True Stories WWII

Cover image: King David, linocut (date unknown), by Sam Herciger

CONTENTS

PART III
AUSCHWITZ AND MAUTHAUSEN

PART IV
WANDERINGS

How did it all begin, from the void you live within?

Through eternities where none but you exist,

From an endless parallel you joined the lines of Cause and Will,

Creating Life from out of the abyss ...

I am mortal. Life will end, but I shall live to live again,

If I am favored whatsoever in your sight,

Give me time enough to live to enjoy the gifts you give,

And finally, let me shine within your light.

(From "The Beneficiary" by Dave Richardson)

For: Sam's children, Annabelle and Louis

His grandchildren, Talia and Gilad

His great-grandchild, Gaia

FOREWORD

I first met Annabelle Herciger in the 1980s, when we were both working at the Anglican School in Jerusalem, I as a teacher of English, Annabelle of French. I had come from Australia, and was fulfilling my dream of living and working in Israel. Annabelle was an Israeli citizen who had been born in Belgium but had made aliyah (immigrated) with her parents some years earlier. We struck up a friendship which endured throughout the following decades, though we both subsequently followed different career paths.

I knew something of the dramatic story of Annabelle's father, Sam – that he was a survivor of Auschwitz, and later had become a successful artist. But my deeper involvement with Sam's journey began two or three years ago, as Annabelle and I sat over coffee at the Café Rimon in Ben Yehuda Street in Jerusalem. It was then that Annabelle told me that Sam had recounted his story to her mother Edith, who had made notes from Sam's dictation, in French. Annabelle had translated these into English, and asked me if I would be willing to turn the notes into a book.

Almost immediately I agreed: it seemed to me a highly worthwhile venture, and one which would be a privilege to undertake. I was touched by Annabelle's belief that I might be able to set down her father's story in a manner that would do him justice. But I also approached the task with some trepidation – one does not write about the Holocaust lightly, for it was then that the darkness that is in the human heart took shape and showed itself openly, in a way that was without precedent. It still confronts us with its mystery and its horror, defying explanation and categorization, and words describing what took place will always fall short.

Nevertheless, the stories must be told, for it is these which help us best to approach the unimaginable, and to contemplate those years when the future of the world, and the whole human race, hung in the balance.

For the past year I have been working on the book, endeavoring to trace the first half of Sam's life as fully as possible. I have developed his story with some imaginative license – while trying to remain true to his character as I conceived it – and have also added historical background. It seemed to me that it was essential to place Sam in his setting, especially as I came to understand his facility for finding himself caught up in some of the most crucial episodes of the war. And I realized, by the time I came to finish the book, that Sam's story had become an epic.

Here I would note that some of the historical sections are a little longer than others, for I felt they were needed to fit Sam's story into the wider background of the war. I have set out these sections in italics, so the reader who wishes to concentrate on the narrative may pass over them quickly.

As I worked on this chronicle of Sam's life, it became an intense journey of the imagination. I found myself caught up with his experiences, sharing in the agonizing depths that soared all too briefly into moments of joy and illumination before plunging once again into a sea of troubles. My desire in this work is to salute him as a man who did not permit his tribulations to overcome or diminish him, but who rather became enlarged in his soul and his creative abilities. I have developed a huge admiration for Sam – his personality, courage, and gifts – and have also learned from him that the human spirit may triumph over adversities of a kind and degree that are beyond comprehension.

I do believe his story is one of the most amazing I have encountered. May you also, my reader, be carried away and enlightened as you follow Sam on his journey, which brought him through so many vicissitudes to eventual fulfillment and joy.

Lesley Ann Richardson

Yom HaShoah, April 8, 2021

PROLOGUE

Arad, Israel, 1979

Sam stood at the doorway of his studio in Arad. A gentle breeze came from the deserts to the south, and he drew in its honeyed breath. It stirred the tamarisk trees lining the street, their leaves fresh and green after the winter rains, and drifted over the wildflowers pushing up at the sides of the road. It was spring in Israel and Passover was drawing near; already Sam's wife Edith was shopping and preparing for the influx of family and friends, some of whom were even now passing Sam's door.

In the development town of Arad, surrounded by the Judean and Negev Deserts, there was a true mingling of all the different groups in the land: Sephardim and Ashkenazim, Ethiopians and Russians and Bedouins. Some soldiers went by in their khaki; across the road religious Jews, black-clad despite the burgeoning heat, were burning the leaven from their homes in deference to the biblical injunction.[1] A handful of fellow artists went by, hastening to the *Eshet Lot* Artists' Quarter. Each greeted Sam as they passed: "*Hag Sameach!*" (Happy Holiday!).

When Sam and Edith had first moved to Arad in 1969 they had opened their gallery on a daily basis and it had soon started to draw like-minded souls. Eventually some 20 other artists joined them and transformed the simple *tzrifim* – the houses of the first settlers of the town. The empty spaces around the barracks were beautified with flowering plants and a small amphitheater was constructed for presentations, and so the Artists' Village named for Lot's Wife was born. It was becoming well known and more and more people were visiting.

Sam stood another moment gazing idly at the scene and enjoying the dazzling clarity of the desert light that lent a magical quality to the unassuming little town. Then he turned and made his way into the studio, the contents of which bore testament to a life of rich, overflowing artistic inspiration. There were landscapes in glowing colors, intense portraits, and black and white lithographs ranging in subject from joyful scenes of Jewish religious life to more somber images of war and captivity. And everywhere there were sculptures, in bronze, stone and wood; some were small, others impressively large.

Sam took up the piece he had been working on, an engraving representing a cathedral-like building flanked by two horses, one on each side. His wife had puzzled over it.

"What is it, Sam? An ascension to heaven?" She stopped before another engraving. "And this?"

In the center was an oval, the shape of an egg, surrounded by abstract, connected lines. "What does it mean?" she asked.

"The egg represents the beginning and end of life," he answered in his deep voice, "and the cosmos."

He began working on the piece, and the transfiguring creative power took its familiar hold of him. The mood was broken when his daughter Annabelle entered the studio to greet him, accompanied by Louis, his son, a few years younger; they had returned from their studies in Jerusalem for the Passover Seder. Annabelle's large dark eyes, mirroring his own, shone with happiness as she embraced her father. After the young people departed, the studio was quiet again.

With the creative spell broken, Sam wandered a little about the room, in a meditative mood. He caressed some of the sculptures, enjoying the living flow of the lines and curves, and the supple feeling of the wood beneath his fingers. On the wall were hung the awards he had received for his artworks and his gaze passed over them as well. A remembrance flashed into his mind: the Dutch art critic Jos Peeters had promised Sam that one day he would be famous – but this fame would come after his death. Sam had laughed and responded:

"In that case I hope I'm not famous for a very long time," he had said.

There was a similar prediction from the man that Sam called in his own mind "the prophet," whom he had met on the banks of the Vistula River in Poland many years earlier. It had been one of the strangest, most enigmatic encounters of his life, and at the time had filled him with elation. And yet the mysterious stranger had not spoken to Sam of one thing of preeminent importance: the price that needed to be paid to create the kind of art that he envisioned. Art, that is, with power to lift mind and spirit into a shining realm of truth and beauty – where suffering is redeemed and transmuted.

So much had happened since that brief meeting ... it had been an epic journey.

His mind flew back over the years.

Sam Herciger with one of his sculptures (early 1970s)

Sam Herciger with one of his sculptures (early 1970s)

Sam Herciger (1917-1981)

1. During Passover, the Jewish people refrain from eating leavened foods such as bread for seven days, as commanded in Exodus 12:15. The practice commemorates the departure of the Children of Israel from Egypt in haste, when they did not have time to wait for their bread to rise. Observant Jews clean their homes thoroughly in the weeks leading up to the holiday; then, just before Passover begins, any leftover leavened food – *chametz* - is burned.

PART I

POLAND

1

ZAWIERCIE

Zawiercie is a small town in the south of Poland, where the Herciger family lived, and where Sam was born in June 1917. From the earliest days of his life, he was surrounded by the enchanted scenery of the region.

The countryside outside the town is dotted with oaks and pines, laced with meadows that in spring and summer are covered by wildflowers, while nearby the winds whisper softly in deep green woods. Here the Warta River finds its source, its clear rippling waters also providing a musical interlude for the small farms clustering on its banks, while further south the snowcapped Carpathians raise majestic peaks. Many of the craggy outcroppings in the area are dominated by picturesque castles, suggesting not so much a romantic aspect, but rather evoking Poland's splendid, if martial, past. It was as perfect a picture of pastoral loveliness as one could hope to find – altogether difficult to reconcile with the knowledge of the events that would shortly take place there.

The little child that came into the world on that June day in the first decades of the 20th century didn't know it, but the most tumultuous 100-year span in historical records had commenced – nor could he have realized that his own life would be profoundly caught up in the unfolding drama. Moreover, the land of his birth, the nation of Poland itself, was destined to be impacted perhaps more than any other by the cataclysmic happenings that, as they came to pass, would shake the whole world. Nevertheless, in the year of Sam's birth, things were looking brighter for Poland in many ways, for the long injustice which had marred her history was about to be remedied.

Over the centuries, Poland's location between the great empires which arose to the east and west had proved somewhat perilous; more than that, it has been truly said that Poland's geography was also her tragedy. The territory periodically served as transit route for the warring armies of Prussia, Russia and Austria, and, in the 1790s, these empires had invaded Poland and divided the nation between them. Once the largest country in Europe, Poland was blotted out from the world map for over a hundred years – yet continued to exist as a spiritual and cultural entity. The hope for independence which burned in the hearts of her people was finally realized at the end of the First World War, when Poland reappeared on the map of Europe like a lost foundling restored to the family bosom.

It was at this auspicious moment that little Sam opened his huge dark eyes and gazed out upon the world. He was born into a Jewish family, the fifth son of Israel and Hannah – for Jews had been an integral part of the fabric of Polish life for almost as long as the nation had existed. On the eighth day he was circumcised and so made his entrance into the covenant established between God and His people; like the other sons of Israel he was drawn even from infancy into the religious life of his community. And although his family was poor – his father was a tanner of animal skins used for shoe-making – his was a home that was filled with love.

Hella, Sam's sister, was 20 years older than he. She had a lovely voice and her singing filled the house with an almost tangible presence of joy; she was the first to nurture Sam's lifelong love of music. Then there were his brothers David and Haim, who shared the family passion for the arts: both played the violin and could recite long passages of poetry. Pinchas came next; he was the most fun, with an outrageous sense of humor, and could keep Sam amused all day with a steady supply of jokes. After him was Yehuda, who was really the genius of the family, with a prodigious memory, but still a candidate for some good-natured teasing because he was a little bit of a dandy. Ten years later Shmiel Szije (Shmuel Yehoshua – Sam's birth name) came into the world, and five years after that Mendele, the little "Benjamin" who was Sam's favorite. He was always laughing, had beautiful eyes, and Sam loved nothing better than to pick him up and cuddle him.

It was as well there was so much warmth and affection in their household. The Hercigers lived on the first floor of their building; they had only three rooms: a kitchen, the parents' bedroom, and the dining room. It was in this latter that the six children slept, two in one bed except for Hella, who had her own bed behind a curtain which separated her from her brothers. Somehow, space was still found for a cupboard filled with books in Yiddish, Hebrew and Polish. All the family shared the traditional Jewish love of learning in full measure.

Although the Hercigers' home had electricity, there was no running water, which was brought to them from the fountain situated in the village; Sam remembered the water carrier as a small man, bowed beneath his heavy load, but very humble and devout. Around the courtyard outside their home were a number of houses; all the families living in them were Jewish and had many children who became playmates for Sam as he grew older. In the midst of the courtyard was a large coal stove where water was boiled in the mornings, and it was here also that all the cooking took place. This was the center of Sam's world as his early years passed, punctuated by the age-old rhythm of Jewish festivals and holy days.

It was the Sabbath, marking the end of the week, which of course arrived more frequently than any of the other occasions. As dusk fell on Friday evening, all the family would gather around the table, having donned their best garments, and take part in the traditional prayers and blessings. Sam's mother Hannah, her air of bustling energy temporarily laid aside, would cover her head with a snow-white scarf and light two candles while uttering the benediction: *"Baruch Atah Adonai Eloheinu"* ("Blessed are You, Lord God, King of the Universe") ... As she prayed the faces of the children would glow in the soft illumination, and the magic of the Sabbath hush would descend upon the home. Finally, the children sang together some of the songs that celebrated the seventh day, and God's gift of rest and refreshment.

Pesach was one of three major feasts of the Jewish year. When it arrived in spring, the family would gather for the recitation of the Haggadah, the dramatic story of the deliverance of the Children of Israel from their bondage in Egypt, and the miraculous crossing of the Red Sea. Fifty days later Shavuot would be ushered in, commemorating the giving of the Law to Moses on Mount Sinai; then, as the summer days began withdrawing their gold and autumn approached, Rosh Hashanah was upon them. The ten High Holy Days proceeded to unfold in awe-filled majesty, culminating in the great fast day of Yom Kippur, a time throughout which the searching questions of the *Unetaneh Tokef* concerning the year to come would echo:

> *On Rosh Hashanah it is written,*
>
> *and on Yom Kippur it is sealed.*
>
> *How many will pass*
>
> *and how many will be created?*
>
> *Who will live and who will die?*
>
> *Who in their time,*
>
> *and who not their time?*
>
> *Who by fire and who by water?....*
>
> *But teshuvah and tefillah and tzedakah*
>
> *(Return and prayer and righteous acts)*

Deflect the evil of the decree.

After this somber period came a dramatic change of religious mood: the eight-day harvest festival of Succot, intended as a time of rejoicing before the Lord. It was the custom for each family to gather branches of leafy trees and build little "tabernacles," verdant green bowers where they would meet together to eat and pray. In this way they recalled the journey of the Children of Israel through the wilderness toward the Promised Land, when they dwelt in tents and were dependent on God's sustaining power alone. Then, as autumn slipped into winter, came the celebration of the Festival of Lights – Hanukkah. It commemorated the exploits of the brave Maccabeean brothers who defeated the forces of the wicked Syrian king Antiochus, and rekindled the lights of the Temple in Jerusalem.

Finally, in the last month of the biblical year, came the Feast of Purim, which honored the brave and lovely Jewish Queen Esther, who had lived in the days of the mighty Persian Empire and who, having won the heart of the king, saved her people from annihilation at the hand of the wicked Haman. There was even supposedly a Polish Queen Esther. She was a Jewess of the 14th century, and the great King Casimir III had fallen in love with her beauty and married her. Like the Persian Esther, it was said that she used her position of influence to save Polish Jews from persecution and have them granted special liberties. Casimir set aside an enclave north of Krakow for the Jews, where one may still find a street named after Queen Esterke, her Yiddish name.

And so Sam's childhood passed in this regular cadence, each "sunrise and sunset"[1] marking the swift passing of the days, which all too soon turned into months and years, themselves to be "carried away like a flood."[2]

---

1. An allusion to the song from the famous musical *Fiddler on the Roof,* written in 1964 by composer Jerry Bock and lyricist Sheldon Harnick. Tevye and Golde sing the poignant, bittersweet lyrics at the wedding of their oldest daughter, Tzeitel, marveling at how quickly time has passed and how swiftly their children have grown up.
2. From Psalm 90, verse 5. All biblical citations in the book unless otherwise noted are taken from the *New King James Version®, Copyright © 1982 by Thomas Nelson, Inc. Used by permission. All rights reserved.*

2

EARLY YEARS

From the ages of three or four the little boys in the Jewish community in Zawiercie attended the *heder* (school), which consisted of a simple room with wooden benches, closely resembling the synagogue. Here they learned the Aleph Bet (or alphabet) of the Hebrew language. The Rebbe would read a word and the children would repeat it with chanting, for all the world like a flock of little sparrows learning to chirp. Once they were able to decipher the letters they would study the prayers, and those performing best were rewarded with sweets. But as summer approached it was hard for the little ones. Through the windows they would hear the birds warbling their throaty songs, and bees humming an irresistible invitation, beckoning them outdoors. But when their attention wandered, the teacher would cuff them.

Sam, like the other children, would watch the turning of the seasons after the winter solstice, longing for the time when the days would lengthen and the first warm breath of summer chase away the cold. As the deep quilt of snow which covered the town began to thaw, as the mountain winds ceased their roaring, and the fields threw off their gauzy veils of mist, the wildflowers would begin to emerge in the meadows: gold and purple crocuses, pale snowdrops, or even the rare lily of the valley. Sometimes Sam would see the storks flying overhead, waving their wings majestically as they returned from their long pilgrimage to the south. He would feel a sudden elated jolt of the heart, and, closing his eyes, wander in imagination to the warm and exotic climes of which he had read. Perhaps – who knows? – the intimation came to him of a dry and hot land, set on the edge of a sparkling sea, the focus of his people's aspirations for so many centuries.

When the long-awaited summer months finally arrived, the children would discard their heavy outer clothing and boots; everyone would go to the park situated outside the town, which had been donated by a Jewish doctor, and bathe in the river. Even more than the swimming, Sam enjoyed the rambles in the dreamy summer countryside. The farms were adorned with hibiscus, sunflowers, and other flowering shrubs, their fragrance mixed in an alchemy, while the meadows were covered in an ocean of white flowers that swayed in the breeze. Under the blue skies the orchards were laden with ripe fruit, and he and the other children would hunt for wild strawberries, blackberries and raspberries, or dig for mushrooms lurking in hidden places beneath their branches.

Most of all, Sam loved the times they ventured into the dark green woods, dense with tall and stately trees: oaks, birches, larch and linden, as well as pines and beeches. The thick undergrowth provided hiding places for shy animals: deer, fox, badgers and hedgehogs – which the children would see peeping at them through the tangled greenery. Sam would listen to the sound of the pines as they whispered in the wind – a noise so common in Poland there is even a word, *szumi*, to describe it. At other times, the wind would sound a sonorous bass note, and he would inhale the scent as the branches shook in the breeze. When no one was watching, Sam would sometimes embrace the supple trunk of a linden, and breathe in the honeyed perfume of the blossoms, experiencing a mysterious sense of transport. But then the smell of chicken soup would come wafting on the air, and he and his companions would scamper home with sharpened appetites from their outdoor adventures.

At the back of the house where Sam lived was another courtyard where a carpenter lived; the children liked to play there among the woodchips strewn over the ground. It was also the ideal place to celebrate Succot, since there was wood in abundance, and it was here that the largest succah in the town was built. Decorated with flowers and colored paper, it was a charming place for the families to dine, and although the weather was often chilly, pious men would also sleep there, Sam's father among them. This meant additional work for the women who had to bring the food into the succah, and Sam noticed other drawbacks as well. Often fronds from the pine trees which covered the roof fell into the soup, and when it rained the succah become soaked and the decorations bedraggled.

All these things never diminished the family's delight in keeping the feast – yet there was another, even more important, reason why Sam loved that carpenter's courtyard so much. During the hot summer months he and his brothers would often sleep there, and he found that the smell of the wood entranced him. He would lie awake as his brothers lay slumbering beside him and breathe in the fragrance of the timber. It evoked for him the mysterious essence of the deep forests near his home and seemed to lift him into another realm, where his imagination could wander with free rein.

Sam also, as he was growing up, had contact with the wider community in his hometown. Thursday was the highlight of the week in Zawiercie; it was market day, when the farmers would bring their produce into the city to sell. They would tramp into town barefoot, their shoes tied around their neck; then, when the market square came in sight, put them on again and resume an air of respectability. The richer farmers arrived in more lordly style in horse and carriage, their butter wrapped in green leaves to preserve its freshness. Once in the marketplace they would pile their goods onto stalls beside the other items being sold, such as leather goods, bolts of cloth, shoes and clothes. Then the townspeople would come to browse, shop and, of course, to gossip.

There were also thieves everywhere, so the farmers needed to watch their merchandise carefully. On Thursdays little Sam would sometimes skip school to go to the market; once there, he would negotiate to guard a stand and earn some coins to buy a cream cake. As he wandered through the market later, nibbling at the rich pastry and letting the sweet unctuous flavor melt in his mouth, his eyes would linger on the brilliant display of produce. The fresh fruits and vegetables spilled out from the stands in lavish profusion, and he delighted in noting the different shapes, colors, and textures. His eye for observation was developing rapidly in relation to the natural world.

Yet Sam was also keenly aware of nuances of expression that chased as fleetingly as summer breezes over the faces of the human subjects he encountered. He often saw the farmers playing card games with itinerant visitors and noticed when the honest open countenance of the countryman flushed with anger. These ruffians would frequently be using rigged cards, which meant that the farmer would lose all his hard-earned money. It was a fascinating glimpse of a larger world ... but, as the day drew to a close, Sam knew he must avoid facing his father. He would somehow manage to sneak home and get into bed without being noticed just as night was falling.

Sometimes also there were parades in town led by a little orchestra; all the children would run behind it to listen. Once, even, a circus came to town; it was magnificent, with wild animals, elephants and camels – for Sam, it was another peek into a beckoning vista, the wide and alluring spaces which, he felt, must exist outside his hometown. On one notable occasion, a black man arrived in Zawiercie, seated at the back of a limousine which had a white driver in the front as chauffeur; it was part of a campaign promoting shoeshine. Sam thought the man, with his white gloves and gleaming teeth, looked superb. But most of all, along with the other children, Sam loved the fairs, to which all the townsfolk would turn out. And at these carnivals he had one favorite thing.

He loved the carousels – those magical rotating platforms with their endless animal creations, whisking the riders around to the accompaniment of loud organ music. One merry-go-round which came yearly possessed a whole menagerie, with assorted animals such as giraffes, pigs, cats, dogs and roosters. But most of all Sam adored the horses, richly colored and caparisoned, with tossing manes and tails, leaping and prancing in their prescribed circle. Their expressions were sometimes proud and dignified, at other times wild and untamed, still others had sweet and gentle faces. Sam knew, with the innate sensitivity of the artist, that they had been carved and painted with love.

There was one especially splendid horse, its mane a wave of beauty, plunging and rocking its way on its endless round. Each time it spun past him, the eyes seemed to rest and linger on him. "Don't you want to ride?" they seemed to ask. Alas … it was hard for him to do so. The children of the town pushed the carousels because there was no motor and afterwards were granted a free ride. But for Sam, being Jewish, it was difficult to get near the merry-go-round for fear of being beaten by the Polish non-Jewish youngsters. It was a reminder of a disturbing reality which existed in his world.

The winds of change were blowing at Sam's birth. If Poland's history was marked by suffering and tragedy, the Jews within Poland, more than any other group, were to be catastrophically affected by the unfolding events of the century. Those stormy blasts that swept through Europe with such ferocity would leave neither branch nor stem, but only a very small root, and that itself not unscathed, to grow up and flourish again in the earth.

3

POLAND AND THE JEWS

It is perhaps no exaggeration to say that religion is at the beating heart of Polish identity. The land surrounding the Vistula had originally been settled by Slavic tribes, but in the 10th century Duke Mieszko I had converted to the Roman Catholic faith, and through his baptism brought Poland into the community of Western nations.

In the same century, a Jewish diplomat from Moorish Spain, Ibrahim Ibn Yakub, recorded his first impressions of the region: "It abounds in food, meat, honey and arable land," he wrote, and the Jews who gave heed to his words soon arrived, traveling along trade routes leading to the east. The lives of the Christianized Slavs and the sons of Jacob would henceforth be interwoven in the land. And, as tradition has it, the name Poland, in Hebrew Polanya, suggested to the Jewish settlers that the territory would be welcoming to them, for it could be broken down into three Hebrew words: po (here), lan (dwells), and yah (God).

Indeed, during those early centuries the country became a haven for Jews fleeing from persecution in the West, beginning from the First Crusade in 1098 and continuing through the expulsion from Spain in 1492. Enlightened kings such as Bolesław III and King Casimir III the Great were resolute in promoting the welfare of the Jewish communities in their midst; they recognized also that the Jews, whose principal occupation in medieval Poland was commerce, brought substantial economic benefits to the land. By the mid-16th century, the majority of the world's Jews lived in Poland, where they enjoyed extensive autonomy and collective prosperity, were Yiddish-speaking, and considered themselves Ashkenazy or West European.

The 16th century was a brilliant age for the Polish-Lithuanian Commonwealth, as the influence of the Renaissance led to developments in the arts and sciences, and astronomer Nicolaus Copernicus formulated the first heliocentric theory of the solar system. Poland was developing a distinctive cultural and spiritual identity and cultivating a tradition of proud and spirited warriors. Meanwhile, Jewish religious life was also thriving, shaped by the spirit of rabbinical learning, an influence which was felt in the home, yeshivas and the synagogue. An impressive galaxy of Talmudic scholars ensured that the culture and intellectual output of the Jewish community in Poland had a profound impact on Judaism as a whole.

Over the years, however, the distinctive faith and accomplishments of the Jewish people often led to friction. From the 17th century onwards, as religious conflict followed in the wake of the Reformation, the blood libel and other calumnies began to circulate for the first time. In 1648, the disastrous Chmielnicki Uprising, during which Cossacks massacred tens of thousands of Poles, both Jews and Catholics, left the Commonwealth in ruins. Nevertheless, in 1683 Polish King John III Sobieski led the allied armies at the Battle of Vienna and, in a legendary battle, saved Europe from a threatened Islamic invasion. New life was also breathed into the devastated Jewish nation through the teachings of the Baal Shem Tov and the birth of Hasidism. Many of the greatest Jewish minds of the generation came to the Polish court of the Besht to learn from him and adopt his mystical ideals: the unceasing, joyful consciousness of God's presence.

Yet turmoil continued to prevail in Poland during the 18th century, and the situation declined until the nadir of the Partition in 1795. Many Poles fled to exile in the West, where a flowering of Romantic literary creativity took place which made a deep impact on Polish national consciousness. This was expressed most fully in the poems of Adam Mickiewicz, who felt his soul to be "incarnate in his country," and the music of Chopin, whose mazurkas and preludes overflowed with patriotic yearning. Throughout the years several valiant uprisings took place, and many Jews also took part in these, and in supporting the cause of Polish independence. The insurrections invariably led to tragic outcomes –but Polish high culture and the attachment to Roman Catholicism endured.

As the long period of instability generated by the French Revolution and Napoleonic wars drew to a close, new ideological movements began sweeping through Europe, including socialism and modern nationalism. In 1791, France had become the first country in Europe to grant the Jews legal equality. As the Age of Enlightenment unfolded, this led to a comparable Jewish movement called Haskalah, which encouraged a process of social and cultural assimilation. Yet the formation of modern nations accompanied other changes in attitudes toward the Jews. Outright persecution might have diminished, but in its place emerged a disturbing new phenomenon: antisemitism,[1] an ideology which sought to place the blame for weakened economic conditions and political instability, all the various troubles which might beset a nation, upon the Jewish people.

In 1772, Catherine II, the Tzarina of Russia, had instituted the Pale of Settlement, restricting Jews to western parts of the empire, eventually including much of Poland. By the late-19th century, living conditions for the many millions of Jews in the Pale began to dramatically worsen, as they were subjected to heavy taxation and repressive laws. After the assassination of Tsar Alexander in 1881 – an action falsely blamed upon the Jews – a large-scale wave of pogroms erupted throughout 1881–1884, and then continued in the early 20th century. Particularly horrific was the 1903 pogrom in Kishinev, about which the Zionist poet Bialik wrote his famous poem "City of Slaughter," while the antisemitic forgery "The Protocols of the Elders of Zion" emerged in the following months.

The pogroms proved a turning point in the history of the Jewish people, prompting a great wave of emigration to the New World and inspiring many Jews to become politically active. A Jewish national movement appeared in the 1870s with the emergence of Hovevei Zion (Lovers of Zion) in Russia and Poland. Jewish philanthropists and organizations began sponsoring agricultural settlements for Russian Jews in Palestine – an area then controlled by the Ottoman Empire – and the First Aliyah (ascent) to the Holy Land took place. The Zionist movement became a politically dynamic force when the charismatic figure of Theodor Herzl burst upon the European stage, and the First Zionist Congress was convened in Basel, Switzerland, in 1897.

At the beginning of his career, Herzl, an Austro-Hungarian journalist, held beliefs in common with those of other European Jewish intellectuals: he nurtured the comfortable conviction that modern enlightened ideals would eventually enable the full integration of Jews within their home countries. But the Dreyfus Affair in France in 1795 – the false accusation of the exemplary Jewish army captain – shattered this illusion. Observing the unfolding events, Herzl became instilled with a passionate persuasion: that, because antisemitism was so deeply ingrained in European society, only the creation of a Jewish state would enable the Jews to join the family of nations and live in peace and safety. And this, he believed, could happen in only one place – Eretz Israel – the Land of Israel.

The precedent for the Jewish people to return to their ancient homeland as a result of God's divine favor and faithful intervention was a central motif in the Hebrew Scriptures: it was Yahweh's mighty hand, the Tanach proclaimed, which had brought about the Exodus from Egypt and ended the exile in Babylon. Moreover, an even greater return in the future, one which would surpass all the earlier homecomings, was the burden of many of the prophetic writings.

Throughout their 2,000-year dispersion among the nations, pious Jews had never ceased to pray for deliverance from galut (exile) and return to the land, a longing highlighted in the conclusion of the Passover liturgy: "Next year in Jerusalem." Herzl called upon this undying hope in the concluding words of The Jewish State of 1896:

"I believe that a wondrous generation of Jews will spring into existence. The Maccabeans will rise again ... we shall live at last as free men on our own soil, and die peacefully in our own homes. The world will be freed by our liberty, enriched by our wealth, magnified by our greatness. And whatever *we attempt there to accomplish for our own welfare, will react powerfully and beneficially for the good of humanity."*

After Herzl's early death, there was little hope for a political breakthrough for the Zionist movement. But then – as the First World War continued to rage – on November 2, 1917, the British Foreign Secretary, Arthur Balfour, one of a long line of Christian Restorationists, made his landmark Declaration, expressing his government's view in favor of "the establishment in Palestine of a national home for the Jewish people." On November 7, five days later, the Bolsheviks seized power in Russia, leading to civil war and the collapse of the western part of the Empire. Meanwhile, British and Australian forces were fighting deep in Palestine, and, in that same momentous month, began their battle for Jerusalem. After the defeat and dismantling of the Ottoman Empire in 1918, the League of Nations endorsed the full text of the Balfour Declaration and established the British Mandate for Palestine.

Poland also was reconstituted as a nation in 1918, and during the Second Republic continued to have the largest concentration of Jews in Europe. The contribution of the Jewish people to Polish life and culture in the inter-War period, whether in the fields of medicine and law, or literature and art, was one of singular richness; Jewish newspapers and theater thrived, while Yiddish authors, most notably Isaac Bashevis Singer, went on to achieve international acclaim. Diverse political parties and Zionist organizations flourished, including the Jewish socialist party, the Bund, and the religious Zionist Mizrahi, as well as any number of youth groups; religious beliefs spanned the range from Orthodox and Hasidic to liberal Judaism.

And yet, as elsewhere in Europe, official policy toward national minorities was hardening. This tendency was exacerbated as the influx of Russian Jews escaping persecution led to an economic instability which worsened with the Great Depression. Matters improved for a time under statesman Josef Pilsudski, who believed in a multi-ethnic Poland, "a home of nations." After his death, however, the antisemitism propounded by the Endecja, a political party based on an ethnically based nationalism, did much to mar Jewish-Gentile relations. This, together with the canard that Jews were disloyal to the Polish nation, increased the attraction of communism and

Zionism among many young Jews. At the same time, persistent boycotts and harassment reduced the standard of living of Polish Jews to such an extent that, during the 1930s, many lived in desperate poverty.

It was during this decade that Zeev Jabotinsky, Zionist activist and writer, became so concerned about the situation of the Jewish community in Eastern Europe that he suggested a plan for the evacuation of the entire Jewish population of Poland, Hungary and Romania to Palestine. This far-sighted proposal was sadly dismissed by both the British Government and the World Zionist Organization. Just before the outbreak of the Second World War, Jabotinsky repeated his warning and described the terrible picture he foresaw. The Polish Jews, he said, were living on the edge of the volcano, one which would soon "spew out its flames of extermination."[2] All the Jews of Europe, he urged, should leave for Palestine at the earliest opportunity to escape the approaching catastrophe.

---

1. The term "antisemitism" was not coined until 1879, but from earliest times the Jewish people have had to contend with opposition and misunderstanding; in fact, antisemitism has been described as "the world's longest hatred" (Robert S. Wistrich, *Anti-Semitism: The Longest Hatred* (New York: Schocken, 1991). But antisemitism is a complex, protean phenomenon, which has taken many different forms over the centuries. After the conquest of Jerusalem by Rome in the first century, and the subsequent dispersal of the Jews, it first was dressed in a religious guise. As the church grew in power and political influence, it began to hold that all of God's promises and blessings were reserved for Christianity, and the curses and punishments for Judaism. During the medieval period, as Jews were debarred from many professions and thus came to specialize in banking and moneylending, the stereotype of the Jew as financial manipulator would emerge, along with other myths such as the blood libel.

   The combination of legal restrictions and deadly suspicion eventually led to a situation where Jews were no longer welcome in Christian society, and consequently were forced into exile, as in the especially traumatic Spanish expulsion of 1492. With the birth of modern nations, antisemitism began to take an essentially nationalist form, and the fact that the Jews often held eminent positions in political, economic and financial spheres caused them to be singled out as potential traitors. In this way, two beliefs that were fundamentally contradictory became merged together: firstly, that Jews were so powerful they should be feared, but also, at the same time, they were so powerless they could be attacked with impunity. After the Enlightenment, antisemitism also took a racial form, the Jews being defined as a people of mysterious eastern origin who could never be assimilated – especially amongst those who considered themselves to belong to a superior Aryan race.

The Holocaust would bring together all the strands of past antisemitism, weave them together, and produce a system devoted to the total annihilation of the Jewish people in Europe. No other prejudice has lasted so long, concocted such demonic fabrications, or had such devastating effects.

2. Taken from a speech by Jabotinsky in Warsaw in July 1938, and quoted by Amotz Asa-El in "Middle Israel: No Place for a Jew," in *The Jerusalem Post*, April 28, 2018.

4

ARTISTIC DREAMS

In the late 1920s, Sam, like all his family, was aware of the complex history of his people, and that there were new and daunting challenges in their political situation. At the same time he was becoming cognizant of the intellectual allure of the societies in the midst of which they lived.

Sam's older brother, Haim, had been the first to introduce books on European culture, art and literature into the Herciger home – but this was done quietly in the hope that Israel wouldn't find out. At the age of 13, Sam ventured into this hazardous realm himself, entering the rich imaginative world opened to him by novels such as *Robinson Crusoe*, *The Three Musketeers* and *The Count of Monte Cristo*. He even tackled some philosophical works, and new questions began shaking the perimeters of his mind. Of course, Israel became aware of the books in which Sam was so often absorbed. But he would remonstrate gently, saying, "My son, do you think the world will disappear if you don't read these books?"

Haim brought home Hebrew literature as well, for he had been caught up with the Zionist ideal and was planning to emigrate to Palestine; he was also learning construction, hoping to work in that trade when he arrived there. Sam was keen to learn of the Jewish settlements springing up in Eretz Israel, with their allusive names – *Petah Tikvah, Rishon LeZion, Tel Aviv* – names that shimmered with the hope in the hearts of the new immigrants, that spurred them to the hard work of rebuilding the land. Moreover, Hebrew itself was being revived there as a modern spoken language, an inconceivable development. Sam thrilled to this news, and also was dreaming of leaving home, but he was gripped by a different vision, and other thoughts and goals had come to occupy his waking hours.

For Sam loved drawing and sculpting, but, for one growing up in an orthodox Jewish household, this created massive problems. Graven images were forbidden by Jewish law in accordance with the Second Commandment which God gave to Moses on Mount Sinai.

There was only one way in which Sam could satisfy this craving to give his ideas pictorial expression. He would regularly slip away from attending classes in the *heder*, make his way into the woods, and there create carvings on the trees. The images seemed to spring fully fledged from his imagination and attain their own separate life on the trunks. Even in winter, when it was bitterly cold, Sam could not resist the lure of the trees. He would tread along snowy paths deep into the woods, where icicles hung like polished swords and frost painted fantastic patterns on the branches, where the wind tinkled its icy breath and set the leaves rustling. At other times there would be a great hush in the forest, and the snowflakes which descended softly from above and swirled silently around him seemed like a pure and solemn benediction. As he carved the pliant wood, wholly absorbed in his creative task, he never felt the cold, but was lifted into a world where a sensation of freedom and purpose seemed of paramount importance.

Sam felt no guilt about the times he missed school, but Israel inevitably found out about his absences, and would spank him, asking, "Where were you? Why weren't you at the *heder*?"

But Sam knew that his father's heart was soft toward all his sons. On one occasion, when Israel came home and Hannah told him, "Shmiel Szija has skipped school again!" Israel became furious.

28

"I am going to give him a beating," he blustered, and stalked into the living room. His eye fell upon all his children, sleeping there soundly, and his heart melted with paternal tenderness. "I will punish him tomorrow," he soliloquized.

This gentleness caused Sam to love his father dearly; he also adored his mother, a small woman who held her household together with common sense, hard work, and unquenchable kindness.

Nevertheless, the idea of running away was coming to him insistently, for he felt stifled in Zawiercie. In 1931, the town had about 30,000 inhabitants, and the economic life of the town was largely based on manufacturing, the result of its location close to the Warsaw-Vienna Railway. This had encouraged the development of coal and iron mines, glass and brick factories, and a large-scale textile industry. The Jews who made up about a quarter of the town's population made their living largely from various trades and the clothing business. It was not, Sam felt, a place where he could nurture the artistic ambitions taking shape in his mind.

There was another associated issue with which the boy, only just in his teens, was grappling: he was becoming less religious, and starting to question and draw away from the teachings of his faith. Neither in Zawiercie was there any possibility of leaving his sheltered Jewish world and embracing an emancipated life, though the occasional conference or lecture held out that hope. There was a group of Jews in his town who listened to the teachings of the Orthodox political group Agudat Israel, as well as the Foreign Leftist Union. But – to the dismay of the Jewish community – they were arrested, accused of being communists, and imprisoned for five years. All Jews in the land were in continual danger of being identified in this way by the government.

Israel was concerned about young Sam and aware of the questions troubling his son. He decided to take a drastic step. Nearby, in the town of Belz in Western Ukraine near the Polish border, was a famous Rabbi of the Belz Hasidic dynasty named Aharon Rokeach.

He was known as a "Wunder Rabbi" for his saintliness and ability to work miracles; many compared him to the Baal Shem Tov and reported extraordinary blessings after he had prayed. Thousands flocked to his court, and at first the Rabbi tried to limit the number of people who sought his counsel. He felt in himself the weight of each problem and the personal burden became very great; eventually, however, he allowed many petitioners to see him nightly. Often they traveled long distances and endured many hardships on the way, and the Polish government had constructed a special railway for them. And now Israel himself made the journey.

The train to Belz was packed with Jews hoping to see the Rebbe; some had come from as far away as Hungary and Russia. All were black-coated, had long sidelocks, and wore the large fur shtreimels on their heads which Hasidic Jews don for special occasions. The train arrived in Belz in the afternoon and Israel joined the line of petitioners which stretched all the way into the town, arriving with them at the synagogue for the evening service. Here the hundreds of worshipers stood swaying in the ecstasy of prayer like a field of wheat rippling in the wind; Israel was caught up in their almost palpable devotion. He had to wait a long time before he could see the Rebbe, but finally he stood in the presence of the great man and poured out his concern for his son Shmiel.

The Rebbe listened carefully, fingering the long beard spread over his chest; his eyes were lustrous with intelligence and compassion, and a visible aura of sanctity clung about him. When Israel came to the end of his petition, the Rebbe gave an answer which assuaged the anguish in his heart: "You'll see – he will change, and you will have *nahes* (joy) from him."[1]

Israel traveled back to Zawiercie, filled with new hope and assurance.

---

1. Later, after the Nazis invaded Poland in 1939, Rabbi Rokeach, as a high-profile Jewish figure, was at the top of the Gestapo's wanted list. Yet somehow, avoiding Gestapo patrols at every turn, Belzer Hasidim managed to spirit him out of the country and into Hungary. At one stage, shaved of beard and sidelocks, the

Rebbe impersonated a Soviet General who had been captured by the Hungarians and was being taken for questioning. His dramatic escape eventually brought him to Israel in 1944 and, although he had lost his entire family to the Nazis, Rabbi Rokeach re-established his Hasidic court in Tel Aviv and devoted the rest of his life to rebuilding the Belzer Hasidic group. Today it is one of the largest groups in Israel and has sizable communities in Europe and North America.

5

FIRST VENTURES

The miracle promised by the saintly Rabbi occurred. Sam decided to focus on his education and stopped skipping school. He became the top scholar in his class and decided to go to yeshiva. Here the boys studied for some three hours each day, with friends or with the director, a pious man who had devoted his life to Torah learning. The students also discussed politics, arguing back and forth about some of the burning issues of the day, playing all the while with their *peyot* (sidelocks).

Sam quickly came to the conclusion that the yeshiva was far preferable to the *heder* – it was less strict. The 15-year-olds were smoking cigarettes in a nonchalant fashion, quite certain they had achieved maturity. Every morning, the students went to the bakery to buy warm bread. As they walked back to the yeshiva, they would tear off chunks of the fragrant dough, talking together and enjoying the companionship. But Sam was also inspired to cultivate the rigorous intellectual methods of the Jewish scholars. One evening, he visited a friend who lived outside the city. It was freezing and the snow crackled under his feet as he made his way, arriving at 10 o'clock. The two boys had decided to study all night long, just as the grown men did. Sam enjoyed it enormously, but the next day was less pleasant. Both were exhausted and still had to go to class.

Gradually Sam began once again to move away from the teachings of his faith, and the idea of studying art renewed its appeal. He knew it was Israel's dream that he would stay in the yeshiva until the age of 18, and then join him in the family business of tanning. Sam understood that this might mean walking a precarious financial tightrope. His family still lived with the memory of the economic crisis of 1926–27, when the checks his father had received in payment for his services were not honored. During this period Ropski, the Minister of Finance, had imposed heavy taxes and many businesses collapsed. Relatives of the Hercigers owned a factory in Lodz, where almost all members of the family worked; this too went bankrupt, while Sam's grandfather and his brother Yehuda lost their jobs. But it was not just the financial uncertainty of this course; he felt it would also sound a death knell to his dreams of studying art.

A year after he had started at the yeshiva a new student arrived from Sosnowiec, a small town close to Zawiercie. This young man had formerly been an apprentice to a furrier, and no sooner had Sam discovered this fact than the idea of learning the same trade jumped into his mind. He felt it might be a stepping-stone to attaining the financial independence for which he yearned, but understood that his plan would bring him into conflict with his father. The disagreement with Israel came earlier than he anticipated – and in a most unexpected way. A friend had lent Sam a porn magazine, and Israel caught him as he was reading it. He seized the offending pages and tore them in disgust.

Sam felt utterly humiliated, but the thought that he would never discover his life purpose if he stayed in his hometown troubled him even more. The situation prompted a fateful decision: he would leave Zawiercie. He took a loan from a friend, bought a small suitcase and stacked it with books and some personal items. Before he left, though, he decided to confide in his mother, Hannah. She had a better understanding of him than his father. "Go, son," she encouraged him, "here you have no future." Her affirmation was like a warm blanket, comforting him.

In February 1931, Sam left home for the first time, with his little black suitcase in his hand. He was 14 years old. His shoulders were broadening, his voice deepening and acquiring the resonant timbre which would mark it all his life. His eyes were his most striking feature, huge and dark, with a compelling quality. Two of Sam's older brothers were by now married and living in Bedzin, some 20 kilometers from Zawiercie. They also had heard of Sam's plans to leave home and had remonstrated with him. "Sam," they had said, "you're too young. Finish your studies, and then you can leave." Nevertheless, they were willing to help their young brother in his new venture, so it was to Bedzin that Sam decided he first would wend his way. Thus he arrived, filled with a mixture of conflicting emotions, at the home of his brother Pinchas.

Pinchas was a gifted businessman who had opened a successful haberdashery store; he was also married to a gorgeous woman. Sam was a little tongue-tied in her presence, for his own home had a predominantly masculine presence. He was also awakening to the power of feminine beauty, and the artist in him perused the face of his brother's wife intently: the delicate modelling of chin and cheek, the lustrous eyes that looked out from penciled brows, her smooth high forehead and tall, graceful form ... *this thy stature is like to a palm tree* ... the lovely line from the Song of Solomon sprang unbidden into his mind. He longed to be able to sketch her. And the houses! The designs were more interesting than in his hometown, and with their soft clear coloring they appeared to him to resemble paintings by Chagall or Ribak.

Chagall was a particular inspiration to Sam at the time. The artist, who was presently achieving a significant level of fame in Europe, had been born into a humble Jewish home in 1887, near Vitebsk, a small city in the Western Russian Empire not far from the Polish frontier. Like Sam he was educated at a small *heder*, where he studied the Hebrew language and scriptures, teachings which would later

34

influence the content and motifs in his work. During those school days, Chagall quickly developed a love for art and chose to pursue it as a career; it was a decision that did not please his parents, but he went on to study painting in St. Petersburg and Paris. In his paintings and stained glass, which soon became widely known, he embraced both Jewish imagery and modern trends and made them uniquely his own – for the charm and simplicity of his work expressed what was in his heart.

And now, gazing at the steep roof of the little house in Bedzin, Sam could almost see a violinist floating over it, beneath a clear sky sprinkled with stars, and a little dog barking at a silver moon. But, alas, Sam's artistic dreams were in abeyance. Pinchas went out on Sam's behalf, searching for furriers. There weren't many, and none of them were ready to take on Sam as an apprentice.

At this juncture, one of their uncles had to go to Dabrowa Gornicza – an even larger city, another 20 kilometers further. Pinchas joined him and took Sam along, also giving the lad some money; he was the very soul of kindness to his young brother. They went to the home of a cousin who lived in the city: she told Sam he couldn't sleep there, but he could come three times a week to eat in return for babysitting. Sam accepted. Where, though, was he to sleep? His situation was so uncertain that he began to regret having left home – yet his pride would not allow him to contemplate returning. Finally he and his brother remembered a great uncle who had once been rich, but had lost most of his fortune. This time they were lucky – the family offered Sam a place to sleep: he would share the bed with his second cousin. It was the same room in which their paralyzed daughter was sleeping.

With this measure of security, Sam set out looking for work. Eventually he found a furrier who would take him as an apprentice, but at the same time he had to pay for this through undertaking various tasks: running errands, cleaning, oiling the appliances. This meant that in actual fact he had very little time to learn the trade and was forced to seize some moments during his midday break to practice on the sewing machine. After two weeks in this situation, Sam realized he wasn't learning anything. He had a hot cooked meal only three times a week at his cousin's house; the rest of the time he lived on bread. Pinchas would occasionally send him money; when he forgot, Sam was reduced to eating scraps of food he found lying around the workshop.

One day, as he was practicing on the sewing machine during his lunch hour, he broke the needle. He tried fixing it and as he did so the handle of the machine fell off, and it stopped working. He sat there for a while, holding the damaged part, and filled with despair. When his boss came back he panicked, and announced that he was returning home for the Purim holidays. He departed without saying anything about the broken machine – and that was how his first apprenticeship ended.

When he returned to Zawiercie he became even more depressed. Those couple of months away had left him estranged from his friends and the town seemed smaller than ever. He would go for long walks alone and dream of leaving again. But it was low season in the fur industry, and work opportunities were unlikely to arise. He started to think of moving to Krakow, the capital ... yet where would he get the money? His funds were nearly all gone, and it was clear that desperate measures were called for.

He decided to buy a train ticket to a destination halfway to Krakow, but then continue on to the city, hoping all the while that he would not be caught. He boarded the big steam engine and found a seat by the window, then gazed out at the view with a nonchalant expression. The train passed his designated stop. After a short while, he became aware that a ticket inspector was making his way through the compartment. Sam's heart came into his mouth, and he slid down into his seat as far as possible – to no avail. The inspector paused before him and asked for his ticket.

Sam looked at the official's face and thought he discerned a gentleness there. He decided to throw himself on the man's mercy.

"Please let me continue to Krakow," he begged. "Please, I don't have money."

He was disappointed. "You are to get off this train at once," ordered the inspector in stentorian tones.

Sam gathered his belongings and stood up miserably, conscious of disapproving looks from the other passengers. But the man bent close to him and added some words in a softer tone.

"I had no choice," he said. "If you told me beforehand in a discreet corner it would have been different. But everyone knows now, and I have to do my job."

While he was writing the fine he gave Sam the address of the Jewish community of the town where the boy would need to disembark. But the idea of begging for money was too much for Sam. Scrabbling in his pockets, he managed to find a few extra coins which enabled him to finally reach Krakow. He arrived there tired and penniless.

6

KRAKOW

It was Sam's first time in the city, and it seemed huge. He walked for several hours until he arrived at the house of an uncle, his father's brother. It was 7 o'clock in the evening and he hadn't eaten all day. Visions of a plate of hot steaming food arose before him as he knocked on the door. Nobody answered, and a sharp wave of disappointment washed through him. What should he do? He wandered a little around the neighborhood and eventually returned and knocked on the door again. This time he was more fortunate. The door opened and two young girls stood there giggling, cousins whom he had not met. Sam introduced himself to them and kissed their hands, thinking they would be impressed by his good manners. They burst out laughing and his face reddened.

The family served him a meal and Sam tried not to appear to be a glutton. Around 10 o'clock his Uncle Jonas came in. Although he remembered Sam he was not particularly warm in his manner toward him; nevertheless, he told the boy that he could stay. He could sleep in the bed of one of his cousins, who was currently in the army. In fact, Sam discovered, all the rooms were furnished with beds, even the kitchen. That it was an eclectic household, he was also to find out. His uncle was a buyer and seller of leather, but because business was irregular he spent most of his time lounging in cafes. His niece Anda, who was barely 20 and worked in a bank, was the one bringing in most of the funds. Sam's aunt had tuberculosis and was away, recovering in the countryside. But that first night Sam was just thankful to tumble into his cousin's bed. He slept soundly, and the next morning when he woke he ventured forth.

Krakow, situated on the Vistula River, is the one of the oldest cities in Poland, and also one of the most beautiful in Europe. At that time it was the official capital, and traditionally had been a center of Polish economic and cultural life. Sam found his way to Krakow's historic center, the Old Town, walking along the cobbled streets through which horse-drawn carriages were plying. He found himself enchanted by his surroundings. The palaces, churches and mansions displayed a rich variety of color and heritage architecture, including Gothic, Renaissance and Baroque, and the charming squares were filled with pavement cafes overflowing with patrons, even at that early hour of the day. High above all, the massive Wawel Castle presided majestically.[1]

Sam passed through the Planty Park, the leafy promenade established in place of the Old Town's ramparts destroyed by the Austrians in the 19th century. Eventually he found himself in the district of Kazimierz, home to one of the largest Jewish Quarters in Eastern Europe, its picturesque streets filled with ancient synagogues. Close by was the famous Vistula, a major waterway which passes through large parts of Poland and provides breathtaking scenery along its length. Sam stood on the bank and gazed at the waters as they reflected the blue vault of heaven, and it seemed one of the loveliest things he had seen. "The Vistula whispers in Yiddish": the fragment of Singer's writing echoed in his mind. On the broad surface of the river kayaks and small leisure boats floated, and there was even a Jewish club called Maccabee which catered for nautical sports.

Sam felt as he wandered that he was treading on air and his feet were wings. The city appeared filled with light and beauty, to which his spirit responded ardently. However, the next day he plummeted rapidly back to earth.

"Have you found work yet?" asked his uncle.

"Not yet," he answered, "but I'm looking."

Sam went to one furrier after another. It was summer and hence low season, he was inexperienced, just 16 years old, and everyone told him, "Come back in three months." He knew it was becoming urgent that he find something. One day, he caught sight of a sign on the first floor of an old apartment building; it bore one word: Furrier. Sam climbed the stairs and met the owner of the establishment. This was Moshe, a pleasant, rather rotund young man, 25 years of age and still single. Moshe took pity on the youngster. As it happened, his apprentice was in prison for communist activities, and he engaged Sam.

Sam soon learned that Moshe was fond of ladies. In his room, hidden behind a curtain, was a couch and a gramophone. When the gramophone was playing very loudly it meant he was making love to one of his girlfriends. One day Moshe asked Sam to go on an errand for him and disappeared behind the curtain with his current flame. On his way out, Sam took the opportunity to peek behind the curtain into this figurative "perfect marriage" and learn something about a subject that had always been taboo at home. Moshe was so engrossed in his amorous activities that he didn't notice.

But Moshe was also unstinting in his kindness to his new young protégé, whom he affectionately called "Baron Sam." Because he was somewhat on the short side, he passed on to Sam some of his used clothes, including the special luxury of a fur coat. Sam attached a collar to this which he sewed together with old bits and pieces of fur he found in the workroom. And there were other benefits in his apprenticeship. His new boss arranged for him to take classes twice a week, studying languages, chemistry and math. Sometimes Moshe even pressed money into Sam's hand and sent him to the cinema, a completely new experience for him; the first movie he saw was

Tarzan. And when the fashionable ladies of Krakow gave him a tip as he delivered their fur coats he would go to a concert or the theater, losing himself in the music of his favorite composers, Mozart, Beethoven and Schubert.

There were other treasures waiting to be discovered in Krakow: the museums and public art galleries, one of which, the Czartoryski Museum, housed paintings by Leonardo da Vinci and Rembrandt. And of course, there were books ... At the Jewish Library, Sam found works by Romain Rolland, Gorki, Victor Hugo and Maupassant which had been translated into Yiddish, while the socialist cultural center offered books in Polish. He started to make friends; most were students and broke. Together they discussed politics and read the turgid poems they had written. With two of his new companions, Jozef and Jenkel, he enjoyed visiting the medieval castle, Wawel, which contained a vast wealth of treasures inside its heavily fortified walls. Through them he also discovered the "wild beach," a secluded, untamed stretch of shore. Its neglected, riotous beauty made him think of surrealist and modernist paintings, the fashion sweeping the art world at the time. Sam loved to swim there in the summer, when it became very hot.

During those steamy months, Sam also loved to hang out at the Jozefat park, a cool green haven where the doves cooed in the overshadowing branches. Benches were scattered throughout the park, and many Jewish young people came together there. Some were communists, some socialists, and others were simply contesting everything. One young man had fled from Russia. Sam listened to his stories about life there but did not believe that the horrors he related were true. At the time he had been influenced by the books of Sokolov and Ehrenburg which showed the Soviets in a very favorable light. Russian movies were also extremely popular with the crowd Sam fraternized with, although their screening always started around 11 at night to prevent the masses from coming to watch. These films also encouraged Sam to embrace positive conceptions about the Soviet regime.

However, during those hot languorous days of summer Sam earned almost nothing. Uncle Jonas was not happy, because he believed his nephew was lazy. "It's not nice what you're doing, Shmiel," he grumbled. "We give you everything and you give us almost nothing."

"In the winter, Uncle, I'll pay you ten times more," Sam promised. "You know it's the slow season now."

He was learning how different his uncle was from his father, despite the fact that they were brothers. In contrast to Israel – who was slender, quiet and somewhat ascetic – Uncle Jonas was heavily built, spoke in a booming voice and enjoyed lavish meals. Still, he wanted to show that he had his brother's interests at heart, and insisted that Sam go to the synagogue on Shabbat. Sam felt that his liberty was being compromised, but there was a compensation: on Saturdays the food was even more delicious than at home. His aunt's sister had come to help in the household and she was an excellent cook. Although gas was available, this thrifty lady felt it was too expensive and cooked with coal. She had also lost an eye but (Sam thought) seemed to see more with that one orb than others with two.

Meanwhile, his aunt had returned to the household, but was getting weaker. At times her manner was extremely kind, but at other times her suffering caused her to become testy. Yet she loved Sam as if he were her own son and used to save leftover scraps for him. Sam felt this was perhaps not very dignified but was secretly happy with the extra rations. He would look with compassion on his aunt's hands as she brought him the morsels; they were black and worn, but to him they had a special beauty and he longed to paint their ruined splendor. He was saddened when his aunt died and things changed yet again. Uncle Jonas remarried not very long afterwards – and this time his new bride was a wealthy woman.

As the months passed, Sam was coming to like Krakow more and more. He visited several churches, many of which were decorated with a Baroque extravagance, featuring colorful swirling paintings on the ceilings, gilded altars, pulpits and balconies, crystal chandeliers and white marble angels. The lavish profusion of the sculptures and paintings in the basilicas were to him new representations of love, suffering ... and death. Religious Jews were not allowed to go inside churches, and he found that the forbidden fruit was especially enjoyable.

Sam especially loved St. Mary's Basilica, the 13th-century Gothic church adjacent to the in the Old Town. On every hour, a trumpet signal known as the *Hejnał Mariacki* was played from a tower of the church. The plaintive melody breaks off midway to commemorate a renowned trumpeter, who sounded the alarm to warn the city of a Mongol invasion but was struck by an arrow before he could finish. But it was the artistic masterpiece in the interior that was the true attraction for Sam, and which drew people from all over Poland, indeed from all over the world, to visit the church.

Inside St. Mary's is the famous wooden altarpiece carved by German master sculptor Veit Stoss, who dedicated 12 years between 1477 and 1489 to the project. Towering behind the high altar, it is the largest Gothic altarpiece in the world, reaching 13 meters in height and 11 meters in width, and containing over 200 realistically carved figures from the Gospels. Composed as a pentaptych (having five wings), it is made of three types of wood: the structure of hard oak, the background of larch, while the figures are sculpted in soft and flexible linden. The piece as a whole has harmony and symmetry, but it was the centerpiece, depicting dramatically the death of the Virgin Mary while surrounded by the 12 Apostles, which made Sam catch his breath.

The central sculptures are almost fully rounded figures, almost three meters high, each hewn from an individual linden tree, and given the character of an expressive individual portrait. Sam did not know the story or the personages, but he was able to read the poignant emotion on each countenance, and grasp the intensity and passion with which Stoss had created the piece. He was dazzled by the German artist's mastery of dimension, the glory of the billowing drapery and his use of vibrant color, all of which added to the powerful impact. The tableau as a whole is gilded with gold, which in the Middle Ages symbolized the eternal light of heaven, and it bathed the scene in soft radiance.[2]

But ... there were other things pressing on Sam's artistic reveries: the unwanted political developments, and the everyday reality of his life in Krakow. They insisted on intruding on his creative dreams, like an unwanted guest who simply will not go away.

---

1. Crowned by its royal castle and the cathedral which was used for the coronation of kings and queens, Wawel is a symbol of Polish national pride, and also the final resting place of former monarchs, including Casimir III who showed such an enlightened solicitude for a peaceful relationship between Jews and Christians, as well as illustrious figures from Polish history, such as the poet Adam Mickiewicz, and Tadeusz Kościuszko. This latter was the military leader who became a national hero in both Poland and the US, having played a key role in the American Revolution, and later leading the Kosciuszko Uprising of 1794, a brave insurrection against foreign rule by Russia and Prussia.
2. Just before the Second World War commenced, and the Germans invaded Poland, the Catholic church authorities foresaw they might lose their priceless treasure. They took the altar apart and stored the individual pieces in crates, dispersed across the country, but the Nazis discovered the hiding places in 1941. Looted and transported to Germany, the crates were placed in deep vaults under Nuremburg Castle, but, as it happened, some captured Polish soldiers were imprisoned there. They discovered the crates and sent a secret message to the Polish Resistance. Despite heavy bombardment of Nuremberg by the Allies, the altar survived the war and was returned to Poland in 1946.

7

MEETING "THE PROPHET"

Krakow had Poland's oldest institution of higher learning: the Jagiellonian University, founded in 1364 by Casimir III; notable alumni include astronomer Nicolaus Copernicus of the class of 1492[1]. The professors at the university were renowned for their learning and usually liberal in their outlook, but a large section of the student body had nationalistic sentiments and antisemitic attitudes. Many embraced Nazi ideology and edited a newspaper which portrayed all Jews as "Judeo-communists." Almost every day violent fights began occurring between Catholics and Jews, and during one of the battles a Catholic student died.

This inevitably precipitated a number of pogroms and antisemitic campaigns; signs began appearing over the city like a terrible black rash: *"Don't buy in Jewish stores," "Entrance forbidden for Jews."* Sometimes Sam joined young people from a Zionist organization who gathered in the basement of a synagogue situated next to the cemetery, though he was too much of a free thinker to accept their left-wing Zionist ideology. He knew that his way of protest would be different.

The sun was beginning its pilgrimage back to the north and the days were lengthening, which meant that the feast of Purim was at hand, engaging the attention of the Jewish community in Krakow. As the story of Esther's triumph over the wicked Haman was retold, the festival often turned into quite a riotous event, with street parties and revelry. The children loved to dress up in costumes, and the small Queen Esthers in their pretty robes and gilt crowns were the stars of the occasion. The boys usually sought a more swashbuckling role and would swagger about as diminutive kings or storybook villains. That particular year many of them were disguised as Hitler, others as Goebbels.

And Sam made his first drawings of the characters from the Purim story. His Haman was very different from that of Rembrandt, who had portrayed a deceptively mild, smooth, northern figure. Sam's arch-villain was dark-avised, brooding, utterly malevolent, and he experienced a fierce joy as he executed the portrait. In the streets of the Jewish quarter there was an atmosphere of celebration, as the people remembered the ways in which God had delivered them in the past and proclaimed their trust for the future.

It was at this point an incident occurred which was to impact Sam profoundly, and which he would remember for the rest of his life. This was the moment when he met someone whom he later named in his mind as "the prophet." It occurred as he was walking along the banks of the lovely Vistula River, just as the first rays of sun had appeared after the long winter. The gentle waves were glinting in the clear air and Sam was gazing at the scene, captivated by its freshness and charm. As he did so, a stranger – a small man – approached him. He seemed to be about 40 years of age, and his face was carved with lines suggestive of suffering and patient endurance. His clothes were old and worn, but it seemed to Sam that he carried himself with an innate dignity. As he drew near to the younger man, he paused, admiring the view that lay before them.

"How beautiful the Vistula looks," he murmured, then continued reflectively, "Nature surely reveals perfection to us." Sam was pondering his words, when the man turned and spoke directly to him. "What do you want to do with your life?" he asked.

46

Sam was still under the influence of a book written by Romain Rolland, *Jean Christophe*, and had wavered in his commitment to art as his first love. He answered, "Either be a composer of music, or a sculptor."

Jean Christophe is a work in ten volumes, for which Rolland won the Nobel Prize in Literature in 1915. The hero of the story is a German musician and composer, a kind of Beethoven of the 20th century. He becomes an exile from his home country, finding refuge first in Paris and then in Switzerland, before returning in triumph to Paris many years later. It shows the progress of a soul in whom the artistic temperament is predominant, and who is devoted to pursuing a lifelong quest for truth. Such a one, in order to give expression to the pure and noble conceptions he espouses, must endure severe hardships and spiritual struggles, before being raised to an elevated moral stature and enabled to bequeath profound works of genius to the world.

After Sam gave his answer, the stranger bent a piercing gaze upon him. "You will become exactly what you want to be," he said.

His words carried an aura of authority, and as they fell on the bright, living air the atmosphere seemed to change, to become charged with a numinous quality, as if the quintessence of the Vistula had surrounded them. It seemed to Sam that he and this mysterious stranger had been enveloped by an ethereal veil, that shut out the world of everyday reality and opened his senses to a new dimension of reality. For a brief, wondrous moment he felt as if he were caught up in another realm, which he had not before known to exist, where shining new truths might be discovered, and where great promises were waiting to be claimed. He was coming to a dim apprehension that this man who had so suddenly appeared was some kind of saint or mystic, and that his statement was a blessing which had a tangible power to create what it uttered, and make good what it pledged.

In silence the stranger and Sam stayed side by side, and when Sam finally looked up he saw that he was alone. He was filled with a hitherto unknown and intense joy – embracing a vision of himself as creator.

8

POZNAN

In 1934 Sam turned 17; he had been living with his uncle for a year. When his employer Moshe left Krakow for Poznan to work with his brother in a large department store, Sam decided to go with him. Poznan is a large city, considerably further north than Krakow, lying equidistant between Berlin and Warsaw. Like Krakow, it had a colorful history and many-layered traditions reaching back to the 10th century. And, at the beginning, business went well.

Moshe had rented three rooms in a family's home, and the rent included food; Sam even had his own room and the evening meals were excellent with lots of pasta and puddings. He didn't get a salary, but he received pocket money, made new friends and felt he had more freedom than before. He also fell in love for the first time, with a young Jewish girl who had come from Germany. Their relationship remained platonic, but Sam found it difficult to concentrate on his work. He was continually gazing out of the window, hoping to see his lady love, lost in dreams. Moshe scolded him, but did it gently.

When Sam had to do the errands, he always seized the opportunity to look at the shops where paintings were displayed, nor could he resist looking at the pictures in front of the movie theaters. He would then be chastised by his boss for taking so long. But he was also able to scan the newspapers displayed on the vendors' stands, and like the other Jews in Europe was watching with disbelief the rise of the little mustachioed Austrian corporal to the heights of power in Germany.

Hitler had come to prominence on the wings of promises to restore German prosperity and greatness. At the end of the First World War, the reparation payments required by the Treaty of Versailles had plunged the nation into economic and social hardship; Hitler and his National Socialist Party promised a strong central government, a restored economy and increased Lebensraum (living space). Using the inflammatory rhetoric of a demagogue, Hitler also presented himself to the German people as a savior, promising to restore national glory and the supremacy of the "Aryan race."

After the federal elections of November 1932, the Nazi Party became the majority party in the Reichstag (Parliament), and, after some political maneuvering, President Paul von Hindenburg appointed Hitler as Chancellor of Germany on January 30, 1933. From this point, Germany began rapidly developing into one of the most terrifying regimes known to history. The nation which had been the most cultured and advanced in Europe, a bastion of enlightenment ideals, began to lay all its accomplishments on the dark altar of fealty to Nazi ideology.

Just a month after Hitler came to power, on February 27, 1933, a mysterious fire broke out in the Reichstag building in Berlin, a central symbol of German sovereignty. Hitler immediately blamed the Nazis' political opponents, the communists, and used the disaster as a pretext to seize emergency powers, suspending civil liberties through a law called the Enabling Act, and deputizing the Sturmabteilung, the Storm Troopers, to arrest those considered political enemies. The secret police force which would become the principal terror mechanism in Hitler's Germany, the feared and hated Gestapo, was created that April by Hermann Göring. It was immediately used to silence Hitler's enemies and to remove from society those he considered detrimental: homosexuals, Jehovah's Witnesses, the mentally handicapped, and members of Christian churches who disagreed with his ideology.

Those arrested for refusing to conform to the new order were sent away for re-education within the confines of a prison, where they would be broken physically, mentally and spiritually – it was the birth of the concentration camp system. The first such prison was Dachau, located near Munich, which was so successful that it became the model for hundreds of similar centers. Upon first entering Dachau, a prisoner passed through an iron gate bearing the slogan: "Arbeit Macht Frei" – work sets free.

A cornerstone of Hitler's ideology was the conviction that the Jewish people were primarily responsible for the nation's misfortunes. In the 1930s, Germany's Jews – some half a million people – made up less than one percent of the German population and most considered themselves loyal patriots. They had made spectacular contributions to the nation in the fields of science, literature and the arts; fully one quarter of Germany's Nobel Prize winners were Jewish. Despite the alarming signs, there was a widespread belief among German Jews that their contributions to German culture and economy would ensure their ultimate protection.

On April 1, 1933, a national boycott of Jewish shops and department stores was organized by Nazis and enforced by brown-shirted Storm Troopers. This was claimed to be retribution for unfavorable newspaper stories appearing in Britain and America concerning Hitler's new regime; the Nazis attributed the bad publicity to "international Jewry." Six days after the boycott, "The Law of the Restoration of the Civil Service" was introduced which made "Aryanism" a necessary requirement to hold a government position. This meant that all Jews were now excluded from holding positions in the civil service, judicial system, public health and education; it was the first racial law attempting to oust Jews from German life.

From that point the Jews of Germany were subjected to a never-ending series of discriminatory laws, and the fountain of Jewish genius that had enriched the country beyond all measure was stopped at its source. Many intellectuals fled the land, including Albert Einstein, the world's leading physicist, who settled in the United States.

Education in Germany would now focus on fitness for military service and the collective pursuit of glory for the "master race," while the quest for truth and objective knowledge, the foundational values of Western civilization, was abandoned. Extensive indoctrination was used to spread the Nazi Party's racist goals and ideals, and in March 1933 Hitler established his Ministry of Propaganda under Joseph Goebbels. The ministry set out to control every form of expression in Germany, and all creative endeavor – music, radio, art, newspapers, even sermons – was crafted to exalt Nazi policies and Hitler himself, and to demonize those whom the Nazis considered enemies.

The era of absolute state censorship was launched on May 6 with a scene reminiscent of the darkest days of the Middle Ages, as students from once-renowned universities gathered in Berlin's Opernplatz to burn books with "un-German" ideas. While giving the Nazi salute and singing party anthems, they tossed to the flames 25,000 volumes of the world's greatest writers and thinkers. Many books were torched solely because their authors were Jews, with Goebbels declaring, "The era of extreme Jewish intellectualism is now at an end." The tragedy of the event could only be summed up in the words of German-Jewish poet, Heinrich Heine: "Wherever books are burned, human beings are destined to be burned too."[1]

The Nazis continued implementing their policies and advancing their political position through physical violence, and the Brownshirts excelled in disrupting the meetings of rival groups and wielding their power of arrest to its fullest measure. In July 1933, Hitler took the step of banning all other political parties: democracy was instantly obliterated, and the country became a centralized, single-party police state. At this point, Hitler began to fear opposition within the Nazi Party itself, suspecting that the Sturmabteilung, whose members outnumbered the German military, were a potential threat to his leadership. On June 30, 1934, in what became known as "The Night of the Long Knives," the SS and Gestapo murdered more than 200 leading Storm Troopers.

This helped Hitler and the Nazi Party to further consolidate their power in Germany and also signaled the rise of the ruthless Nazi SS (Schutzstaffel), a paramilitary organization under the leadership of Heinrich Himmler and Reinhard Heydrich. It acquired command of the Gestapo and took control of all the concentration camps in Germany, and thereafter would function as *the principal agent in executing the Nazi policies of oppression, violence and death.*

On August 2, 1934, President Hindenburg died. Hitler then abolished the office of President and declared himself Führer of the German Reich; this was in addition to his position as Chancellor. He had now become the absolute dictator of Germany. The German army took an oath of allegiance to its new commander-in-chief, and the Führer assured his people that the Third Reich would last for a thousand years.

The shadows were lengthening and foretelling a threat more ominous than any the Jewish people had faced before – yet neither Sam nor his companions were able to recognize the scorching degree of danger.

Moshe's former apprentice, a young man named Oscar, was released from his year in prison and came to Poznan, and he and Sam became friends. Together they bought a second-hand bicycle and went swimming every day in a pool which was open to the public. Other times they would lie in the sun on the grassy banks of the River Warta, before dipping themselves in the cool waters. Oscar's father was working in a bakery, and he got brown and white bread for free. The two boys were poor, and sometimes had only bread to eat for their lunch. They would make themselves a "sandwich": two white slices with a brown one in the middle for filling. Mmm … delicious!

Oscar was very mature for his age, and had had some experiences which were beyond Sam's comprehension at the time. One of his brothers was still in prison for communist activities and Sam went with Oscar to visit him. It was Sam's first contact with a jail (but unfortunately not his last). Families and friends brought food and clean clothes to the prisoners, and would take away the dirty laundry. Inside the clothes secret notes were often hidden, and Sam trembled when he saw how Oscar opened the seam of a shirt to insert a message written on cigarette paper. He stored away the incident in his mind, but his intellectual and artistic pursuits were still uppermost in his thoughts.

On one occasion the great classical pianist Artur Rubenstein came to Poznan and gave a recital, playing works by Mozart, Beethoven and Chopin; he was considered a master interpreter of the latter's work. Sam attended the recital, and noted that although Rubinstein was Jewish he was nevertheless received rapturously by the audience, who gave him standing ovations. This lent an added measure of shock to his emotions when he stepped outside the theater and noticed a poster reading: *"Jews – Get Out – Go to Palestine."* On another occasion he saw Rubinstein walking in the street, dressed very elegantly and wearing cream-colored gloves. Sam burned with the desire to approach him but was too timid.

This was a period when music attracted him even more than art. When his trousers wore out, instead of buying new ones he spent his funds on a violin. His musical endeavors were not pleasing to his neighbors, while his friends teasingly called him "Paganini." Music and art would remain the two greatest passions of his life.

As the months passed, work was becoming scarce in Poznan, and having saved a small sum of money San decided to return to Krakow. He boarded the train in the evening on the last day of the year, December 31, 1934. It was a cold and bleak night. The train was almost empty and another young man who worked in the fur trade was with him. He had brought a record player with him, and the two friends whiled away the hours listening to music. As they did so, they were heedless of the clocks ticking away the final second of the year at the stroke of midnight, with a thud as definite as the fall of Haman's dice. The momentous 1934 had passed, during which the world had been edged toward a fate more dark and sad than any the malice of the Persian minister could desire.[2]

---

1. The line is taken from Heine's 1821 play *Almansor*. Copies of Heine's books were among those burned in Berlin that day, and to commemorate the event the line

is now engraved at the site: *"Dort wo man Bücher verbrennt, verbrennt man am Ende auch Menschen."*

2. An allusion to Stanza 24 of "Daphnis and Chloe," written by 17th-century English poet Andrew Marvell: *Fate I come, as dark, as sad, As thy Malice could desire; Yet bring with me all the Fire That Love in his Torches had.*

9

SECRET PLANS

Moshe arrived in Krakow a couple of days after Sam. His amorous adventures had finally caught up with him, and he had been fired because he had slept with the daughter of his German Jewish employer. She was a simple girl, small and gentle, who worked as secretary for her father. After making love to her, Moshe had been caught *in flagrante delicto* with the maid as well! He was unable to continue employing Sam, but recommended him to another furrier. In Krakow it was a time of economic hardship and it was difficult to find work, so Sam was thankful. He was not well paid, but was able to put aside the money he had made in Poznan.

He also managed to find a room to rent in the house of a divorced woman. Her husband had been quite a famous artist, and, like Picasso, one of whose early great paintings was *Family of Saltimbanques*, he had become fascinated with circus performers. He had subsequently fallen in love with one of the girl *artistes*, and left his wife and child. The lady of the house taught piano and Sam began to take lessons from her; since he was renting a room she gave him a very good price. His room was spacious and filled with paintings, but they were too modern for his taste.

Meanwhile, the antisemitism in Krakow was becoming more

pronounced, and riots involving Jewish and non-Jewish students increased in frequency. The assailants were usually members of the National Democratic Party, Endecja. Disturbing news from Germany continued to filter through, and Sam helped members of an illegal anti-Fascist organization to distribute the "brown book," which published documents and pictures relating to the camp in Dachau. The approaching hoofbeats were drumming, but Sam was still focused on his artistic dreams.[1] He had heard that in Russia it was possible to learn art and music for free, and the idea of somehow making his way into Soviet territory began to haunt him. He had been convinced by the left-wing literature pressed upon him by his friends that Russia was a paradise on earth for aspiring artists and thinkers.

Although this hope was with him day and night, Sam kept it a secret. He knew that Russia's border was very well guarded and was afraid he might be betrayed. After buying a map, he began his clandestine study of the routes. The demarcation line, he discovered, was situated on the other side of Poland, on the River Zbruch, a tributary of the Dniester. Historically, this had formed a border between the Austrian Monarchy and the Russian Empire, but after the Treaty of Riga was re-established as the Polish-Soviet border. The checkpoint was at a town named Podvolochisk; this was to be his target. Sam realized he had to save money, work out a plan, and wait for the right moment.

He decided he would go to Russia in the mid-winter month of January, right after the fur season had ended, so he could earn as much money as possible before leaving. For an entire year he put funds aside, stopped going to concerts, finished piano lessons and tried to spend as little as possible on food. He had heard that the Jewish sports club Maccabee was arranging for train tickets at reduced prices for those taking part in winter sports, so he became a member. Knowing the rigors of the Russian winter, he did part with some of his funds to purchase warm clothes, and also began to buy rubles. He was certain that once he was in Soviet territory he would find work immediately; after all, there could be no unemployment in this utopia! He imagined his life there: he would work during the daytime, and in the evenings he would study music and art.

When he visited his parents' house, he confided his plans only to Mendele, who was barely ten years old. "Mendele, you can't tell anyone," Sam impressed sternly upon his young brother. "Do you swear to keep this a secret?"

Mendele's eyes were round with excitement. "Shmiel, I'll be like a fish," he promised. "I won't say a word." He was very impressed with the idea that his big brother was about to undertake such a grand adventure.

Sam then devised a strategy for his parents. "My boss is sending me throughout Poland to buy fur," he said to his father. "By the way," he added casually, "I remember you once worked with a fur merchant who lived in Podvolochisk."

Israel gave him a card with the address and looked at his son with pride. "You're doing well, Shmiel Szija. I'm happy you're finally becoming a merchant."

When Sam left, Mendele began crying. The secret was too heavy a burden for the small boy to carry. "I'll never see my brother again," he blurted out. "He's going to Russia."

But Israel and Hannah didn't believe him. "A child's fantasy," they said.

Sam took the evening train in the direction of Podvolochisk. In his pocket was a ticket given to him by Maccabee, which was valid for 1,000 kilometers. He had a small bag with him, more like a child's suitcase; the contents comprised a toothbrush, a towel, a shirt, a razor, and his tefillin (phylacteries).[2] He wasn't religious, but the tefillin were like a talisman. He had confided his plans to a friend. "Please send a picture of me to my parents in six weeks," he asked.

He spent the night in a lodging house halfway to his destination. As he lay down to sleep he realized how tense he was, thinking of the undertaking ahead. Suddenly it dawned upon him that this was a dangerous enterprise which might well cost him his life. He didn't sleep much during those long hours of darkness. The next morning, Thursday, he took the train to Podvolochisk, located adjacent to the Russian border and close to the River Zbruch which separated the two countries. On the platform a number of secret police were sauntering, posing as passengers. Fortunately, they paid little attention to Sam and his unimpressive luggage.

He arrived at the house of the fur merchant with whom his father had done business and gave him the same story. "I'm coming to buy fur. Would I be able to stay with you a couple of days? I'll gladly pay."

The merchant's family were pleasant and welcoming. On Friday evening he went to the synagogue with them, and on the Sabbath he went out with a bunch of boys and girls who were members of a Zionist organization. He enjoyed their company, but his main purpose was to get to know the surroundings. He was hoping against hope that the river would be frozen – that would make crossing easier.

"Before returning home," he said to them nonchalantly, "I would like to see the exact place where the border is."

"Come on, bro," was the reply. "It's not very interesting. It's just a river, and every day people get killed there."

The hair on the back of Sam's neck prickled, but he continued to feign an airy curiosity, and finally, in order to please him, his new friends took him to the border. The river was far wider than he had expected, and the waters that rushed and tumbled along were carried by a strong current. There was a band of shifting sand at the river's edge and it was freezing. Sam stared at the swirling waves, trying to hide his dismay. All his misgivings were beginning to return in full force, but he continued with the masquerade so his companions would not become suspicious.

"What time is there a train early tomorrow morning for Lemberg?" he asked.

"At 5 o'clock."

Sam decided to get up at 4. The furrier gave him a little alarm clock for a present. "If you put it on a small plate," he said, "it will make even more noise."

It was the first time Sam had seen such a clock. But long before the jangling notes fell on the quiet air he was awake, and listening to the beating of his heart. He rose, dressed silently, gathered his belongings and left the house.

---

1. A reference to the four horses of the Apocalypse – Book of Revelation, Chapter 6.
2. Tefillin are the small black leather boxes containing scrolls of parchment inscribed with verses from the Torah, worn by observant Jews while praying.

10

RUSSIA

When the inconceivable happened at the end of the First World War, and the powers that had partitioned Poland for so long collapsed, the reborn nation experienced a period of euphoria. Welcoming its return to the map of Europe, Polish-born English novelist Joseph Conrad singled out what he saw as his nation's greatest achievement during a century of captivity: "Under a destructive pressure, of which Western Europe can have no notion, applied by forces that were not only crushing but corrupting, we have preserved our sanity."[1]

And yet the road ahead was bound to be difficult. Nearly half a million Poles had perished in the three imperial armies, and the different regions that had been separated economically, politically and socially for so long had yet to be forged again into a single entity. A hundred years of living within one or other of three entirely different cultures had distanced social groups within the land, and there were other challenges as well: extensive war damage, a shattered economy, and the need to recreate all the structures of a state. Above all, there was the matter of frontiers – and, of all these, it was the issue of the border with Russia which proved most "burning and intractable".[2]

When Lenin had become leader of the new communist government in Russia in 1917, he embraced a grand vision: to carry his proletarian revolution into the very heart of Europe. According to Trotsky, this triumphal procession would take place "over the corpse of bourgeois Poland."[3] In 1919, he amassed the soldiers of the Red Army and they charged toward Warsaw, but were met and routed by Polish forces under the command of Josef Pilsudski in a David and Goliath battle situation. Later known as the "Miracle on the Vistula," it was a victory hailed by many military analysts as saving Western civilization. Eventually a peace treaty was signed between the two combatants at Riga in 1921, dividing the disputed territories of Belarus and Ukraine between them.

In January 1936, at the time Sam was making his attempt at escape, Poland had long borders with two powerful dictatorships, Hitler's Germany to the west, and Stalin's USSR to the east. Yet, while Poland had attempted to maintain some degree of concord with Nazi Germany, the Soviet Union was regarded with unremitting hostility. Relations between Poland and Russia at that point were cold indeed, colder even than the icy air which enwrapped Sam as he left the little house in Podvolochisk in the pre-dawn darkness. He began making his way through the silent streets toward the river and soon reached wet fields at the outskirts of the town, but his progress alerted some dogs, which began barking. The noise seemed to Sam to shatter the stillness like the shriek of an express train. One of the animals even approached and circled about him, sniffing at his heels. He pushed ineffectually at the creature with his little suitcase, but it continued to impede his progress.

Finally the river appeared, rising out of the gloom. In the darkness the waters seemed black and threatening and it was impossible to see the far side. Sam squelched his way through the sludgy sand at the river's edge, wondering all the while how deep it was. He wished desperately that it had been frozen over. Arriving at the first small waves which lapped the shore, he divested himself of socks and boots and strung them around his neck, then pulled his trouser legs as high as they would go. He took a deep breath and entered the waters, discovering with a shock how absolutely frigid they were. As he waded forward they rose around his knees and then his thighs until he was waist deep, and still the ground was shelving. The river was deeper than he had anticipated, and seemed to possess a mysterious, frightening power all of its own, magnified by the darkness and cold, and the icy wind that whistled about his head.

Soon he had lost touch with the bottom and was forced to strike out clumsily, hampered by his case and sodden clothes. The water swirled and eddied about him, and still he could see no sight of the farther shore. His body became ice cold, and he felt as if needles were piercing his flesh. But he urged himself on: "Come on – courage! Just another 50 meters, and you'll be in Russia."

Exhausted and panting heavily he finally arrived at the other side. He sat on the bank and pulled on his shoes and socks, feeling a profound happiness. He had succeeded; he was now in a free country! At that same moment, he heard footsteps approaching. The rags of night were fleeing and in the tenuous light which was beginning to envelop the scene Sam saw a tall, strongly built man standing before him. The stranger was looking down on him, surveying him. It was evident that Sam, in his soaking jacket, had crossed the river illegally and was a foreigner.

"Come with me, lad," said the man in Polish. "You're wet, and I'll bring you to a warm place where you can rest."

Sam followed the Russian without fear, but soon received a stunning blow to his hopes. He was ushered into a small building with a low ceiling and barred windows: it could be nothing other than a KGB office. The man he had followed with such innocence and alacrity, then, belonged to the Russian secret service, notorious for its harshness and cruelty. Sam was led to a dark room which smelled of damp and mold; three men were sitting there behind a table. Stolid and heavily built, with faces impassive as gargoyles, they were altogether intimidating. They looked with cold eyes upon Sam, then produced a newspaper and showed it to him, pointing to a picture.

"Who is it?" grunted one of the men. It was clear what he was asking.

"Stalin," answered Sam.

They seemed satisfied and nodded to one another. Sam began to relax, but suddenly a hood was whisked over his head and he was plunged into darkness. Two soldiers led him away, their guns prodding his side. They didn't walk a long distance – it seemed to Sam they passed through a courtyard with rough stones, over which he stumbled, and he sensed they were then passing through an iron gate, which creaked behind them. He was thrust into a cell, the door was swung to with a thud of great finality, and he was left alone. Sam tore off the hood and gazed around at his bleak confines. Fear threatened to swamp him, but he tried to boost his morale. "They will surely find out the truth, and then they will let me go," he assured himself.

All that day he saw no one; he sustained himself by nibbling on some of the rations in his case. At 2 o'clock in the morning the cell door burst open as he lay half-dozing, conscious only of hunger, weariness, thirst and cold. An armed soldier kicked his legs, forcing him to stand. He was taken to another office where a tall blond man was seated behind a desk; he reeked of vodka. This, Sam discovered later, was the police superintendent. He spoke to Sam in Russian, but the boy shook his head and spread his hands to indicate his lack of comprehension.

This seemed to infuriate the officer, who shouted at him in heavily accented Polish. "You understand Russian," he said, "you're a spy!"

Sam started to laugh. The idea that they thought he was a spy was so preposterous! The Russian became even more incensed and continued shouting; after half an hour, Sam was led back to his cell. He remained optimistic. Tomorrow he would be free, he thought to himself. But he had only a light blanket that gave little warmth and wasn't able to sleep. An hour later, at 4 o'clock, his jailers came for him again. They didn't let him have time to put his shoes on properly before he was taken to a large room with an ugly, worn-out carpet on the floor. Here a small, thickset man began to interrogate him once again – in Russian. Sam once again shook his head.

"For God's sake, what languages do you speak?" shouted the man.

Sam understood what he was asking. "I speak Yiddish and Polish."

It was somehow impressed upon him that he would have to give them his home address, and he was led back to his cell. During the day he saw only his jailer – a skinny man, with lines of bitterness carved into his face. He brought Sam a herring, minus any bread. Sam still had a piece of dry crust, and he started to eat the fish; it wasn't fresh and was terribly salty. He made gestures to try and make the jailer understand he was thirsty, but the man merely shrugged his shoulders. In the evening his replacement arrived and noticed the half-eaten herring.

"You'll soon be happy with such a meal," he sneered. "You spoiled brat."

Sam did not want to imagine that this present situation might become an enduring reality. His thirst had become excruciating, and his throat was burning. In the middle of the night he was taken for another interrogation. This time it was easier. The session was led by a small fat man with a moustache who spoke Yiddish. He even offered Sam a cigarette which the boy refused – he didn't smoke. The interrogation took three hours:

"Where are you from?"; "How many brothers and sisters do you have?"; "What do your parents do?"; "Are you a communist?"; "Do you sympathize with communism?"; "Why are you in Russia?"

Sam insisted forcefully, "I've come because I want to study art and music. I've heard that all lessons are free here, and there are excellent teachers."

He found it hard to understand that another Jew would believe him to be a spy. Finally they gave him something to drink. The coffee was disgusting, but it didn't matter – he cared only that he could slake his thirst. He was put back in his cell and fell asleep, deadly tired. Three-quarters of an hour later he was woken, and the same procedure started again. Sam was so weary he could hardly speak.

"Who did you work for?"

Sam gave the names and addresses of his employers.

"Well, well, we found a card from Maccabee ... so you were part of a Jewish organization. Hmmm."

Finally he was allowed back in his cell. They had taken all his money – for which he had worked so hard for a whole year – as well as his imitation gold watch and wet tefillin. Inside this they discovered the parchment with the Hebrew script, and were convinced they had discovered secret documents. If he hadn't been so undone by events, Sam would have laughed at the absurdity of it. Next morning, he got cold tea with a small lump of sugar and a piece of dry bread. It was freezing.

All day he was left alone, but at night the cross-examinations were repeated; this time his interrogators came armed with an official statement. A thin man with an eagle's beak of a nose spread the document before him and told him to sign it.

"How can I sign it?" he asked. "I don't know what's written in it!"

Eagle-Beak became furious. "You'll do as you're told! Sign wherever you see it's crossed."

Sam signed. He was so exhausted that he was past caring, and thought that if he did so they would cease interrogating him. He was wrong. Three hours later he had to answer the same questions all over again.

The situation went on for four weeks.

---

1. Cited by Zamoyski, (2009) *Poland: A History*, London: William Collins, p 296.
2. From Lukowski, J., & Zawadzki, H., (2019) Independence Regained and Lost, 1914–1945. In *A Concise History of Poland* (Cambridge Concise Histories), Cambridge: Cambridge University Press, pp 279-359.
3. From "The War with Poland: Death to the Polish Bourgeoisie." *The Military Writings of Leon Trotsky*, Vol 3 (1920).

11

SKETCHING IN SOLITARY

Sam felt that he had become an automaton. He hardly heard either the questions or the answers he gave to them. He wasn't beaten, but he was physically and mentally at the end of his tether. The lack of sleep was a continual torture, and he felt terribly lonely in his cell.

After a month had passed, some soldiers entered his room and put a hood over his head. He thought they might let him go, but instead he was taken to a nearby prison. Compared to his previous place of incarceration, it seemed like a palace. There was a bed and a chair, and on the floor of the cell reposed a bucket. Every day he was given some water to wash himself, which he would pour out in the bucket, and then empty in the bathroom in the little courtyard opposite his cell. The door of the courtyard had to remain open, however, and he found this humiliating. There was a guard looking at him day and night through the small, barred window.

But the food was better and there were no further interrogations. One day a guard he had not seen before came to cut his hair – very short – and in the end decided to shave him as well; this fellow was much more good-humored than any of the other soldiers Sam had encountered. *Are barbers just naturally happier people*, he wondered, with a touch of his old insouciance. There was no such thing as a mirror of course, but he felt less unkempt – the destruction of his sense of humanity in the cell had been insidious. But the isolation and loneliness became more intolerable for the 17-year-old than anything else. He asked the soldier who brought him the food, "Could I please get some books?"

"In which language? Yiddish or Polish?"

He was given some books in Polish. One was about the 19th-century revolutionary Russian poet Aleksey Pleshcheyev. He had been arrested along with the writer Dostoyevsky, given a death sentence, and taken to Semyonovksy Square in St. Petersburg to face a firing squad. At the last minute the prisoners were given a reprieve by Emperor Nicholas I; the scene was later recalled by Dostoyevsky in his novel *The Idiot*. Pleshcheyev's death penalty was commuted to a sentence of hard labor in Siberia, where he spent ten years in exile. Sam learned his poems, translated into Polish, by heart:

> *Mayst thou not lose in the hard struggle with evil,*
>
> *All of which at present thy soul is so full;*
>
> *And the life-giving lamp of faith and love*
>
> *May the wave of life not extinguish in thee.*[1]

The title of each of the poems appeared in majuscule letters in Russian, beneath which was the translation into Polish. To pass the time, Sam copied the letters and started to decipher the Russian alphabet. He was exceedingly pleased with himself when he succeeded in writing his name in this new language, and from then on used the piece of paper with his name in Russian as a bookmark. But the guard found the piece of paper, pounced on it like a tiger, and his face glowed with satisfaction.

"Aha! You claimed all this time to be innocent, didn't you? You pretended not to know Russian."

"It was just a game," protested Sam. "I was bored."

But the guard went out triumphantly holding the piece of paper in his hand, like a guerdon of war. Surveillance became tighter; Sam was now a suspect. Days passed, each a dreary repetition of the one that had gone before. The young man felt consigned to some infernal region where a vista of endless loneliness yawned drearily before him. He asked the guard, "Could I please get some drawing paper?"

They gave him dirty scrap paper and he drew for hours. The faces of his mother and father – how he longed for them! Scenes of his native town and the deep green woods near his home where the wind sang in the pines. Krakow and its celestially blue river, and the mysterious man who had seemed like a prophet and had predicted fame – a man who would reappear in many of his later art works.

But Sam's jailers would not allow him to keep his drawings, and he felt he was being robbed. These were his first expressionist drawings, and each stroke was alive with passionate feeling, but he didn't say anything. He knew that without the scrap paper and pencils he might lose his mind.

Eleven weeks passed. They never changed his linen, and every day he asked the guard bringing him his food the same question: "Please, when can I take a bath?"

He never received an answer. One day, he had had enough. Angrily he announced, "If I can't take a bath I'm starting a hunger strike."

The guard looked at him in amazement. Hunger strikes were strictly forbidden in Russian prisons, but Sam started to leave his food untouched. After three days an officer entered his cell.

"If you won't eat, we'll force you to. Tell me the truth – do you do this only to get a bath?"

"Yes."

The officer regarded him with wonder and a hint of respect. "Okay," he said. "You'll be permitted to take a bath."

Sam agreed that he would eat again. An armed soldier put the customary hood over his face; they crossed the courtyard and he was taken to a dark room boasting a bath which looked reasonably clean. Sam submerged himself in the warm waters, which seemed to caress rather than lave his whole weary body. This was definitely the best moment he had spent in Russia. But the pleasure was short-lived and after ten minutes he was forced by a brisk command to get out. Before he could put on his clothes he was checked thoroughly. The hood was put back on and he was returned to his cell. From this point on, for the next two months, a guard would examine his cell every night.

They let him know that his file had been sent to Moscow. As he waited, his loneliness became even more acute; he felt that he was completely cut off from life, nature, beauty, humanity. Even in the courtyard he saw no one.

One night he was woken up and informed curtly, "You have to go back to Poland."

"Please, Officer," he entreated. "Let me stay here. I've gone through all this to follow my dreams. You know now that is the truth; you know I'm not a spy. There is no reason to send me back to Poland."

His supplications were to no avail. His clothes were returned, but not his money, nor his watch.

"Please give me back my drawings," he requested, but again he was ignored, and didn't dare insist. He was broken-hearted to lose them, for into them he had poured his soul, his pain, his yearnings. But there was a flash of pride that the sketches were considered good enough to be stolen.

Sam got dressed; this time the hood wasn't used. He walked outside and looked back at the tall building, where a dim glow showed through narrow windows; it looked surreal. The soldiers stared with astonishment at the high boots Sam was wearing; in Russia only the nobility had that kind of footwear. The night was dark and cold, and he was pushed into a military car. His new-found liberty didn't bring him any joy; in this corner of Russia he had known only pain and disillusionment. He wondered in a disinterested way where they were going; it was as if he was a distant spectator of the scene.

The car stopped at the river, the same place where he had entered Russia all those weary months before.

"This is where you have to cross," was the abrupt announcement.

Sam got out of the car and it drove off. He was left standing alone on the bank of the river.

---

1. B. A. Rudzinsky (1917) *Selections from Russian Poetry*, Edited with Biographical Sketches, English Translations and Notes. London: Robert Cunningham. Digitized from the Library of the University of California, Riverside. According to Rudzinsky, the poems of Pleshcheyev "bear the imprint of melancholy, disappointment, and renunciation, but they are also filled with the aspirations of his youth. He was the most cultivated and the most sympathetic poet of his time" (p 78).

12

AN ABYSS

It was the month of March and it was freezing. As Sam stood on the bank, with the noise of the rushing waters dinning in his ears, it was not so much the thought of the crossing that made him feel so miserable, but rather the sense of betrayal. He waded into the ice-cold water. The river seemed even deeper than the first time he had braved it, and he arrived on the other side covered with mud and shivering. The long months in the Russian jail had undermined his health.

But he was back in Poland! And there, shining out of the darkness like a star, he beheld a light, beckoning him. He made his way toward it and saw it was coming from a windmill, one of those structures so commonplace in Poland which also served as a dwelling. He knocked hard upon the thick wooden door at the entrance, hoping he would find a sturdy Polish farmer, someone who would offer warmth and hospitality despite the lateness of the hour. He heard footsteps, then the sound of bolts being drawn back, and the door opened, but there was no welcome in the face of the man who stood before him. Sam could hear his wife calling in the background, "Don't let anyone in!"

Sam's wet clothes and the mud which filled his boots made it obvious that he had just crossed the river, and the fellow exclaimed as he noticed these things, "Come lad, I'm taking you to a warm place where you can rest and get dry."

Sam followed the man without fear; the knowledge that he was in his homeland filled him with a sense of overwhelming relief. In his imagination he pictured the place to which he was being taken: a cozy house with a blazing stove and a motherly landlady. But there before them, through the darkness, loomed a square-set building, and as he caught sight of it Sam knew exactly what it was. With its gray walls and squat design, it was clearly not built for any aesthetic purpose, but for one reason only: incarceration. The thought of trying to escape crossed his mind, but it was fleeting. He told himself that they would soon see his papers and all would be well.

The peasant knocked at the door for a long time until the heavy door was opened. "For God's sake," shouted the guard. "What's happening?"

Sam's latest betrayer gestured toward him, presented a voluble explanation, and departed. The young man was taken to a large room furnished only with a rickety table and four chairs; an ancient print of Krakow, yellow with age, hung askew upon the wall. What happened next profoundly shocked him.

The commander – or perhaps it was a junior officer – came near to him and hit him in the face. Blood immediately filled his mouth.

"Dirty Jew ... filthy communist spy!" spat the man. "We'll teach you a lesson. Come on, give me your papers."

Sam fumbled in his case; his hands shook as he drew out his documents. He felt that he was close to fainting. After examining the papers, the officer began to write a report; he waved Sam away into the hands of some guards, and he was dragged into a basement. Here there was only a wooden board without a blanket and it was bitterly cold. With his last strength Sam wrung out his pants and started moving to get a little bit of warmth. That was how he passed the night, continuously chafing his limbs to keep the circulation going. At dawn two rough-looking guards came in. He quickly pulled on his still-wet pants.

"Am I free to go?" he asked.

"What are you complaining about? You're getting free food and lodging."

They laughed uproariously, then pushed him outside and bundled him into a car. Sam closed his eyes. His cheek hurt, a burning sensation enveloped him, and he felt light-headed. The car eventually stopped at a small house outside the city.

"Where am I?" he asked.

"A five-star hotel." They laughed again.

It was the headquarters of the secret police. Sam was taken into a room, decently furnished, where three men were sitting behind a long wooden table. A middle-aged man who seemed to be the one in charge began the interrogation.

"Where do you come from? Why are you here?"

"I'm from Poland. I went to Russia because I wanted to study there."

From nowhere, out of left field and beyond his line of vision, the punch came, and pain exploded in his jaw.

"Who sent you from Russia to spy on us?"

The questions came relentlessly and with every answer Sam gave they continued to punch him. He was in despair: how could he make them understand that he was telling the truth?

"You wait, you dirty Jew. We know how to make you talk," they threatened, and this time he was punched so hard that he fainted.

When he regained consciousness he saw that he was in a basement faintly lit by a lamp; his feet were loosely chained together. In a corner of the room he saw a bald muscular man who had a boxer's nose and blank eyes bulging from their sockets. As Sam gazed

74

around his new surroundings a wave of unspeakable dread washed through him. Hanging on the wall was a variety of grotesque implements; they were clearly instruments of torture.

Sam closed his eyes. *Hopefully I'll faint again and won't see these horrors*, he thought to himself, and felt the bile rising in his gorge. The bald man pointed to a bucket, but Sam couldn't make it on time and vomited copiously on the floor. He asked for a rag to clean the mess, fearing he would be beaten. But the jailer seemed to think it was amusing and handed Sam some old cloths and a bucket of water.

At this moment, a good-looking, tanned young man, clearly an officer, entered the room. He cast a brief look at Sam, then rapped out a command. "Get started," he said.

The bald man started to laugh, displaying a row of golden teeth. He grasped Sam with an iron grip and made him lie down on the floor. He took off the boy's chains, and put new ones on his ankles and wrists, tying him down with metallic rings attached to an electrical device.

The officer spoke to him soothingly. "Just tell the truth and nothing will happen to you."

"I went to Russia because I wanted to study art, but they sent me back to Poland. I'm not a spy."

"Go ahead," said the officer to the waiting man. "Don't overdo it."

With alacrity the brute grasped and turned a wheel, and exquisitely painful electric shocks pierced through Sam's body. The pain was unbearable. "I haven't done anything," he mumbled desperately.

"Faster," commanded the officer.

The pain became even more intense. "Well, you bandit, why have you come to Poland?"

Almost inaudibly, Sam whispered, "I've told you the truth. I'm not a spy."

"Faster."

Sam's throat began to emit shrill cries; he felt as if he was being was torn apart. His eyes bulged. "Stop," he screamed. "Please, just kill me. Let me die now – just stop."

The tempo was diminished.

"Once more," ordered the officer.

God, please let me die, Sam prayed. The pain was excruciating. Didn't they have enough proof? Didn't they now realize he was innocent?

Finally the agony came to an end. Two soldiers dragged him into a room where a fire had been lit and put him on a bed. Did he stay there minutes or hours? He didn't know. He was floating in and out of consciousness.

When Sam came to himself, the pain was gone. He got up and took his pants, which were still wet, and put them next to the fire. He lay down again and heard music. It was probably the soldiers, singing Ukrainian songs to the accompaniment of a guitar. Their voices were melodious and Sam closed his eyes. He didn't feel alone any more; the music gave him a sense of peace. He slumbered and dreamed of the Vistula River. The weather was fair; the little waves sparkled in the sunlight as he strolled along its banks, and a light breeze played through his hair. He saw the man who had spoken to him, "the prophet," hovering in the air and descending slowly. He smiled and repeated his words to Sam: "You will become a great man. You will achieve fame."

Startled by a sudden noise, Sam woke up. A soldier shoved food inside – it was a complete meal, the first he had had in months. Would they liberate him? He was filled with hope. A small skinny man entered the room and asked Sam questions in a monotone. He wrote a report, then beckoned to the young man. "Come," he said.

Sam's optimism soon evaporated. Instead of the large, comparatively warm room, where he had been lost in reverie, he was locked in a tiny cell, where the bed took up almost all the space. Every day thereafter he was transferred to a different room, and the same skinny creature would ask the same monotonous questions: "Are you a spy?" "Why did you come to Poland from Russia?"

As incredible as it may sound, the interrogations took him out of his numbness; they provided a diversion. The loneliness seemed a different form of torture, and his body continued to ache. After eight days some soldiers came for him and put him in a military vehicle.

"Where are you taking me?" he asked.

"To the Tarnopol Prison."

"What's it like there?"

They didn't bother to answer such a stupid question.

13

TARNOPOL

The city of Tarnopol had a checkered history which might serve as a microcosm of the fluctuating fortunes of Poland itself during the early-20th century. Originally founded in the 16th century by a Polish commander as a military stronghold, it had come under Austrian rule during the Partition era, but in the early days of the First World War was seized by the Russians, and thereafter changed hands a number of times. Eventually, by the terms of the Riga treaty, the Soviets and Poles partitioned the Ukraine between them, and for the next 19 years the ethnically mixed Tarnopol region remained under Polish control.

The city was to remain at the epicenter of shattering events which took place in Eastern Europe in the years prior to the Second World War, when the Soviet Union forced farmers in the Ukrainian territories lying just east of the city to give up their land in a process of collectivization. It was a program which proved ruinous: the Ukrainian farmers were left with nothing to eat, all their food either remaining unharvested or being transported to other parts of the Soviet Union. During the Second Ukrainian Famine of 1932–33 some three million perished, and a new word was coined to describe the anguish endured by the people: *Holodomor*, a combination of the

Ukrainian words for hunger (*holod*) and extermination (*mor*). The period coincided with Hitler's rise to power in Germany, which helped to conceal the extent of the disaster.[1]

As Sam traveled with his captors they passed through green fields, and he gazed with longing at the peaceful old farms and villages which lay dreaming in the sunlight. He thought of his parents and brothers, and the joy he would feel if he could only find himself sitting at the family table sharing a meal with them. The car stopped; they had arrived. Sam was used to the sinister appearance of jails by now and Tarnopol Prison was no exception, with a heavy iron door, high walls, and small barred apertures.

He was taken to a room which differed from others he had encountered during his periods of incarceration. The furniture was modern, and lamps with reflectors were scattered about; two men were seated behind a desk with a typewriter on it. One of the men was clearly in charge; the other had a repellent appearance, with small-veined eyes, soft wide ears and a large, turned-up nose. But Sam's instinctive revulsion was overtaken by a more powerful emotion: dread. The thought sprang into his mind: *Is this my fate? To live in never-ending fear?*

The reflectors were switched on, and a harsh light was directed onto him while the rest of the room remained in shadow. The interrogation began, and Sam broke out in a cold sweat which covered his entire body.

"You're a Russian spy," asserted the commanding officer. "You've come here to resume your work!" He continued with a string of forceful allegations.

Every time Sam answered "No," the pig-like man would hit him with a club. Blood commenced flowing from his nose and mouth.

"Sign this paper and it all will be over!"

Somehow, whether through stoicism, stubbornness, or with a sheer brazen courage born in the midst of the circumstances, Sam refused to sign. Later he discovered how fortunate this was. The treatment continued for half an hour, until he was about to faint. The projector was shut down, but the session had not come to an end.

"Take off your pants," he was ordered.

For Sam this was terribly degrading, but he obeyed. Now the heavy club was landing on different parts of his body, with all the force of the pig-man behind it. The pain was excruciating. Sam noticed that, while he was enduring this punishment, the officer was eating chocolate.

Finally the torture ceased and Sam was taken by two soldiers to the cellar. For two days in a row the scene was repeated, and his battered body became unrecognizable, his flesh covered with running sores.

There were many other prisoners in the cellar, but they all kept to themselves. The highlight of each day came as they were permitted to go for a few minutes to a room with wash basins and running water; this was also the place where interaction with other inmates could take place. As Sam stood one day sluicing his weeping sores at the basin, a Russian man with an impressive red beard drew near him. "When you get out of here, inform the Russian Embassy," he whispered. "My name is Kirilenko."

Sam didn't answer. *He too thinks I am a spy*, he thought.

After another week he was taken to a hall lined with wooden benches; it looked like some sort of courtroom, and he wondered if he would now hear a decision on his case. A man with an aloof manner – Sam presumed he was the judge – pronounced his verdict.

"You have been condemned to three months' imprisonment for having illegally crossed the border," he intoned.

Sam closed his eyes and a wave of relief washed through him: he would live! If he had been convicted for espionage it would have meant the death penalty.

He was taken outside, shoved into a car, and driven to another jail. Here they walked him through long echoing corridors, and finally pushed him into a cell with many beds lined up next to one another. There were 20 prisoners incarcerated there and it was very clean. Sam swiftly learned about the chain of command that existed in the cell, and the correct protocol. An elderly man approached him and whispered to him about the prisoner-in-charge, who, he alleged, was a forger. "Be careful," he warned. "He's a sneak."

Every morning, the prisoners had to tidy and clean the cell; the beds were moved from one place to the other so that the red-painted floor could be scrubbed until it shone. There was no toilet, but in a corner a sort of barrel with a cover. Nonetheless, life was now bearable; after what Sam had been through it seemed almost pleasant. He was not lonely and his life was not in danger. Every day they had some moments in an open courtyard. Someone taught him how to play chess; the pawns were made out of chewed black and white bread. Sam was a lousy chess player, but his pawns were beautiful.

After eight days, he was transferred to a less pleasant cell. There were 15 inmates and it wasn't clean; the only resemblance was the stinking barrel. The prisoners had to peel potatoes which were mostly rotten, and the food was disgusting.

A day came when he was summoned to the Superintendent's office. With a fast-beating heart he entered a luxuriously furnished room. A gentleman of middle years with a cultured voice spoke to him.

"The police have made an investigation regarding your case in Zawiercie – your native town. Do you wish to add any information? Were you a member of an organization?"

"Yes," Sam replied. "I was a member of Mizrachi, a religious Zionist organization."

"That will be all for today," he was informed. "We have notified your parents of your whereabouts."

The three months passed and the date for Sam's release drew near, but the other prisoners gave him warnings about life "on the outside" which filled him with trepidation. If you had no funds, they told him, you were treated like a tramp and could be re-arrested. Sam had no money and no idea how he would be able to reach his home.

One day a guard collected him and took him back through the long corridors into a room furnished with an old leather couch, where some dusty plastic flowers drooping in a vase provided a sad attempt at adornment. But Sam scarcely noticed these things. In a corner someone was standing. It was Israel!

Sam's heart filled with gladness. "Father, oh Father," he mumbled.

Israel had been intending to speak sternly to his son, but when he saw him standing there, barely recognizable, just skin and bones, his heart overflowed with pity. This was his child, whom suffering had turned into a man.

His first words were, "You really deserve a spanking."

But then he hugged his son close to him. "My God," he continued, "what have they done to you? What have they done?" Still clasping Sam to his breast, he murmured, "I'm so happy to see you."

Sam also was happy; he put his hand in his father's. His eyes welled up with tears, and for the first time in his life he wept for joy. He was grateful to Israel, who had undertaken the long trip across the land to fetch his son, though he knew hardly any Polish. Sam was suffused with admiration for his courage.

They took the train to Zawiercie; it was spring and the weather was gorgeous. As he gazed at the woods and fields they passed, Sam experienced a hitherto unknown rapture – that of newly regained freedom.

---

1. At Tarnopol Prison Sam was to experience a little of what his countrymen and fellow religionists would suffer in that unfortunate region only a few years later. In the 20th century, the territories of Poland, Belarus, and the Ukraine became

the setting for a series of atrocious events which combined genocides, ethnic purges and wars, and eventually climaxed in the Holocaust. During little more than a decade, between 1932 and the end of the First World War, some 14 million people living in this area lost their lives. Caught between two rival totalitarian regimes, people (mostly civilians) were murdered in Stalinist purges – from Holodomor (1932–1935), through Stalin's Polish operation (1937), and the massive extermination of Belarusian and Polish intelligentsia (Katyń, 1940). These harrowing events were followed by the ravages of the world war, making it one of the most tragic periods in history. (See the 2010 account by American historian Timothy Snyder, *Bloodlands: Europe Between Hitler and Stalin*).

14

BACK TO KRAKOW

Finally, Sam was home. His mother pampered him like a newborn babe and he found the food even more delicious than he remembered. He also found himself something of a celebrity. Rumors of the dramatic events in which he had been caught up filtered through the small community like wildfire, and everybody was eager to press questions on him. But Sam would always answer repressively, "There is not much to tell."

Leftist sympathizers were the most curious of all. Nothing could shake their firm belief in the superiority of the socialist ideology, and they yearned to know more about life over the border. Sam would smile, shake his head and say, "About Russia, I know only prisons." He was afraid to divulge anything more and perhaps find himself in trouble.

Under the ministrations of his mother, Sam recovered from his wounds and regained his health. He was growing taller and reached his full height, developed a powerful breadth of chest and a strong physique. His eyes remained his best feature; they were dark and intense, and his voice had a singular depth and resonance. Although possessing a natural reserve, his intelligence combined with his gentleness of manner and courtesy gave him a charisma that quickly attracted others.

The searing experiences through which Sam had passed thrust him early into maturity. He had caught a glimpse of an abyss in human nature, and had come to understand that a limitless and unfathomable evil might manifest itself within the circumscribed sphere of the individual psyche. He could not yet say, "I will fear no evil."[1] But the events that had transpired in his life had given rise to a concomitant determination that he, in the timespan allotted to him, would continue to pursue the beautiful, true and good, as the highest goal of human endeavor.

Once again Sam was growing restless, and knew he would not stay long in Zawiercie. His father was aware of his son's plans for departure, but didn't protest. Instead, he said, "Shmiel Szija, I want to have a suit made for you. Let's go to the tailor."

Sam was duly measured and fitted; when completed, the garment was of a quality, material and cut which surpassed anything he had worn before. He put it on, and his father looked at his handsome, dignified son with pride, but then tears rushed to his eyes. Sam remembered the moment long afterwards. Did his father have an inkling, he wondered, that after his child left he would never see him again?

Sam had decided he would return to Krakow to look for work, and once again set out on the journey to the capital, this time without any misadventures. He discovered that his former employer was unable to provide him with a position, but he did recommend Sam to another furrier, who agreed to take him on.

By now it was 1936. The decades since the First World War had been a time of great upheaval in European society generally, with the emergence of racist and fascist ideologies, frequent riots and constitutional crises. In Poland, the democracy had endured, but not without the challenges that came as the result of the ethnically mixed population. A significant proportion of the peoples in the land were of Belarusian, Ukrainian, Jewish, or German backgrounds, and while the Paris Peace Conference of 1919 had required Poland to sign a pledge guaranteeing minority rights, this demand was somewhat resented by the Poles. They could point with pride to the nation's long history of toleration, and yet the antisemitism in Poland did increase throughout the years leading up to the Second World War.

In the 1930s there were over three million Jews in Poland, representing ten percent of the population, the largest Jewish community in Europe. Many had assimilated into Polish society, but the majority were somewhat conspicuous. The religious Jews wore black gabardines, had sidelocks and beards, spoke Yiddish rather than Polish and made their living by trade instead of agriculture. The Jews also represented a disproportionate presence in professions such as law and medicine, thus incurring a measure of envy. And while many supported Polish aspirations and had fought in Pilsudski's Legions, many others embraced socialist ideology, making it difficult for the Catholic hierarchy to distinguish between Jews and Bolsheviks.

So, although relations between Poles and Jews varied enormously, there was a deeply ingrained antisemitism in some areas of Polish society. Beginning in the 1930s, limits were placed on Jewish enrollment in universities, ownership of Jewish shops and businesses, and admission to the medical and legal professions. Following the death of Piłsudski in 1935, members of the far-right Endjeca increased their efforts to remove Jews from all spheres of social, economic and cultural life in Poland. They organized anti-Jewish boycotts, and provoked violence which in some cases led to pogroms in smaller towns.

As the Great Depression worsened in the 1930s, the fortunes of many Jewish families fluctuated dramatically, forcing them to rely on local charities or Jewish agencies in the United States. Polish representatives in the League of Nations urgently pressed for the lifting of restrictions on immigration into Palestine and the West. Meanwhile, in Germany, Hitler was building up his military resources. Poland's long yearned-for independence had been under threat since it was attained in 1918, and the same powers that had helped restore Poland to the map of Europe seemed reluctant to commit themselves to her survival. The specter of another war was looming, and it was evident that Poland did not stand a chance on her own.

This time, Sam could hear the approaching thunder, and came to the decision that he would leave Poland. It might have been thought that the traumatic events of the past winter would have crushed his spirit, but no! He was still aflame with the desire to study art and fulfill his creative dreams. Once again, though, he was faced with his old nemesis: money. The low season had brought a halt to the fur trade, but friends suggested that he should look for work at the Jewish hospital where they were looking for a doorman. The administrator, an older man, told Sam that he was accepted for the position.

"Well, my lad," he said, "you'll get food and lodgings. You can sleep in the shed in the garden. You won't get an actual salary, but you'll get pocket money."

Unemployment had risen in Poland, and Sam knew that many envied him his good fortune. All he could do would be to try and save some of his pocket money for the journey he was planning. But he would never forget his introduction to life as a hospital employee. During his first days there he had to accompany the coroner to the morgue for the examination of a new-born baby; it was the first time in his life he had been confronted with death. He was profoundly shocked by the sight of the tiny form lying still and waxen on the cold gray steel of the table, feeling a pang of sorrow for this little one who hadn't been granted the gift of life.

Still, Sam's interaction with the other members of the hospital staff was pleasant enough. He worked from 8 o'clock in the morning to eight in the evening, and his superior during these hours was the chief doorman. He was a huge fellow who thought he was king, relished the authority his position gave him, and didn't let anyone in after official hours unless they bribed him. Most of the personnel were Jewish, although there were some Christian surgeons, and people came from all over Poland because the medical services were so highly reputed. Sam's job also involved answering the phone, but whenever it rang he felt nervous, aware of his inexperience. Most of all, he was conscious of being drawn into a hitherto unknown realm: confronted by the countless dramas, tragedies and agonies played out every day in the rooms and corridors of a hospital.

Sam shared the garden shed with a nice young fellow from the country, who was in charge of heating in the hospital, and secretly enamored with one of the nurses. He didn't dare to tell her of his feelings, and in the evenings would pour out his expressions of lovelorn longing. Sam listened sympathetically, but also on other occasions managed to escape the hospital grounds, together with his old friend Jozef, who also worked at the hospital. The garden where he stayed was surrounded by a high wall – a sight Sam hated, because it reminded him of prison. At 10 o'clock, when the hospital closed its doors, Sam and Jozef would climb over the wall using a ladder, like thieves. They visited friends and went to concerts; it was all like a game to them. Returning to the hospital was more complicated because they had to clamber up a tall tree before scaling the wall. But Sam loved to breathe an air that seemed free, far from the patients and their woes.

Sam was still uncertain as to which country he should travel to study art. One day, however, as he sat in the small cafeteria at the hospital, his eye fell upon a brochure lying on the middle of the table. He picked it up idly and turned it over, then gazed in surprise at what he saw. The brochure was featuring the Royal Academy of Art of Antwerp in Belgium, which it described as one of the most distinguished centers of learning in Europe.

Sam read further, his attention totally absorbed. The Academy, he learned, had been founded in 1663 after Dutch artist David Teniers the Younger had been granted a charter by Philip IV of Spain, then sovereign of the Netherlands. Since that time, it had attracted students from all over Europe – from Ireland to Poland – and provided a solid classical training to the young aspiring artists who entered its hallowed doors. The incomparable Vincent van Gogh had also studied there prior to his departure for France.

Sam's heart seemed to glow as he read. He had no idea how the brochure came to be there, but it seemed to be more than fortuitous. He lay the pages down and closed his eyes. A picture rose before his mind – a low-lying country set on the edge of the gray North Sea. A center of European culture, rich in learning, with a cosmopolitan history, a confluence of trade, ideas, great events. And, most of all, conspicuous for its art.

He remembered that, from the late Middle Ages until the 18th century, the Low Countries, comprising modern day Belgium and Holland, were a leading force in the art of northern Europe; indeed, it was one of the most profoundly important periods in the whole of Western art history. The illustrious figures who had lived and worked in the Netherlands during this epoch had produced countless masterpieces, across every category of painting. Sam was familiar with the works of the Dutch and Flemish masters, but now he wondered: *what was it that had prompted their vast outpouring of creativity?* The area seemed to be beckoning him, and he decided he would spend some time researching its history and influence.

One Saturday afternoon he had some hours free, and decided to make his way to the Jagiellonian Library on Mickiewicz Avenue, Krakow's academic library and the oldest in Poland. He entered the doors, found his way to the art section and gathered a collection of books. These he spread out on a table in the reading room, under the light which poured through windows in the high ceiling and made rainbow ribbons on the texts. He was soon immersed in his reading, trusting that, as he did so, the paintings themselves would speak to his heart and provide him with the direction he so earnestly desired.

---

1. Psalm 23:4b. *Fear No Evil* is the title of the 1988 biography by Soviet-Israeli activist and politician Natan (Anatoly) Sharansky, detailing his struggle to emigrate to Israel from the former Soviet Union.

15

THE DUTCH AND FLEMISH MASTERS

The lands that lie along the coast of the North Sea were, long ago, on the frontier of the Roman Empire, and eventually became part of a Frankish empire ruled by the dukes of Burgundy. They were great patrons of the arts, and in the early-15th century presided over a period of prosperity which led to flourishing cities and artistic innovation. Formerly, artworks such as illuminated manuscripts, stained glass and tapestries had occupied the creative energies of artists, but at this point a new form emerged: panel painting. Founded by Jan van Eyck and others, it was noted for its observation of detail and enamel-like surface achieved by built-up layers of oil paint.

Toward the end of the 15th century, the Italian Renaissance increasingly came to influence the culture of the Low Countries. The classical ruins of Rome attracted painters and sculptors from the region and when, in the early-16th century, Raphael and Michelangelo completed their famous frescos in the Vatican, these and works of other masters such as Caravaggio and Titian provided further inspiration. The ideals of humanism were gaining traction in the large centers of northern Europe, while the spread of printing promoted cultural literacy. Under these influences Antwerp became a cultivated and cosmopolitan city; as the leading port in Europe during this period, its economic importance also led to cultural and artistic dominance.

Meanwhile, the region was caught up in the religious ferment that had gripped the whole of Europe since Martin Luther had nailed his Ninety-One Theses to the door of the church at Wittenberg in 1517. Luther's ideas took hold early in the Low Countries, despite the fact that during the 16th century the Netherlands had come under the rule of Philip II, the Catholic monarch of Spain. Many thousands of his subjects fled to England and Germany, and the prince of Orange, William of Nassau, called for freedom of religious belief before declaring war against Spain. This long-drawn-out battle, the Eighty Years War (1568–1648), eventually brought independence to the northern Netherlands, but Belgica Regia and Flanders remained loyal to the Spanish king. Both regions would continue to nurture some of the greatest artists of the 17th century, but the religious differences between north and south meant that the art they produced was markedly different.

As part of the Counter Reformation, the Roman Catholic Church decided that the arts should serve to communicate religious themes by making an overt emotional and sensory appeal. Meanwhile, the broadening of intellectual horizons, spurred by developments in science and exploration of the globe, encouraged a more naturalistic treatment of sacred images. The Baroque art that evolved from this fusion of ideas was primarily intended to evoke emotion and passion, rather than appeal to the calm rationality prized during the classical era. To this end, the Baroque artists often chose to portray the most dramatic moment of a biblical story, which would be set forth on a grand scale and embellished by rich color; while the use of chiaroscuro, the interplay of intense light and dark shadows, could also produce a highly charged scene.

It was very different in the north. The new Dutch Republic emerged at the end of the Eighty Years War, and swiftly began prospering as a result of the wealth gained from colonial ventures. It was a unique era of political and cultural greatness, during which the little nation on the edge of the North Sea ranked among the most powerful in the world. Dutch religious freedom was unprecedented in early modern Europe, and in the volatile religious climate the nation proved a haven for people of diverse faith attitudes, as *well as innovative thinkers. The extraordinary season of the Dutch Golden Age was commencing, the age of Descartes, Spinoza, Locke – and, most especially, of art.*

The rising Dutch upper middle class of wealthy merchants delighted in decorating their homes with artworks, and, although religious paintings were forbidden in churches, a whole new range of subjects was realized through the Dutch creative genius. Genre painting – the depiction of everyday life in beautiful detail – was accomplished by artists such as Vermeer, and a more realistic Dutch landscape style developed, as seen in the work of painters such as Ruysdael. The sea was a favored topic as well since the Low Countries depended on it for trade and exploration, and the region itself was a lattice of rivers and canals. In the absence of religious images, the Dutch still life masterpieces nevertheless often conveyed a salutary moral: "memento mori."[1]

Sam looked up from his reading, which had evoked for him all the color and gorgeousness of the world of art in which he longed to immerse himself. It struck him that this was perhaps the creative gift par excellence, recording the ongoing story of humankind in each age, with its different challenges and achievements, all the tragedies and triumphs of the human spirit. Two individual painters seemed to him to stand out in all this panoply, and to embody the two realms of the Netherlands; they were Rubens in Antwerp in the south, and Rembrandt van Rijn in the Dutch Republic. He reached for the books that contained lavish color reproductions of their works.

The Flemish painter Peter Paul Rubens was one of the best-known artists of the 17th century, and a foremost exponent of Baroque painting. As court painter in Antwerp to Archduke Albert and Archduchess Isabelle, regents of the Southern Netherlands, Rubens utilized religious and allegorical themes inspired by the great masters of Italy; he also painted landscapes, portraits and historical subjects in a unique style that made him a legend during his own lifetime. No other artist could equal him in the number and variety of the works he produced, and Rubens himself was able to truthfully aver: *"My talent is such that no enterprise, however vast in number and in diversity of subjects, has surpassed my courage."*[2]

Sam began leafing through the color plates depicting some of Rubens' best-known paintings. He found himself staggered by the artist's seemingly boundless imagination, the breadth of his subject matter, and the breathtaking confidence with which he selected each scene to garner the greatest emotional impact. These things, combined with masterful ease with which he handled the most challenging of compositions, the richness of color, and the sheer verve of the dramatic action were more than capable of sweeping away the viewer.

"My passion comes from the heavens, not from earthly musings."[3] Sam read the words of Rubens' declaration, and they seemed to reach out to him through the centuries. He knew that this hunger, this passion for artistic expression that resided in his heart, came not from himself.

He turned then to the art of Rembrandt, the greatest painter of the Dutch Golden Age. During the 17th century, Rembrandt had lived in Amsterdam, where he created astonishingly life-like portraits of the city's leading figures, and, of course, his own self-portraits. As the eyes of the Dutch master gazed out at the young man over the centuries, the years fell away – and here, Sam knew, was another mentor speaking to him. All Rembrandt's technical mastery, he reflected, was to this end: to unveil the depths of the human heart.

Sam knew of Rembrandt's close association and affinity with the Jews of Amsterdam. The painter had lived on Breestraat in the Vlooienburgh neighborhood, where dwelt members of the great Portuguese Sephardic community. They had begun settling in the Netherlands after 1600, fleeing persecution in Spain and Portugal. The painter's love for his Jewish friends, his understanding for their history, their tragedy, his admiration for their gifts, is evident throughout his work. And although there was no longer any demand in Dutch churches for Christian art, it was the scriptures of both Testaments which were the mainspring of his work.

Sam paused at Rembrandt's painting *Moses Holding the Tablets of the Law*, the depiction of the prophet descending Mount Sinai, holding aloft the two stone tablets with the Ten Commandments engraved in Hebrew. *How different was this picture*, mused Sam, to Michelangelo's famous statue. There, the Lawgiver was depicted as a man set apart, one towering over others, with a countenance stern and intimidating. Rembrandt's Moses could not be more different. His face was marked with gentleness and meekness; this was a man conscious of his closeness to other men, in anguish over the sin of the people he was shepherding. As Moses held the tablets of the law high to smash them, it was not in anger or indignation, but through suffering and empathy with Yahweh, the God he was coming to know.

Finally, Sam looked at Rembrandt's last great painting, completed shortly before his death, one which surpasses all other Baroque works in its evocation of religious truth – *The Return of the Prodigal Son*. It was based on Christ's parable in the Gospel of Luke, and shows the moment that the young man returns to the father he had earlier abandoned in pursuit of worldly goals and endeavors. Now, after long wanderings and many vicissitudes, he comes to his father's house, dressed in rags and with shaven head, while the cracked soles of his feet and his one broken shoe tell mutely the story of his travels and suffering. The prodigal is a picture of the most abject ruin and defeat as he falls at the feet of the richly dressed father who has come to meet him.

But his parent bends over him, his face illuminated with love and forgiveness. His hands rest with ineffable tenderness on the son's back, and the prodigal leans into his father's breast, where he finds such unexpected forgiveness and acceptance; meanwhile, the red wrap over the old man's shoulders forms a canopy above the pair. Emanating from the tableau is an eternal quality of stillness, of compassion, a sense of homecoming. The figures of father and son stand out in light against a dark background; only from out of the darkest depths, Rembrandt seems to suggest, emerges redemption.

Sam laid the book gently down on the table. Tears pricked at his eyes as he remembered how his own father, Israel, had come to meet him in the prison and take him home after the most harrowing experience of his young life, during which he had not known whether he would live or die. He felt that Rembrandt's picture was speaking to him; that perhaps also it was in this part of Europe he would experience another kind of homecoming, one in which his artist's soul would be recognized, welcomed and nurtured.

---

1. Latin for "Remember death." The phrase is traced to the spectacular Roman parades called "triumphs" which honored a victorious general. As the celebrated commander received the plaudits of the crowd, a servant would stand behind him to whisper in his ear: "Remember you are but a man, and you will die!" In the art genre of *vanitas*, symbolic objects such as human skulls, hourglasses and wilting flowers signified the brevity of human life and the fleeting nature of time.
2. Rooses, M. (2015) *Rubens, Volume 2*, Palala Press, p 350.
3. Quoted by Willard Spiegelman. "Finding Inspiration in the Flesh," *Wall Street Journal*, August 20, 2011.

16

PASSOVER 1937

Sam's mind was made up: to Antwerp he would go! He confided his plans to his friend Jenkel Englander, who told him, "My sister lives in Antwerp. I'll give you her address if you want."

"Of course."

"It's Zurenborgstreet Number 5."

"Thank you."

The fact that this was Sam's only contact in that faraway land did not deter him.

Now that he had made his decision, he was filled with an electric energy. He started to learn French, and once again began poring over maps to plot his journey to artistic freedom. This time, however, he would be traveling west, not east, and there was a formidable obstacle in his way – *Germany*. It lay in his path like an iron anvil, which he must somehow skate across before the hammer came crashing down. But he made his plans with a sublime insouciance. He remembered he had an aunt living in a town called Olesnica, close to Poland's border with Germany, and decided that from there it might be easier to slip into the territory of the Third Reich without being apprehended. Then he would make his way across the country until he reached the Netherlands.

The Jewish holiday of Passover came toward the end of March that year. Because of his commitments at the hospital, Sam was unable to travel to Zawiercie to be with his family, but he celebrated the holiday with a group of friends in Krakow. They gathered around the table, and the Seder began: *"Ma nishtana ... Why is this night different from all other nights?"* The Haggadah was recited, the ceremonial foods eaten, and as the company relaxed over the lengthy meal the conversation eventually moved to the burning topics of the day. But it was the ancient story of the bondage that the Children of Israel endured in Egypt, and their miraculous deliverance from Pharaoh and his armies, which formed the backdrop to the discussion around the table, and added a new dimension and poignancy.

The ritual of the Seder has been followed for almost two thousand years in an enormous variety of settings: throughout the Mediterranean world in Roman times, in Spain during the Golden Age of Sephardic Jewry, in the Ottoman Empire and the shtetls in Russia, in palaces, mansions, villas, and humble cottages throughout the diaspora. Each time the Haggadah is recited, the Passover story remembered, there is an almost mystic participation in past observances of the ritual, a sharing in the thoughts and feelings that must have occupied the minds of millions of Jews who have kept the feast in former generations, in infinitely varied circumstances.

How often had the Haggadah been recited when the Jews had been in great peril through one or another would-be dictator and oppressor! Sometimes the matza had been eaten in silence and with bitter tears, at other times with the joy of experienced deliverance, with songs on the lips. Yet where were the conquerors of the past? Assyria, Babylon, Rome – all had vanished; the eternal people yet remained. And so, reflected Sam, the Passover story was like a many-layered lapis lazuli; each year the retelling evokes some of the "magic, suspense, danger and wonder"[1] of that long-ago night – and each generation adds its own patina of beauty and meaning to the story through the drama of its own times.

The situation that confronted the Jewish faithful who were gathering around the table that night was no less dire than any experienced by previous generations: matters were critical, not just in Germany, but also in Palestine. After the Balfour Declaration of 1917, the goal of establishing a Jewish national home had become an internationally binding treaty through the San Remo Resolution of 1920. Britain was given the Mandate to facilitate Jewish immigration to Palestine, and since that time Jewish settlements had sprung up all over the land – on the coastal plains, in the Judean foothills, the Negev and the north – in the midst of places associated with a majestic biblical past. Their agricultural projects brought a remolding of Jewish cultural traditions: the people who had worked primarily in commerce and academia were now engaged in coaxing the land to produce the cornucopia promised in the Bible: "a land of milk and honey ... of wheat, barley, vines, fig trees and pomegranates and olive oil."[2]

The cultivation of the Hebrew language took place alongside the cultivation of the land, and a considerable Hebrew literature sprang up, from the masterly dictionary of Ben Yehuda to the daily newspapers. From the beginning, the Jewish settlement (Yishuv) in Palestine considered itself a political entity, creating governmental institutions based on the principles of Western democracy and establishing its own economy as well as social welfare programs. The members of this autonomous community demonstrated qualities such as national pride, resourcefulness and courage, and during the 1920s and early 1930s great numbers of new Jewish immigrants arrived, while the cities – Jerusalem, Haifa, Tel Aviv – grew apace.

After Hitler's accession to power in Germany in 1933, however, dark clouds developed on this bright horizon. Many German and Eastern European Jews were anxious to seek escape from a steadily worsening situation, but all the Western countries, including the US, Britain, and its dominions, closed their doors to significant Jewish immigration. That left the land of Palestine as the only potential safe haven for the Jewish people. In 1933, however, Palestine's Arabs, led by the Haj Amin al-Husseini, the Grand

Mufti of Jerusalem, mounted a campaign to pressure the British to bar all Jews from entering the country, which culminated in 1936 in a full-scale anti-British and anti-Zionist rebellion.

The violence unleashed, including murders, ambushes, plunder and arson, quickly spread throughout the country, and although the British sent thousands of troops into Palestine in an ineffectual attempt to quell the disorder, and the Zionists armed their own defense organizations, hundreds of Jewish lives were lost. As a result of the political chaos, the British sharply restricted Jewish immigration to Palestine.

In Poland, matters were deteriorating also. After Pilsudski died in 1935, responsibility for Jewish affairs was transferred from the Ministry of Internal Affairs to the Ministry of Foreign Affairs, suggesting that Jews were no longer citizens to be protected by the state. The National Democrats pushed their campaign of popular antisemitism and organized pogroms, while the new Camp of National Unity, OZON, announced its preference for the emigration of about ninety percent of Poland's Jews. Foreign Minister Beck proposed they be sent to Madagascar, even while calling on the British to ease immigration restrictions to Palestine. It was a betrayal of Poland's most vaunted traditions.

Sam watched the faces of his countrymen and women as they talked in the candlelight, their voices low and intense. Every countenance without exception was alive with intelligence, passionate and animated, but anxiety over the escalation of antisemitism in neighboring Germany, and also in Poland, was plainly to be read there. All present had in some way felt the metaphorical lash and sting of corrosive attitudes, and endured the small or larger insults and humiliations directed against them on a daily basis. Sam pondered *the riddle wrapped in a mystery inside an enigma* of this enmity toward his people and felt the injustice clutch at his heart. The talk ranged back and forth as options were weighed and discarded.

"Run the gauntlet of the British army ... join the Haganah ... hopeless to try to get an entry visa ... Madagascar – the thought is madness ... the loopholes are tightening everywhere ... powder keg ... Polish Jews in Kibbutz Sh'aar HaGolan ... Ben Gurion ...."

When and how their deliverance would come – that was unknown. But no one, on that cool spring evening in Krakow, could have foreseen the cataclysm about to burst over their heads. As the evening drew to a close the company regrouped for the closing songs and the traditional affirmation: *Shana haba'ah b'Yerushalayim* (Next year in Jerusalem)!

Many of those around the dinner table that night would never live to see Jerusalem.

---

1. Raphael, C. (1972) *A Feast of History: The Drama of Passover Through the Ages*, London: Weidenfeld & Nicholson.
2. From Deuteronomy 8:8.

17

A PERILOUS PLAN

Sam was pondering when it might be best to make his departure, and again the answer came in a seemingly fortuitous way. He had a rare day off from his work at the hospital and was visiting one of his favorite haunts, Wawel Castle.

A work by Jan Matejko, Poland's most famous painter, was on temporary loan to the Castle and Sam, together with Jozef, paused before it. Entitled *The Constitution of May 3, 1791*, it was a large and crowded canvas, filled with depictions of well-known figures from Polish history. But it was not the artistic merit which arrested Sam; it was rather the date, May 3, which seemed auspicious, and he decided that he would make his own bid for independence on that day. *Besides* (he thought practically) *there would be so much happening.* The Constitution Day holiday was only reinstituted after Poland regained its freedom in 1918, and marked with ceremonies, picnics and other festivities throughout Poland. It would be a good day to make an unobtrusive exit!

April was drawing to a close, and there was but one week to go before his scheduled departure when another event occurred on the international stage which appeared to threaten his plans and heighten the danger of travel across Europe.

Civil war had broken out in Spain in 1936, when Nationalist rebels under General Franco launched an uprising against the country's democratically elected Republic. Franco was unable to break the spirited resistance of the people in the mountainous Basque region of northern Spain, and called on Germany's aid. On April 26, 1937, the Luftwaffe's Condor Legion[1] dropped 30 tons of munitions on the Basque town of Guernica, killing hundreds of people and destroying most of its buildings. Guernica, according to horrified international observers, had no strategic value as a military target, but rather had served as the testing ground for a new Nazi military tactic – a strategy known as terror bombing.[2]

Sam tried to dismiss the volatile situation from his mind. The day fixed for his departure arrived, and he put his meager possessions in a cloth bag, went to the railway station and bought a ticket to Olesnica. The train traveled through Upper Silesia, and as it did so Sam's ears became attuned to a new accent. Silesia had formerly been under German rule and was only handed to Poland after the First World War; the inhabitants of the region were known as Wass Polacker (Water Poles). Their Polish had subtle differences and was sprinkled with German expressions. Sam felt he was being prepared for what lay ahead.

After four hours' travel, he reached Olesnica and disembarked; he passed through the marketplace where many people were dancing and reached his aunt's house. Although she was not wealthy, her home was open to all and he was grateful to be warmly received. Nevertheless, the thought of his prospective journey was weighing upon him, and as soon as he could he drew aside his cousin Eli. His plans for departure came tumbling out, as his cousin listened in wide-eyed sympathy. Sam was hoping that Eli might be able to give him guidance about entering Germany.

"Where would be the best place to cross the border undetected?" he asked.

"You need to go to the cemetery, and then climb over the wall behind it," Eli answered.

"Will you show me the way?"

But his cousin was reluctant to help. "It will look suspicious," he demurred, looking anxious.

"Can you just explain the directions?"

"Well, you go down this road" – Eli drew a diagram – "until you see a farmhouse with a thatched roof. Then turn left, continue straight, and you'll soon be at the cemetery. There you'll see a high wall; Germany is on the other side. Do you have German money?"

"Yes, I changed all my money."

Sam stayed at his aunt's place for two more days. During this time he reflected on all that he had read about the Nazis and the situation of the Jewish people in Germany since Hitler had come to power. It was a sobering assessment.

The Nazis had adopted a worldview in which myth displaced rational theory; they believed the Germanic peoples to be heirs of an ethnic group, the Aryans, which they considered the master race with a destiny of world rulership. The creation of the myth of the Aryan as noble and strong went hand in hand with another: the stereotype of the Jew as antitype to this ideal, embodying all that was contrary to it; hence antisemitism became a central ideological plank of the regime. The Jews, in Hitler's mind, were the "eternal enemies" of the German Volk, and he used them as a scapegoat for all the nation's economic and social problems.

The new masters in Germany drew renewed inspiration for their neo-pagan ideologies from annual rallies at the magnificent medieval city of Nuremberg. Each September, many thousands gathered from all over the nation to participate in torchlight marches and occultic ceremonies which created a kind of religious fervor among the participants. The dramatic appearance of the Führer was the climax of the occasion. Hitler's words, which cast an intoxicating spell over the audience, affirmed their mystical understanding of the mission of the Reich, and of history as the theater of the eternal struggle between Aryan and Jew. At the infamous Nuremberg Rally of 1935 special laws were announced which forbade intermarriage and sexual relations between Jews and Germans – an ultimate denial of Jewish personhood.

However, the main thrust of the anti-Jewish policy in the earlier years of the Nazi regime was to encourage German Jewry to leave their homeland. This strategy operated on two levels: firstly, through legal measures intended to isolate Jews from society and strip them of rights and property; at the same time, there was the covert encouragement of campaigns of incitement and violence against them. Adolf Eichmann had joined the Sicherheitsdienst (SD, Security Service) in 1933, and assigned to investigate possible "solutions to the Jewish question." His efforts at first focused on encouraging emigration, and he would soon become adept at extorting wealth from Jewish citizens in return for safe passage out of the country.

For the Nazis, at this stage, it was still necessary to refrain from actions against the Jews that would undermine their credibility on the world stage. Hitler began to focus his attention on military rearmament and to seize any opportunity to expand the Reich. The first steps toward Lebensraum occurred in 1935 when he reintroduced military conscription and began rapidly rebuilding the German army – in open violation of the Treaty of Versailles – even while proclaiming his desire for peace and offering assurances that the buildup was solely defensive. A year later, in March 1936, three battalions of the German army crossed the bridges over the Rhine and entered the demilitarized area of the Rhineland. But France and Britain, parties to the Treaty, failed to respond.

The next item on Hitler's program, intended to demonstrate to the world the superiority of his new order, was the Summer Olympics. The Nazi administration built an impressive sports complex just west of Berlin, with a huge stadium which had a special seating area for Hitler and top Nazis. Huge controversy erupted over the exclusion of Jewish athletes from Germany's Olympic team, but eventually the Games proceeded and the *omnipresent "Jews Not Welcome" signs were temporarily removed from public places. The Games were a spectacular success, remembered most of all for the performance by African-American track star Jesse Owens, who became an instant celebrity in Berlin – though it was noticeable that Hitler never acknowledged his victory. But there would be no more Olympic Games for a dozen years; rather, during that time, the young people from many countries would be battling on different fields.*

The Nazi regime had gained a measure of international approbation through the staging of the Olympics, but by 1937 life had become still more difficult for the Jews of Germany. Their exclusion from public or private employment left many without a means of livelihood, and extreme pressure was being placed on them to leave German territory – even though, at the Evian Conference in France in July 1935, most countries refused to accept more Jewish refugees. The vise was slowly being tightened. Nevertheless, Herschel Grynszpan had not yet made his fateful journey to the German embassy in Paris,[3] and the events of Kristallnacht were not to occur for over a year.

So, it was time for Sam to set out.

Around 6 o'clock in the evening on the third day of his stay at his aunt's house, he casually remarked that he was going for a walk. He swung his bag over his shoulder and set out in the twilight through the quiet streets, following the route his cousin had traced for him. Soon he reached the cemetery, which appeared at that hour to be deserted, and began threading his way through the tombstones. All his senses were alert, and as he gazed about it seemed to him that he had been thrust into a gloomy stage setting for a comic opera.

The moon had risen, sailing like a "ghostly galleon"[4] above the tall trees, and throwing a fitful light through dark clouds. Its pale gleams illumined the white marble of the gravestones, which stood out starkly in black and white relief. His feet crunched on the pebbled paths that wound between the tombstones, and he could hear the rustling of small animals and soft calls of birds in the branches. Then, suddenly, there was another noise close by – the sound of footsteps. Such was the eerie nature of the scene that Sam felt the hair rise on the back of his neck. In front of him yawned the dark mouth of an open grave, freshly dug and clearly ready for a coffin. Without hesitation he scrambled silently down into its dank embrace.

He waited, crouching there while the minutes ticked by, but still could hear the murmur of voices. As he continued his vigil the cold began gradually to penetrate his body, but he closed his eyes and thought wryly, *Better alive here than dead.* His sense of humor would rarely desert him.

It started raining, puddles began to form around him, and soon he began to shiver. He stayed for a couple of hours in the dark cavity and when he emerged he was soaking. But the moon had vanished, it was pitch black and very quiet. He made his way to the wall which loomed ahead of him, climbed over it, and landed in Germany.

---

1. The Condor Legion was commanded by Colonel Wolfram von Richthofen, cousin of the infamous Red Baron of the First World War. After the Spanish campaigns, he was promoted to a leading role in the future invasion of Poland in 1939, and then in France in 1940, utilizing the Luftwaffe in the German Blitzkrieg tactics that appalled the world.

2. Guernica's ordeal was memorialized by Spanish artist Pablo Picasso, who debuted his famous mural at an international arts exhibition in Paris in July of the same year. According to art critic Robert Hughes: "*Guernica* was the last great history painting ... It was also the last modern painting of major importance that took its subject from politics with the intention of changing the way large numbers of people thought and felt about power ... Picasso could imagine more suffering in a horse's head than Rubens normally put into a whole Crucifixion." Hughes, R. (2013) *The Shock of the New, The Hundred-Year History of Modern Art*, p 73. New York: Alfred A. Knopf.

3. In 1938, Herschel Grynszpan was a 17-year-old Jewish refugee who had fled from his home in Nazi Germany and was living in Paris. When news came to him that his family had been arrested by the Nazis, deprived of their property, and herded aboard trains destined for the Polish border, he became determined to draw attention to their plight. On the morning of November 7 he bought a gun, went to the German embassy in Paris, and asked as a German citizen to see an

embassy official. Grynszpan was ushered into the office of a junior diplomat, Ernst vom Rath, and proceeded to shoot him several times. Two days later vom Rath lay dead, and the Third Reich used the murder as justification for unleashing the violent riots of *Kristallnacht,* which took place on November 9 and 10.

4. From the 1906 ballad by English poet Alfred Noyes, "The Highwayman."

18

THROUGH THE LION'S DEN

The rain stopped, and Sam tried to scrape the mud from his clothes. It took him an hour before he started looking presentable, but his body was frozen. He was in Breslau. The city was one of the three largest in Germany, together with Berlin and Frankfurt, and had been a famous center of Jewish scholarship.

But now. as Sam made his way to the center of the city, he saw large inscriptions everywhere which read *"Entrance forbidden for Jews,"* or *"Don't buy from Jews."* He didn't want to linger. People were emerging from their houses on their way to work, and the shops started to open. He bought a postcard and posted it to his aunt; he wanted to thank her for her kindness and explain his disappearance. He was intrigued by the stamps which featured the portrait of Hindenburg, Germany's last President, who four years earlier had transferred power to Hitler.

Sam asked a young boy for directions to the train station; because Yiddish was related to German he was able to converse quite easily. He made his way to the station, a huge terminal with a golden façade, but its beauty was diminished, he thought, by the ubiquitous signs reading "Heil Hitler" and the swastika armbands on the sleeves of the passersby. Sam could overhear the greetings on every side also; "Heil Hitler" they were saying to one another. The abrupt staccato syllables reverberated unpleasantly in his ears.

He bought a ticket for Berlin, climbed aboard the train and searched for a corner where he could be as inconspicuous as possible. He lowered himself into a seat next to an elderly couple, and the man acknowledged him with the same jarring phrase, "Heil Hitler." Sam stared neutrally ahead; he wished he could become invisible. Suddenly he realized he was heading in the wrong direction, and managed to jump out just as the train was starting to move. This happened a second time, but the third train he entered appeared to be the right one. He found a seat and decided he would feign sleep to avoid conversation.

Berlin ... it seemed enormous! Sam had never seen so many people. He took a room in a hotel next to the train station and was so tired he fell immediately into a dreamless slumber. In the morning he didn't have enough money for breakfast in the hotel; leaving early, he bought a loaf of bread and some butter and drank tap water. Then he returned to the terminal and took the train for Dusseldorf, situated 40 kilometers from the Dutch border. This time he took the right train, and once again pretended to be sleeping, regretting all the while that he was unable to look at the scenery.

Arriving at his destination, he decided that 40 kilometers was not such a great distance, and that he would make his way to the border on foot. He trudged sturdily through the blossoming spring countryside, but after a while the road seemed to go on forever. Finally he spied a road sign that read *"Achtung Zoll"* (Beware Customs) but was soon disappointed; there were still 15 kilometers to go. It started raining, and it seemed that he would have to spend another night in Germany.

Walking a little further, Sam reached a village, and his eye was caught by a bistro where some tables and chairs had been placed outside under a brightly striped awning. Suddenly, he found himself longing for a cup of coffee. Wrestling with his common sense, which told him to press on as fast as possible, he entered the café, gave his order, then savored each mouthful of the hot, fragrant brew when it came. Reluctantly rising to his feet, he went to pay, and as he drew out his money asked the proprietor where he might find cheap lodgings for the night. At that point the man noticed Sam's Yiddish accent. Throwing down the towel with which he had been wiping the counter, he shouted viciously, "Get out of here, you dirty Jew."

Sam was profoundly shocked but knew he had to remain calm. Choking back words of protest, he laid the money on the counter and silently departed. It was still raining, a small drizzle which soon became quite a heavy shower and drenched his clothes. He began hoping desperately for some kind of shelter. Reaching the outskirts of the village, he noticed a barn, looked around, but could see no one. He entered, and the bovine smell immediately assaulted him. At the back of the barn was a door; he passed through it and discovered a toolshed, with a ladder inside, which he climbed. Was he dreaming? There in the attic was a worn-out mattress propped against the wall. He placed it on the rough wooden floor, stretched out with a sigh of relief, and fell asleep. At dawn he crept out again like a thief and reached the street, then continued walking in the direction of the border.

The terrain was very flat, and the fields and meadows through which he passed were wrapped in different shades of emerald and verdigris; sleek-looking cattle were munching contentedly on the grass. Sam was walking as if in a dream, compounded of fatigue, apprehension and anticipation; as he gazed at the peaceful landscape it appeared to him that he was looking at the paintings of the Dutch masters. But the idyll was about to be broken. The road entered a wood, and there was a bend. Sam passed around it, and straight away almost bumped into a young German soldier.

"Halt," shouted the soldier instantly, his hand flying to the gun at his side.

Sam froze.

"Where are you from? Who are you?" The questions came like bullets.

"My name is Sam," answered the boy. His heavy Yiddish accent didn't leave any room for doubt about his background.

"Show me your papers," came the demand. "Come. Don't try to get away or I'll shoot!"

A third player suddenly appeared on the scene. It was a policeman, and the soldier, proud as a peacock with his important capture, handed Sam over.

The officer was an older man, who looked at Sam intently and gestured for the boy to walk beside him. "Well, lad," he said eventually, "are you going to Spain to join the communists?"

"No," Sam answered. "I left Poland and I'm on my way to Belgium via Holland. I want to work there, and I want to study art." For some indefinable reason he felt he could trust the man.

As Sam unfolded a little more of his story, the two reached a gas station, the outskirts of another town.

The policeman appeared to be lost in thought. Finally he said, "There is a Jewish family in this town. Walk ahead and take the first street to your left. It's the street which leads through the center of the town. But keep walking until you come to the last house; that is the one you need. But don't tell anyone I've released you."

Sam walked quickly along the street the policeman had indicated. It was Sunday, and people were dressed in their best clothes, going to church. Everywhere he saw signs reading "*Juden Verboten*" (Forbidden for Jews).

He reached the last house and knocked at the door. There was some delay, and finally the door opened. In front of him stood a man with deep lines carved into his face; after some hesitation he invited Sam in. "What do you want?" he asked.

"To cross the border," Sam replied. "Can you help me?"

The man shook his head. "I can't ..." He took a piece of paper, wrote something and handed it to Sam. "This is the address of a Jewish family. They live on Market Square Number 5, on the second floor. Here, take ten *pfennig*."

Sam felt humiliated. It was the first time in his life he had accepted charity. He put the coin in his pocket and made his way to the second address, where he found a warm and welcoming Jewish family. They gave him food and drink; it was all delicious. Sam told them the story of how he had come from Poland hoping to study art, and asked their advice about crossing the border.

"Well, lad," replied the *paterfamilias*. "We will show you the way there. Once you've crossed it, you will find yourself in a town called Enschede, where there is an organization which helps German refugees. This you must apply to join." He handed Sam a paper. "Here is the name and address of a man who will help you with the procedures."

Early the next morning, just as dawn was breaking, they led him out of the town and pointed out the way to the border; it was very close.

"May God guard you! And be careful the address doesn't fall into the hands of the Germans!"

Sam thanked his benefactors and started to walk, his heart beating fast. It was a still, quiet morning, and there seemed as yet no traffic on the road. He reached the checkpoint, saw that it was clear, and came to the barrier. Just as he did so, he saw a sentry emerge from a small guardhouse. Fear lent wings to Sam's feet, and he started running.

"Halt!" shouted the guard. "Halt, or I'm shooting."

Sam continued running. The bullet whizzed past his head and his feet landed on the soil of Holland.

He had passed into the lion's den and come out safe on the other side! His mind flew to Rubens' painting of Daniel, which he had so recently been studying. It showed the prophet after the long night he had spent in the company of the wild beasts, his gaze steadfastly turned to heaven; all about him prowled the monumental, savage creatures – but he had been kept safe and unscathed, sheltered by a mysterious power.

PART II
BELGIUM

19

A SENSE OF HOMECOMING

Sam was elated. He had made it to Holland, on the westernmost coast of Europe! But his euphoria was to be short-lived. For there were, of course, authorities to face on the other side of the border as well, and even now two policemen were advancing upon him.

"Papers, please," came the dry, official demand.

Sam had only his Polish passport to show them. They glanced at one another, conferred, and were obviously disapproving.

"Come," they said to him. Sam was taken outside the building and pushed into a car.

As he traveled with them to an unknown destination, Sam suddenly remembered the piece of paper on which was written the address that had been given him – which he had been warned to guard. He surreptitiously fished the paper out of his pocket, placed it in his mouth and tried to swallow it, but one of the policemen noticed what he was doing and pulled it out of his mouth. The officers clearly thought this was further grounds for suspicion.

He was taken to an old building that belonged to the national gendarmerie, and conducted to the top floor, where he was given a large room with a high ceiling. Evening came and he tried to sleep, but the building was right next to a church with a high tower, and a bell that rang every 15 minutes. To Sam, the noise seemed deafening. He put his head under the blankets and the pillow, but nothing helped. His head was bursting, his ears were ringing, and the night seemed of infinite duration. In the morning, though, he was given some black coffee, bread and Dutch biscuits.

Once again, Sam was thankful for the richness of his native language, Yiddish, which had some affinities with the Dutch language, enabling him to understand the policemen. "We will take you to the organization for German refugees," he was informed.

Sam thought he was dreaming. No prison! A refugee was treated here like a human being, not a criminal.

The car stopped in front of a neat-looking house, with a bright display of flowering red and white geraniums in pots on the window sills. Sam entered an attractively furnished room, where he was greeted by the president of the organization, Mr. Van Damme, who shook his hand.

"Please, sir," he said, with great courtesy, "do sit down. Now tell me, do you come from Germany?"

"No," said Sam. "From Poland."

"From Poland!" He was clearly astonished. "This is preposterous. There is absolutely no reason for you to escape from there."

Sam launched into a description of the growing danger in his home country, but Mr. Van Damme shook his head in disbelief.

"This surely isn't possible, Mr. Herciger," he said, "Please take this money and return to Poland."

It was Sam's turn to look at the director with astonishment, dismayed by his ignorance of what was taking place in Eastern Europe. Nevertheless, he was invited to stay at the house for a few days and found the atmosphere very pleasant, enabling him to relax a little after the tensions of the journey through Germany. Some of the young people he met there were hoping to emigrate to Palestine, but Sam didn't waver in his own plans. He was given some money by the organization, and knew immediately what he would do with it. It was the exact amount that he needed to go to Maastricht – a city in the southern tip of the Netherlands, right beside the Belgian border.

Once again Sam set out, and this time he wasn't afraid. The people were friendly, the policemen were not intimidating, and for the first time in his life he wasn't aware of antisemitism. He had also been given the name and address of a man who, he was told, would be able to help him find the way to the Belgian border. He arrived in Maastricht and was lucky – the street he was looking for was near the train station. He rang the bell and a servant opened the door; she looked at him with a measure of suspicion, but let him in.

"Mr. Frans hasn't come home yet," she said. "He'll be here in an hour; you can wait in here for him."

She showed him into a comfortable sitting room. He was very thirsty. "Could I have something to drink, please?" he asked.

The maid brought him coffee with milk and sugar, clearly reluctantly. Sam was also very hungry, but couldn't bring himself to beg for a slice of bread. Finally the owner of the house arrived, a man who appeared to overflow with kindness and warmth. When he heard Sam's story, he said immediately, "Come, lad, I'll show you the way you need to go. I've helped others before in your situation."

The two set out together and walked for an hour. His hunger was still bothering Sam, and his thirst had returned. They passed a bridge where a soldier stood on guard. Sam felt his heart start beating fast again, but the soldier made no move toward him.

"Young man – you are now in Belgium," said Frans. They passed a shop. "Wait," he said, and came out of the store with a packet of chocolate. "This is for the trip."

Sam knew he was being treated like a kid but accepted the chocolate with pleasure. "Thank you," he said.

"Ah yes," said his benefactor, "and here is money for the train to Antwerp."

Sam was given the exact amount he needed for the ticket. He took the train to Liege, where he had to wait three hours for the connection to Antwerp. He wandered about the city, listening to the people chatting in French, then entered a park – but when he saw a policeman he left hastily. Once again, his hunger became intense; the chocolate bar was long since gone. He returned to the station and took the train to Antwerp, arriving at his destination famished and exhausted.

The central station at Antwerp had high, arched ceilings with glass domes through which the sunlight filtered in myriad points of light. It was beautiful. The concourse was lined with restaurants thronged with people, and the scent of grilled meat and French fries came wafting out enticingly. He took the stairs to go out of the station into Pelican Street. Each of the steps were shining, it seemed with thousands of small diamonds which dazzled his eyes. *My God*, thought Sam, *what a rich country*.

Emerging into Pelican Street, he immediately felt secure. Orthodox Jews with long beards, sidelocks and black gabardine garments were walking there, and he could overhear their conversations in Yiddish. He showed one of them the address he had been given, the home of his friend's sister in Zurenborgstreet, and asked for directions. That was the only contact he had in Antwerp, and his only hope. In his pocket he had one franc left – just enough to pay for the tram.

He arrived in front of the house, and with his heart pounding rang the bell. An attractive young woman opened the door. "Can I help you?" she asked.

Sam introduced himself. "I'm a friend of your brother, Jenkel," he said.

"Come in," she said, opening the door and gesturing for him to enter.

They went up the stairs and into the kitchen, where the young woman busied herself opening a can of sardines and putting bread on the table. Sam discovered her name was Esther Polarski; her husband was working in a bakery and wasn't yet home. The fresh bread was delicious and he devoured slice after slice; Esther started to cut the second loaf. Sam continued steadily eating until finally his hunger was satisfied.

At that point, Mr. Polarski came home and Esther introduced Sam to him. The three began talking. Sam told of the adventures and privations of his journey as his new friends, clearly highly cultured and intelligent, listened sympathetically. Together they began to thrash out the challenges of his situation now that he had arrived in Belgium.

"It will be difficult for you to obtain official papers or even a temporary permit," warned Mr. Polarski, "but you need that in order to work."

They conversed together a little longer, until Esther insisted that Sam should take some rest.

"You must be tired after your long journey," she said, then added, "and we will be happy to have you stay with us until you find your feet." Mr. Polarski nodded in agreement, smiling.

In the evening, after a delicious supper, Sam lay down in his bed in a small room in the attic. The cool sheets draped over his weary body were imbued with the fragrance of fresh lavender and his taut nerves began relaxing. He realized that the road ahead would not be easy, but he was encouraged. Although he was a stranger, he had been received as a member of the family, and he slept feeling safe.

20

ANTWERP

When Sam woke the next morning his heart was brimming with happiness. At breakfast, Esther told him, "Take tram number 11 and go to the Old City." She pressed some money into his hand.

He made his way downtown and emerged from the tram in front of a medieval stone fortress called Het Steen. After entering the picturesque turreted building, he climbed some winding stone steps, and came out on a wide platform. As he took in his surroundings, he stood motionless for a moment. *My God*, he thought again, *it must be one of the great views of the world.*

There before him was spread the broad expanse of the waterway which had determined Antwerp's fortunes for more than half a millennium. The city is situated above a large bend of the Scheldt River, which, together with the Meuse and the Rhine, forms the biggest estuary in Western Europe. This fortuitous location caused Antwerp to blossom into one of the leading seaports of the continent – despite the fact that the city is some 80 kilometers distant from the North Sea. During the 15th and 16th centuries, Spanish and Portuguese merchants bringing precious goods from their colonial possessions established Antwerp as one of their main trading bases. The Scheldt was navigable for ships of wide burden, and on its slate gray waters was built a line of magnificent quays. Against them could be found vessels laden with products from the far corners of the world – spices from Asia, cloth from Italy, wines from France and Spain, silk from Turkey – and diamonds from Africa.

Antwerp was then the richest and most cosmopolitan city in Europe. It was governed by an oligarchy of banker-aristocrats; merchants from across the continent came there to trade, and the city's tolerant policies attracted a large Jewish community composed of migrants from Spain and Portugal. But this prosperity began to decline with the accession of Philip II of Spain and his furtherance of the Inquisition, which drove thousands of inhabitants to seek asylum elsewhere. The Dutch then blockaded the Scheldt from 1585, when Antwerp surrendered to Spain during the Eighty Years War, until 1795. But, although Antwerp's golden age was short-lived, it forged the city's rich and enduring cultural life, especially in the great works of art produced there.

This, Sam was to discover, was the key to the allure of Antwerp. On the one hand, the city radiates an aura of charm and romance which is quintessentially European, in its medieval cobblestone streets, Flemish Renaissance buildings and stunning Baroque artworks. At the same time, it breathes an air of wealth and sophistication through its link to the global shipping routes entered by way of the North Sea – encapsulated in the priceless gems glittering in the storefront windows of the diamond district.

As Sam stood on the waterfront and breathed in the salt-laden air he felt strong, light, and free, as if champagne were fizzing in his veins. The river was a scene of unceasing activity, with every variety of sea-going vessel under heaven moored at the docks or floating on the wide canopy of water. It was another magical day, like that first time in Krakow, a day not of golden light but of a softer northern hue, its radiance shot through with pale gleams of sunlight that danced on the gray expanse of the river. A breeze came in freshly with the tide, the waters ruffled like silk taffeta and the seagulls wheeled above with mournful cries, tossed on gusts of wind, while the shadows of the clouds raced over the estuary.

The waterfront was alive also with all the sound effects of a maritime city. Sam listened to the shouts of the deckhands, the creak of the boats as they tugged at their moorings, the clang of anchors and tackle, the deep sonorous horns. He noticed numerous cargo vessels from the Congo and his artist's eye was arrested by the rhythmic grace of the workers as they heaved great pallets filled with coffee to the docks, then piled them high onto small horse-drawn carts. The play of muscles under the black, glossy skin of their bare shoulders and arms evoked for him the movements of a ballet, and he longed for a sketch book. The flags on the ships streaming in the breeze flaunted all the colors of their countries of origin, and set him dreaming of the tropical lands from which they had come.

Eventually he tore himself away from the waterfront,[1] and found himself entering the heart of the Old Town. He passed through the Groenplaats or Green Place, a classic European square with Flemish gabled houses and baroque architecture, dominated by the bronze statue of Rubens, Antwerp's most famous son. The 16th-century architecture continued at the adjoining medieval square of Grote Markt, where the Flemish guild houses topped with gold statues shed abroad an aura of prosperity as they watched over the comings and goings of the Antwerpers. The smart, busy citizens, impeccably dressed, swirled past him.

Almost in a reverie, Sam found himself standing before a great church with one lovely, soaring spire – the Cathedral of Notre Dame, one of the largest and most beautiful examples of Gothic architecture in the Netherlands. He felt compelled to go in. A small entrance fee was required, and he still had some funds left over from Esther's gift. He handed over the money, and the son of Israel then trod firmly into the sanctuary named for the Jewish maiden, Miriam. Once past the doors, he found the interior to be simple and imposing, with a lofty choir and triple aisles on each side uninterrupted by partitions or screens, giving an effect of vastness.

But the all-surpassing attraction in the cathedral was "the great Antwerp pair," two altarpieces of Rubens depicting the crucifixion and death of Christ. A curtain hung before each, and a guard drew them aside.

Each altarpiece was in a triptych format, executed in oil paints on wood, and enormous in size. Sam fixed his gaze on the first, *The Elevation of the Cross*. He could recognize all the artistic influences that had contributed to the work, but it seemed to him that it was Rubens' own emotional breadth and genius that was incarnated in the painting, and sweeping him away with irresistible force. He gazed, exalted in spirit, at the crowded, passionate, *living* canvas, and the infinite suffering of that luminous, perfectly rendered central figure. It was the same with the second triptych, *The Descent from the Cross*. All the richness of Rubens' artistic vision and creative power compressed into the painting suggested to Sam he was in the presence of something more than mortal, and lifted him into a realm which he himself longed to access through his art.

For some time, he remained speechless at the sight of such exquisite beauty. The reality was so much more impressive than the reproductions he had seen; the perfection of each piece beyond anything he had imagined.[2] How long did he stand there? He didn't know. Then, suddenly, soft notes of music started to waft about the space where he was standing. At first they were low, then became stronger, until he felt the music was engulfing the apse. Was he dreaming, or was it a miracle?

No, it was the organist rehearsing.

That was Sam's first day in Antwerp. He felt a love for the city which would never fade.

---

1. As Sam wandered along the waterfront, he may have caught sight of the buildings of the famous Red Star Line. From the early 1870s, some two million men, women and children from all over Europe had left their homes to travel to Antwerp, where they embarked on Red Star Line ships for a journey to Ellis Island, the gateway to America. More than a quarter of these emigrants were

Jewish – largely from Eastern Europe until the exodus driven by the rise of Nazi Germany – and notable travelers had included Irving Berlin and Albert Einstein. Sadly, the buildings were then deserted, for the US Congress had introduced a bill to limit the number of immigrants and the line had recently abandoned its journeys.

2. As Rubens' biographer Samuel Edwards stated concerning *The Elevation of the Cross*, "... the finished work would be hailed as one of the most magnificent ever painted by any artist ... in which suffering and fury, horror and pain and passion were expressed with such dynamic force and lyricism." Edwards, S. (1973) *Peter Paul Rubens, Biography of a Giant*. Philadelphia: David McKay, Co. In a charmingly written 1872 novella called *A Dog of Flanders* by Ouida (English author Marie Louise de la Ramée), a boy and his dog freeze to death in front of the altar, simply content to have seen the masterpieces.

21

HENNIE

Sam returned to Esther's home still treading on air. He realized also that he had walked through the city all that day without dreading any veiled anti-Jewish hostility. Esther had prepared a delectable meal, and Polarski made for him a list of all the furriers in Antwerp. He accompanied Sam the next day as he visited them.

It was May, the low season in the trade, and Sam could find no one ready to take him on. He knew, however, that in the low season certain furriers would trim white ermine with paws of black Astrakhan lamb, as in the robes worn by the royalty of several European nations. It was delicate work, and the pieces had to be assembled together somewhat like a jigsaw puzzle. Sam had no experience whatsoever in the skill but fortune favored him: one of the shop-owners in Vanneau Street was related to Sam's former employer in Krakow, and he accepted Sam for a trial period.

The work was not well paid, and did not have such an auspicious beginning. On the first day Sam laboriously assembled the paws together with the ermine; the piece then had to be dried and turned on the other side so that all parts could be sewn properly together. His first attempt was a disaster, and the seamstress working with him was furious, but her anger soon cooled, and she and Sam eventually became fast friends. She was actually the first person to call him Sam instead of Shmuel or Shmiel, and that became his nickname for the rest of his life.

Sam soon learned the new skills, but knew he couldn't stay forever at the Polarskis. When he started to look for a furnished room, Esther's sister invited Sam to stay with her family for a time. They were kind and welcoming people, who were keen to learn more about life in Poland.

"Sam," they said in horror, "how did you dare cross Germany to get to Belgium? You know, if the Germans had arrested you, they would have sent you to a concentration camp!"

This thought had never occurred to Sam, and he wondered idly whether a concentration camp could possibly be worse than a prison.

But there was an extra joy in his life right now. He had met a young girl, only 16, but very feminine; she was petite and blonde and had sparkling blue eyes – Sam couldn't tear his gaze away from her. Her name was Henriette but everyone called her Hennie. She spoke perfect Flemish, French and Yiddish and loved reading. She and Sam began meeting once or twice a week, but her parents, Zalman and Zuvia Teichteil, were not very happy about the relationship. They thought Hennie was too young to have a boyfriend, and to make matters worse Sam was only a poor, illegal youngster.

Renting a room also proved harder than he had expected, because he had no papers and Belgian law required the landlord to give the authorities information concerning their tenants. Sam was constantly aware of the danger of being found out and expelled from the country. Finally, however, he found a furnished attic situated next to a candle factory in Plantijn Moretus Avenue. The stench was terrible but Sam was happy. He now had a room, a little money, and he was in love with Hennie. After a couple of months Hennie went up with him to his room. Her parents, of course, had no idea of what was taking place.

So there were small waves rocking Sam's little boat in his new land, but he took them with equanimity – until one day a larger, more violent swell brought back vivid memories of previous traumatic experiences. Sam had invited Hennie to the Majestic Theater on Carnot Street, and when the movie ended they went out into the street hand in hand, smiling and happy and talking together in Yiddish. From nowhere, a group of thugs materialized, about 12 young men in all, and surrounded the pair. They had overhead Sam and Hennie conversing in Yiddish and made them a target. One of the group, tall and cadaverous, approached Sam, thrust his face close, and shouted: "You're the one who wanted to beat up my brother, aren't you?"

Sam kept silent. He thought only of Hennie who, when he glanced at her, was white as chalk. He too was very frightened but tried not to show it. The street about them was deserted and the thugs began throwing punches at him, beating him about the head and chest. Hennie's hand was in front of her mouth as she watched, terrified. Sam couldn't defend himself; there were too many, and their rage was so explosive he feared that if he resisted it might be courting death. A heavily muscled gang member grabbed him and knocked his forehead with such force against Sam's face that blood came gushing from his nose. He shouted at Hennie, "Run away, run away!"

But the sight of the blood had sobered the gang members, and one by one they began melting away into the darkness. Hennie and Sam were left alone together; she had stayed at his side. A passerby came upon the scene and was concerned. "Poor guy," he said, looking at Sam's bleeding face. "You should go immediately to the police. They'll find them!"

But that was impossible: Sam had no papers. His nose was broken, but he didn't go to a doctor either: not enough money.

The year 1938 dawned, and Sam turned 21. He had to leave his little furnished room, and followed up an advertisement mentioning a room for rent in a private home. The landlady was a middle-aged spinster, somewhat myopic. She peered at Sam when he appeared on the doorstep and asked about lodging.

"I'm a student," he told her, "but I don't have an ID card yet."

"Okay," she said sternly, "but you must understand that I rent the room out for board and lodging only, and you must pay one week in advance. Oh, yes, and no feminine visitors allowed!"

The *propriétaire* asked only a small sum of money and seemed to develop maternal feelings for Sam. In the backyard she kept some chickens and every day Sam got a fresh egg, hard boiled. After a while he got fed up with the monotonous little sphere that appeared every day on his plate, and seized the opportunity to teach his landlady how to prepare an omelette with onions. After that the omelette reappeared at every meal ... *she doesn't seem to realize that people like variety once in a while,* he mused. But she did make for him a tomato soup with cress sauce, and for the first time Sam got a taste of the delicious Flemish cuisine.

When the Belgian national holiday came around, his landlady prepared a more elaborate dinner. She knew that Sam loved tomatoes and had stuffed some as an impressive first course. Sam took a huge bite but felt a strange, unpleasant texture on his tongue. With his fork he delved into the tomatoes on his plate, and saw what seemed to be large worms. He pushed them aside.

His hostess became apoplectic. "What?" she screeched, "you don' t eat crayfish? Do you have any idea how expensive they are?"

"I'm sorry, but I can't eat it."

The landlady looked down her nose with supercilious disdain at Sam, and his popularity dwindled.

But Sam's domestic woes were not affecting his essential focus. Now that he was somewhat settled in the city, he felt he could finally approach the Academy of Art to enroll there as a student – his whole reason for choosing to come to Antwerp in the first place.

22

AT THE ACADEMY AT LAST

Sam made his way to the campus of the Art Academy at Mutsaardstraat 31 and wandered through the time-honored buildings. Three paintings in the large entrance hall arrested his gaze: there were portraits of Rubens and van Dyck, and the third, the allegorical *Antwerp, Nurse of Painters*, by Flemish painter Theodor Boeyermans, depicts young students presenting their creative work to Lady Antwerp. The river god Scaldis, a personification of the River Scheldt, reclines beside her holding a cornucopia suggesting the wealth and bounty of the city's artistic heritage. Sam was on fire to begin his studies, and soon he was seated opposite the Director of the Academy, Mr. Opsomer.

Without further ado, he was asked, "Show me your drawings, please."

Sam spread a selection of his artworks on the desk but was disappointed – Mr. Opsomer hardly glanced at them.

"I'll put you in the introductory class," he said dismissively.

Sam could not remain downcast for long, and felt as if he was in a dream as he made his way to his first classes. These were given in the evenings, in French, and focused on drawing; his teacher was a man by the name of Peter Colfs. Although Sam's first desire was to be a sculptor, he understood that he had to become proficient in basic techniques and worked very hard. He also made new friends among his classmates. There were many young Jewish people at the Academy, and they often went to exhibitions together.

At the same time, Sam continued his work in the fur trade; it was an occupation he had wisely decided to keep from his landlady. She knew that he went to the Art Academy because she sometimes received letters which said, "Your son has missed classes." She also, when Sam was out, went snooping in his room where he kept many drawings. One day, however, as he returned home, a small piece of fur fell from his pocket. The landlady pounced on it. "Now what is this supposed to mean?" she demanded. She examined Sam's nails, that were not too clean, and looked up triumphantly. "So that's what you are – a furrier!" she pronounced in tones of lugubrious doom. His popularity took another blow.

The last straw was not long in coming. One evening Madame la Propriétaire returned home late and heard the voice of a young woman coming from Sam's room. She opened the door and slipped inside; the young couple were making love.

"Aha!" she said furiously, "young man, you know very well that it's strictly forbidden to bring ladies here. I won't tolerate it!"

Sam had to leave. There was another tenant who didn't take his meals there, and once a week slept with a prostitute in his room. That she did tolerate. Was she jealous? Sam didn't know.

He found another room not far away but regretted the change; he missed the good food – even the omelette – and the rent had been very low. Nor did he realize that his new landlord had notified the authorities of his presence. One day there was a knock at the door, and when he opened it a policeman was standing there. Sam began shaking. *That's it*, he thought to himself. *It's all over.*

But the policeman was civil and polite, causing Sam to wonder if he had landed on another planet.

"Would you please follow me, sir?" he asked. "It is only a formality, but you do need to register."

The policeman took him to the townhall of Borgerhout-Antwerp, where the clerk began asking him a series of questions: "What do you live on? Do you work?" he asked.

Since Sam was employed illegally he answered, "My parents send me money."

"Why don't you have a visa?"

Sam kept silent. He was registered, but had to come back the following week to show his documents. It was a precarious situation and he discussed it with his friends.

"Don't do it," said Camille. "You'll get expelled." According to Leonard: "You only have one chance out of a thousand to get a work permit."

Sam didn't return. He rented another room where they didn't ask him to register, and stayed there for a year.

It was now high season in the fur trade, and since this lasted only four months Sam worked between 85 to 90 hours a week, but he was happy to make a living. He earned six francs an hour for his work, which was relatively good money: a cheap meal cost eight francs. He regularly sent a little money to his parents in Poland. In order not to lose time but also to prevent any kind of inquisition he ate at work, which meant he didn't see daylight at all. At 11 o'clock at night he went home, avidly inhaling the fresh air. During this period he wasn't able to go to classes at the Academy.

In January 1939, however, Sam's workload was reduced to one or two days a week, and finally he could return to the school. But the money he had saved during the high season simply wasn't enough to sustain him. In order to skip lunch he would sleep late, and when he ate outside he ordered only half portions – sometimes only a first course or soup with bread. He often went to a Jewish restaurant in Mercator Street where the owner was generous; when Sam had finished his meager meal he would bring him applesauce with bread. But the secret police came there often. Sam used to eat in a little room next to the kitchen with a door leading to the garden; every time he saw an officer he would slip out.

Soon Sam didn't have even enough money to pay for half meals. He bought some dates in a grocery store; they were cheap and nutritious and he would eat them with bread in place of sugar. Clothes were also becoming a problem. He had worn the suit his father gave him before he left Poland a great deal, and every evening he placed his pants under the mattress to keep them pressed. They had definitely started to wear out, but he was too engaged in his studies to let such mundane matters trouble him too much.

Because he now had more free time, Sam went often to museums, and registered at the library in Aveugles Street where he could admire the art books available in several languages. At the library Sam met a man named Efraim Shmidt, who was a tailor. Together they discussed Flemish art and music, and during one of their meetings Sam mentioned to Efraim, "I would love to buy a violin."

"We happen to have one at home!" said Efraim. "I am happy to sell it."

Sam went to examine the violin; it was in a good state. He ignored the thought of his woefully low funds and said apologetically, "I'm sorry I don't have a lot of money right now. But I could give you a small sum now and pay the rest monthly."

Efraim agreed, and Sam left carrying the violin, feeling happy. The neighbors were less ecstatic. Sam continued to walk around in his worn-out trousers, and every month he paid Efraim.

More than two years had passed since he had arrived in Antwerp and taken up his art studies. He had sometimes found the courses at the school aggravating, for he was longing to throw himself into studying sculpture – but he took the delay philosophically, realizing he had first to gain proficiency in drawing, color and composition. He knew he was making progress, began experimenting with new techniques, and gained third place in his year. He couldn't help feeling a thrill of pride; after all, his attendance at the classes had so often been curtailed because he had to work.

The teacher, Mr. Colfs, showed some of Sam's drawings to the director of the Academy, Mr. Opsomer. Sam never knew what was said between them, but learned that his work would be exhibited in the festival hall of the city council, together with works of other outstanding students. A grand ceremony was held there at the end of the academic year, and the Mayor of Antwerp, Camille Huysmans, gave a speech. Sam was more impressed by the elaborate costumes that the dignitaries present were wearing, with their high starched collars, than the fulsome words that were spoken.

When it came time for the courses to commence in the new academic year, Sam was finally granted permission to begin his studies in sculpture. Together with 15 other students, he entered the introductory class, and seated himself at a desk. In front of him had been placed a plaster bust, and he took it in his hands and closed his eyes, feeling an almost childish joy springing in his heart. He examined the tools which would be used for the task, weighing them in his hands with reverence. It was a long-held dream at last coming true.

Sam's new teacher was a man named Willie Kreitz, who was not only an accomplished sculptor but also an excellent instructor. The atmosphere in the class was very cosmopolitan – there were other Poles, Czechs, even a student from the Congo. On one occasion Mr. Kreitz organized a visit to Brussels for an exhibition dedicated to "One Hundred Years of French Sculpture." The students crammed into two cars, and as they traveled to the capital they shared jokes and a lot of laughter. Finally, accompanied by the guidance of Mr. Kreitz, Sam was able to admire the grand masters such as Rodin, Maillol, Despiau, Zadkine, Lipchitz, Chanah Orlova, and others.

Sam was fascinated and inspired by the exhibition, but also felt humbled. He made a silent pledge to himself: "I'll work and work, and will try to arrive at their level. I'll make the material live, will bring it my soul and my passions." The vow seemed to produce in him a purifying, ennobling effect. Before his mind rose up the vision of a great classical bust he would create.

The group returned to Antwerp, tired but happy. Willie invited the students to his home, where his wife had prepared a small repast of sandwiches and cold drinks; after the meal they visited Willie's workshop. This should have been for Sam one of the happiest days of his life. But there was one great thing which was marring his joy.

It was September 1939, and Poland had just been invaded by Germany.

23

ONSLAUGHT ON POLAND

Since Sam had arrived in Belgium in 1937, he and his friends had followed the political developments taking place just to their east with foreboding. Germany – one of Europe's most enlightened societies, the land of Bach and Beethoven, Goethe and Kant – was held fast in the grip of an unprepossessing tyrant with messianic pretensions. While he was weaving a web of sinister demagoguery, rearmament was proceeding apace under Göring's Four Year Plan, and Germany's youth were being hardened like steel for sacrifice for Führer and Fatherland.

First in Hitler's line of sight was his homeland of Austria, and in early March 1938, German troops crossed the border without resistance; Hitler's declared rationale was that he was protecting the millions of Germans in Austria from a communist uprising. Two days later the unification (Anschluss) of Germany and Austria was a fait accompli, and the triumphant Führer entered Vienna to the acclaim of many.

It was Hitler's first move beyond Germany's frontiers and now, having conquered Austria, he had Czechoslovakia surrounded on three sides. This country, created by the Treaty signed at Versailles, was dominated by two different ethnic groups, Czechs and Slovaks, but in the highly industrialized area known as the Sudetenland Germans were a majority. Many of these erstwhile Germans were now desiring political autonomy and, once again,

Hitler made a show of concern for their welfare as a pretext for demanding territorial concessions.

The Czech government ordered the mobilization of its army and called upon its allies, France and Britain, to honor their Treaty commitments. Pursuant to their goals of maintaining peace in Europe, Britain's prime minister, Neville Chamberlain, and France's premier, Daladier, agreed to meet with Hitler and Mussolini on September 29 in Munich. And thus began a disastrous diplomatic dance.

By the time of the Munich Conference neither Britain nor France felt militarily prepared to fight against Nazi Germany, while after the devastation of the "war to end all wars" the idea of another conflict seemed insupportable. In this climate, they chose to accede to the German request for occupation of the Czech border regions, and, with his actions thus sanctioned by the Allies, Hitler sent his troops into the Sudetenland on October 1. Chamberlain had spoken of "peace in our time." In the House of Commons, Winston Churchill gave his prophetic riposte: "Britain and France had to choose between war and dishonor. They chose dishonor. They will have war."

On November 9, 1938, the true face of the Nazi regime began to show itself. During the horrific events of Kristallnacht, the Jewish community in Germany was brutally attacked in an unparalleled orgy of mayhem, murder and violence that took the lives of hundreds, and saw many thousands of others sent to concentration camps. According to appalled onlookers in Britain and America, the manifestation of such savagery demonstrated that Germany had returned to the Dark Ages. The year 1939 dawned, with a sky smeared red from horizon to horizon for those with eyes to discern the signs of the times.

Having seized Austria and Czechoslovakia, Hitler was now desirous of expanding German living space still further east – to Poland. Under the Treaty of Versailles the former German provinces of West Prussia, Poznan and Upper Silesia had been added to Poland, but for the Germans there was an even more galling issue. The ethnically German city of Danzig located on the Baltic Sea coast had been established as a Free City under the League of Nations, while the Polish Corridor, along the lower course of the Vistula, *ensured that Poland had access to the Baltic. However, it also separated East Prussia from the rest of Germany, and, in January 1939, the Führer informed Polish Foreign Minister Josef Beck, "Danzig was German, would always remain German, and sooner or later would return to Germany."*

Hitler predicted that the German army would be able to defeat the Poles within a few days; Chamberlain's accommodating stance in the 1938 negotiations had convinced him that the British and French would not resist the further annexations. The deadly danse macabre intensified throughout the year until, in August, an event took place which bemused international observers: the historic enemies, the Soviet Union and Germany, signed a non-aggression pact known as the Molotov-Ribbentrop agreement. Stalin had entered negotiations with Hitler because he feared that the Führer would attempt to annex parts of the Soviet Union and the Allies would refuse to come to his aid, whereas Germany wished to attack Poland without fear of Russian intervention. It was also a blow to the Allies, who had counted on the Soviet threat to check Hitler's territorial ambitions. Nor did London and Paris know that the deal included secret provisions outlining how the two powers would divide up the smaller nations that lay between them into "spheres of interest."

On the night of August 31, the SS staged a phony Polish attack on a German radio station, leaving behind a handful of dead concentration camp prisoners in Polish uniforms to serve as evidence of a supposed Polish invasion – Hitler's casus belli for the war he was about to launch. The first attack of the war took place on September 1, 1939, with a symbolic gesture: the German battleship Schleswig-Holstein opened fire on a fortress in Danzig while a handful of Polish soldiers held out as a suicide squad.

Simultaneously, at dawn, one and a half million German troops launched a ferocious assault on Poland all along its border with German-controlled territory. Using panzer tanks preceded by Stuka dive-bombers, the German forces advanced at a dizzying pace – the Blitzkrieg had begun. Meanwhile, the sophisticated German Air Force, the Luftwaffe, sent its bombers and fighters to attack airfields, railways and troop concentrations, while dumping tons of explosive on cities the length and breadth of Poland, in an effort to create a fleeing mass of terror-stricken civilians, disrupt communications and target Polish morale.

Poland was determined to resist Germany's invasion, and her troops were highly motivated, but her forces mobilized late, with an air force one-tenth the size of Germany's, and no mechanized divisions. As soon as the hostilities commenced, Poland requested immediate assistance from France and Britain, and on September 3 both declared war on Germany. With Hitler's invasion of Poland there was no longer any political support for appeasement. On the same day Churchill addressed the House of Commons: "This is not a question of fighting for Danzig or Poland," he said. "We are fighting to save the whole world from the pestilence of Nazi tyranny and in defense of all that is most sacred to man."

The Polish armed forces hoped to hold out long enough so that an offensive could be mounted against Germany by British and French forces. Although the Western military commanders were strong in principle, they were accustomed to the strategies of the First World War and unprepared for the rapid invasion of Poland. The British had no way of reaching Poland with an army, while the French were digging in behind the Maginot Line – it was the beginning of the "phoney war."[1] And so, despite fighting valiantly and inflicting serious casualties on the enemy forces, the Poles began to be overwhelmed.

On October 17, the situation became even more desperate. In the east, the Red Army soldiers poured across the Polish border into the territory that fell into the Soviet "sphere of influence" as agreed in the Molotov-Ribbentrop pact. The Russian government announced it was protecting the Ukrainians and Belarusians who lived in the eastern part of Poland. Any prospect of Poland's survival now ended, and the next day her government and military leaders fled the country through Romania.

From the very first hours of the war, Warsaw, the capital of Poland, was subjected to huge aerial bombardments. The Germans wanted to cause panic by striking at the cultured city in the very heart of Poland. On September 8, the first German armored units reached the outskirts of the city and soon afterwards Warsaw was placed under siege. As the war progressed, the German High Command directed a relentless onslaught

against the city, especially the historical Old Town, the Warsaw Royal Castle and other iconic monuments. Apart from the military facilities, the German pilots also targeted civilian facilities such as hospitals, markets and schools, which resulted in heavy human casualties.

The assault culminated on September 25 in what was then the biggest air raid the world had ever seen. On this infamous "Black Monday," the already shattered city was pummeled by hundreds of tons of high explosives and heavy artillery fire. The Warsaw army fought ferociously, but against overwhelming odds, while the situation of the civilian inhabitants of Warsaw became increasingly tragic. After the brutal siege ended on September 27, when the city capitulated, some 140,000 Polish soldiers were herded out of the city as prisoners of war, while the bodies of many thousands of dead civilians – men, women and children – lay entombed under the rubble of collapsed buildings.

On the following day, Germany and the USSR outlined their zones of occupation. Once again Poland was partitioned by its more powerful neighbors and ceased to exist as a country. Germany directly annexed Western Poland and Danzig, while the portion in the middle of the land, including Warsaw, was placed under the administration of the newly established General Government. It was ruled from the city of Krakow by Hans Frank, Hitler's former attorney and an enthusiastic proponent of Nazi ideology. The Russians absorbed the eastern portion of Poland including Byelorussia and West Ukraine, and immediately started a program of Sovietization.

The curtain had rung up on the most tragic six-act drama the world had ever witnessed, and each year would bring horrifying new revelations about the possibilities of "man's inhumanity to man."

---

1. This was the name given to the eight-month period at the start of the Second World War, during which little warfare occurred in Western Europe. It began after the declaration of war by Britain and France against Nazi Germany on September 3, 1939, and continued until the German invasion of France and the Low Countries on May 10, 1940.

24

PRISON AGAIN

As Sam read the news reports about the situation in Poland he wondered in anguish how his parents and siblings were faring. But, like the other Jews in Europe, his own life would now be caught up in the unfolding events.

Sam had been forced to change lodgings yet again, and had taken a room in the Rue Philomene where he made some new acquaintances. On the floor below him lived a German refugee named Asher who was an outstanding artist, while in a nearby house dwelt a tall, red-bearded Russian called Nicolas. He had fought in his homeland in support of the Revolution but left there in 1923, escaping from Stalin. Sam and Asher often visited him. However, the Belgian police had started to track down persons they considered suspicious, and they came for Nicolas, who managed to flee just in time. The police set a guard on his house, and when Sam came to visit him – having no idea what had transpired – he was arrested.

"Papers, please," they asked him. Sam had nothing to show and was taken to the Courthouse. The Commissioner was civil.

"Name and address, please ... Why don't you have any papers?"

But Sam could see they were more interested in his relationship with the Russian than with his residential status. "Why were you in contact with him?" they asked.

Nicolas was married and had a 16-year-old daughter. "I came to visit his daughter," said Sam.

The interrogation was short and he was pushed into a car and brought to the prison in Begijne Street. Sam shivered involuntarily when he was led inside. His cell seemed familiar: small and dark, with a chamber pot to relieve himself. But there was running water, and in the afternoon he could go out for half an hour in the paved courtyard. The prisoners had to walk one after another in single file and were forbidden to talk. It reminded Sam of a work by van Gogh, *Prisoners Exercising*, which the artist had created while shut up in an asylum in Saint-Rémy and longing passionately for release. The painting depicts a group of men shuffling in a suffocating round beneath the high brick walls of a prison courtyard. It evokes a sense of silent despair, and the horror of incarceration is accentuated by the glimpse of two small-winged creatures fluttering high above.

Nevertheless, this half hour was the best moment of Sam's day; it was when he felt less lonely. And once a week Hennie was given permission to see him. They met for her first visit under the watchful eye of a guard who, thought Sam, with his heavy jowls and bulldog stare had a distinct resemblance to Cerberus, gatekeeper to the Underworld.

"How are you?" Hennie asked him across the table that separated them.

"Really, very well," he answered. "I sleep ... I eat ... I drink, and I read books."

Hennie was wearing a red skirt and a tight white blouse; she was an incongruous bright flower blooming in the drab gray surroundings. *She's so pretty*, Sam thought. He gazed at her hungrily, imprinting the image of her face and delicate form on his mind, and reached out to take her hands.

Cerberus sprang at once into growling action. "That's forbidden," he shouted.

With a sigh Sam let go of her small hands ... but he knew he wasn't alone in this trial and carried the thought like a talisman in his heart. The days passed slowly. Hennie had brought him paper and he made several drawings – faces and some nudes. Finally, after five weeks, he was liberated. Hennie waited for him at the gate, and they walked away from the prison doors in silence. They didn't feel the need to speak, and in their wordless communication rejoiced in each other's company.

Life resumed for a time on its old course. Sam bought a second-hand bicycle, and on the weekends he and Hennie rode with friends – Jozef, Camille, Leonard, Rosa – to the Schoten-Wijnegem Forest, about 15 kilometers from Antwerp, where they would go swimming. Sam became a member of the Friends of Nature Society. When the young woman behind the desk asked for his ID card, he answered, "Sorry, I forgot it, but this is my student card from the Academy of Art." To his elation, he was accepted without further ado. This meant that he could also sleep in the youth hostels which were dotted about the countryside.

At one point the group of Antwerpers decided to spend a few days in the seaside resort of Scheveningen in Holland. When they arrived at the hostel they discovered, to their dismay, that a group of young Nazis was also staying there. They were all without exception sporting and handsome, they sang with fine voices, and their bathing suits were imprinted with swastikas. The presence of the young Germans in the hostel was used as a means of propaganda by the Nazis, and the manager turned a blind eye to their swagger, loud banter and pretensions of superiority.

"Jews are vile and lazy creatures," remarked one laconically. "The world would be a much better place without them."

A wave of horror washed through Sam as he listened, and he longed to protest. But his friend Camille met his eyes and shook his head lightly. Camille was a calm and gentle young man, a born peacemaker. Yet Sam was not simply indignant about the slander – for all Jewish people had heard many such words before. It was rather that, at that moment, he sensed a premonition of what the future would bring, and also felt a sense of helplessness: he was a poor, illegal immigrant who still had no papers. He and his friends decided to return home; their joy was gone, and in their ears still rang the words laced with so much poison. The beautiful weather also changed; it became windy and rainy, and as they cycled back to Antwerp they battled with the elements all the way. They arrived exhausted, but there was worse to come: Sam's premonition already began to prove prophetic.

One day, as he and Hennie were cycling side by side through the streets of Antwerp, he reached out and put his arm on her shoulder. A policeman who was passing by waved at them, ordering them to stop, and Sam was overtaken by sudden panic. He started pedaling as fast as he could, trying to escape, but a tram came hurtling in front of him like a silver nemesis, and he was forced to swerve and stop. The policeman caught up with him, by now very angry. He wrote a report with three damning indictments: *No ID card, Infraction of Traffic Regulations, Attempt to Escape Arrest.*

Sam had shown his student card from the Academy, but the policeman simply shrugged his shoulders. Hennie accompanied Sam to the police station but wasn't allowed in.

"Please," she pleaded. "Let him go; we'll pay the fine."

The Teichteil family did pay the fines; they also contacted a lawyer who tried to have Sam released as soon as possible. Meanwhile he was treated harshly, interrogated at length, made to remove the belt of his pants and his shoelaces, and once again found himself shut up in the prison of Begijne Street. In his cell there were three other men, imprisoned for the same offense of having no papers; together they endured the bad food. Every Friday they had to polish brass objects and clean the cell thoroughly. Sam got books from the library and also glued bags – it helped pass the time and he earned some pennies. After one month he was liberated.

The sense that war was imminent became more tangible. The Director of the Academy received an order to transmit the names of non-Belgian students to the authorities, and it became increasingly difficult to find a room without being registered. The Polarskis, now living in Cuperus Street, agreed that Sam could sleep in their attic; they didn't want payment but Sam insisted. At first he wasn't able to sleep because of the sound of the nearby railway, but quickly got used to it. Then, one Friday morning at 6 o'clock, two men rang the doorbell; it was the secret police, who had got the address through the Academy. Esther was pale with fear; Sam stayed calm.

They won't arrest me, he thought. *After all, I'm a student at the Academy …*

He was wrong. He was taken again to the Begijne Street prison. For the third time he underwent the same interrogation, and again was incarcerated. The Teichteil family was contacted and made a statement to the effect that Sam had a place to live and wasn't working. He stayed imprisoned for six weeks, and afterwards was granted an official temporary permit for a period of six months – the coveted "white card." Sam put it in his inside pocket with a smile. The relief at not having to hide any more was intense. *From now on, life will be good*, he thought.

The six months passed. Hennie was in Sam's room, and looking out of the window saw two men approaching the building. It wasn't difficult to recognize their identity and purpose. "Sam," she cried urgently, "two strangers are coming to the house. I think it's the secret police. Quickly, hide!"

Sam ran down the stairs and went out through the back door; he hid in a shed where a rusted bicycle and other derelict items were stored. The men rang at the apartment of the neighbors downstairs, who indicated the way to the attic. Hennie opened the door when the peremptory knock came.

"Shmiel Szija Herciger, please."

"He's not here." Hennie was shaking.

They pushed her abruptly aside and looked around the small lodging. "His coat is here!"

"No, it's my brother's," said Hennie.

They left, and after waiting 20 minutes Hennie went to get Sam. She was still trembling, but Sam remained calm and embraced her. "It's nothing," he told Hennie. "But it might be easier if I just got a season ticket for the Begijne Street prison."

He smiled, but it was a sad smile.

25

GERMANY'S WESTERN CAMPAIGN

The German invasion of Poland, in September 1939, took place almost 25 years to the day after the Great War began in 1914. Memories of that conflict were still vivid as the peoples of Britain and the Low Countries began living in expectation of a German advance westward. During the winter months, nearly half a million soldiers of the British Expeditionary Force (BEF) deployed alongside Allied troops in France and Belgium – yet there was still no action on the Western Front.[1] Then, on May 10, 1940, the phoney war came to an abrupt end.

On that day, Hitler began his Western offensive with the radio code word "Danzig," launching a concentrated air and land attack on Belgium, Luxembourg and the Netherlands. The Germans justified their actions with an egregious falsehood, alleging that British and French armies were planning to march through the Low Countries to attack the Ruhr. In Britain, news of the German invasion was received with dismay, yet it did have one effect of incalculable significance: Prime Minister Chamberlain, who had lost the confidence of the British people, resigned office in the evening of May 10 and the mantle of leadership passed to Winston Churchill.

The battle in the Second World War would now unfold much more swiftly than in the First, both on ground and in the air. In their Western campaigns, the Germans were planning two major operations – Fal Gelb (Case Yellow), to be followed by Fal Rot (Case Red), both dependent upon their tactic of Blitzkrieg, or "Lightning War."[2]

In the early morning of May 10, watchers on the Dutch coastline saw bombers from the Luftwaffe flying in the direction of the North Sea and assumed they were heading for England – but once out of sight the planes circled around and flew back to the continent. At 6 o'clock in the morning, they let their bombs fall on the port of Antwerp, and soon airfields throughout Belgium, Holland and Luxembourg – nations which had declared their neutrality in the event of a pan-European conflict – were being pummeled by waves of German aircraft. Meanwhile, thousands of German airborne troops were parachuting into cities and strategic locations scattered the length and breadth of the Low Countries.

Belgium had suffered greatly in the First World War, and her citizens had no desire to be caught up in another such conflict. In the 1930s, the Belgian military had been reorganized as an exclusively defensive force, and the country's ring of forts situated around Liege and Namur were considered part of Europe's most advanced protective network. The mighty fortress of Eben Emael, which guarded the Albert Canal, was thought to be impregnable – until the German invaders came gliding in from the skies. Despite mounting a valiant counterattack the Belgian soldiers were soon overcome; and it was not long before German divisions were racing across Belgium, while bombing raids struck terror into the hearts of the populace.

On May 11, the second day of the offensive, the Belgian front was broken. That same day, the roads leading westwards, away from the fighting, were filled with panic-stricken refugees fleeing from the onslaught; as many as two million civilians jammed the highways, hampering the movement of defending troops. The Belgian forces continued to fight against the overwhelming odds, but were gradually pushed into a small pocket in the northeast of the country. On May 28, King Leopold III ordered a surrender, and most of the surviving Belgian defenders were made prisoners of war.

The lethal German assault had also focused upon the Netherlands, where Rotterdam especially was suffering, with much of the city set on fire and hundreds killed. The Dutch and Belgian governments appealed to Britain for help as soon as the war broke out, and the BEF as well as French troops were rushed into the northern half of Belgium and toward Holland. But this action was to have disastrous consequences for the Allies. The German invasion of the Low Countries, comprehensive and terrible as it was, had been largely a diversionary measure, part of a wider blueprint for the invasion of France. When they made their advance into the Low Countries, the Allies were in fact facilitating an operation for the conquering of la République Française which had been planned in meticulous detail by the Germans.

The Allied commanders were still steeped in the military doctrines of the First World War, with its long-drawn-out trench warfare and slow attritional fighting. The nation of France, shattered by that earlier conflict, was determined to prepare for any future war with strong defensive measures. During the 1930s, the French Government had constructed an enormous barrier along its eastern border, a sophisticated chain of fortifications known as the Maginot Line. But while the French confidently expected that it would protect their nation from Switzerland to the sea, the portion on the Belgian border was extremely weak, and there was another stretch which was nearly undefended.

This section of the line was beside the Ardennes Forest, a heavily wooded region with a rough and hilly terrain, located primarily in Belgium and Luxembourg. The French considered the region impassable to tanks, and impossible for a large force to cross quickly. As a result, the Allies were expecting the Germans to focus on invading France through central Belgium as they had in the First World War ... but the German divisions had been elaborately rehearsed in the Black Forest for the campaign in which they were now to take part.

Over the course of May 11, German tanks and infantry streamed through Luxembourg under the cloak of the Ardennes Forest and protected from above by the Luftwaffe, completely bypassing the Maginot Line. The area which the French believed impénétrable was penetrated by the German army with relative ease as they proceeded with their main offensive into the heart of France. They reached the River Meuse by the evening of May 12 and soon broke through the French defenses into open country. Turning *westward, they began to race through the valley of the River Somme toward the English Channel, aided by the German aircraft that now ruled the skies. The German panzer division under the command of General Erwin Rommel – the future "Desert Fox" – advanced so quickly that it was dubbed a "ghost division."*

As the Germans moved rapidly toward the coast, the BEF decided on a counterattack, code-named Frankforce, to take place near the town of Arras. The surprise assault on May 21, executed by just two infantry battalions totaling around 2,000 men, and reinforced by 74 tanks, initially made rapid progress – but the lack of supporting infantry made it difficult for the British to consolidate their gains. The German panzer divisions regrouped quickly, Operation Frankforce came to an end, and the next day the Germans continued their advance. But that little, bravely acquitted battle at Arras would later have a profound effect on the course of the war.

Soon the German tanks were sweeping up past Boulogne and Calais, capturing all the French and Belgian ports north of the river Somme – apart from Dunkirk. With German troops advancing against them through Belgium, and the panzers pressing up from the south, the Allies were now trapped between the two German armies, being pushed back toward the coast under heavy bombardment. It had become clear to the British High Command that the only option which could possibly save the Allied troops was that of evacuation – but the single port from which such an operation could take place was Dunkirk, and that was already being seriously threatened by the Germans. By May 23, the German panzer groups had reached the canal defense line close to the port, while the bulk of the BEF was still far distant.

More than a quarter of a million British and Allied troops were encircled by the Germans and threatened with complete annihilation by the German High Command. Their plight was desperate and, over in England, Churchill feared he soon would be announcing the single greatest military disaster in the nation's history.

1. Although thought of as the calm before the storm, the period was hardly uneventful. On the same day that Britain announced they were at war a German submarine torpedoed the passenger liner *SS Athenia* near the Irish coast, killing 117. German vessels laid vast numbers of mines in the English Channel, leading to the loss of hundreds of tons of merchant shipping, while their U-boat campaign took a huge toll, destroying the British aircraft carrier *HMS Courageous* and the battleship *HMS Royal Oak*, and causing the death of hundreds. The situation in the West then began to escalate as German forces invaded Denmark and Norway in April 1940 with the objective of preventing the Royal Navy from controlling the North Atlantic.

2. This name, Lightning War, was fully justified: a surprising and violent attack in a crucial location, employing speed and the use of overwhelming force, often aimed at encircling the opposing forces in what was known as a *Kessel* or cauldron. The strategy was designed to create havoc and maximum psychological shock among the defenders – ideally leading to a quick victory.

26

MAY 1940: DUNKIRK

Sam and his fellow Antwerpers watched appalled as the defenses of Belgium crumbled before the relentless German advance during that awful month of May 1940. War had made its murderous appearance in the land, and this meant, for Sam, that all the sweet dreams of the Academy evaporated. He knew that the repercussions of Nazi rule would be terrible; nor was it lost upon him that the difficulty of his situation, as a Jew with no papers or citizenship rights in Belgium, was especially acute.

After the surrender of the Belgian military on May 28, Sam visited two of his friends, Camille and Lenard, who were in similar predicaments. They discussed their options and eventually decided to take their bikes and cycle to Koksijde, a beachside town on the North Sea in the Flemish province of Flanders, adjacent to the French border. From there, they would try to make their way into France.

After coming to this decision, Sam went to see Hennie's parents, the Teichteils. He was hoping desperately they would realize the seriousness of the situation and allow Hennie to join him; he planned to urge them to come as well. "I'm leaving for France," he told them and outlined his plans. "What are your thoughts?"

Salman and his wife shook their heads. "We're not going anywhere; we are staying here."

As they talked together, Hennie was gazing at Sam all the while, fear written plainly on her countenance. She didn't say a word, but suddenly her face crumpled, and she turned and ran from the room. Sam started to go after her but her father stopped him. "Don't you understand that you're only making things worse?" he said. "Just leave!"

Sam departed, his head bowed. In his mind's eye he could see only the picture of Hennie's face with the tears running down her cheeks. He was utterly torn, but his decision was made, and the same day he left Antwerp on his bike with his two friends for the 150-kilometer ride to the sea.

The roads out of the city were like rivers, overflowing with refugees fleeing from the chaos in Belgium and making their way to France. Every variety of transportation was being called into use: some were traveling in cars, others on horseback, in carriages, or on bicycles like Sam and his friends. A vast number were trudging on foot, laden with pitiful bundles, and many pushed baby carriages. Men who were 18 years and over were required to go to Roeselare to enroll in the militia and they also swelled the long column on its move southward. Sam felt a pang for the older men and women who sat or lay exhausted on the sides of the road. Some were holding their heads in their hands in despair, and he knew that for many their quest to find freedom would prove fatal.

In the evening his group reached a village which was filled with the refugees; every lodging place was taken but a young couple with a child agreed to let them share their room. All night the thunder of falling bombs rattled the windows. Early next morning they rose and set off again on their bikes until they reached the border. It was a chaotic scene: the French had closed the crossing point and were not allowing anyone to pass. Children were crying, some were begging, others trying to bribe the border police, all to no avail.

The long day dragged by and night fell again; it was bitterly cold. People lay huddled next to one another for warmth. Morning dawned; again the hours passed slowly, while the queue in front of the border became steadily longer. Suddenly, in the afternoon, the police left their positions and the long line in front of the checkpoint galvanized itself and began thrusting toward the empty border post, like rolling waves crashing on a hard shingle. After reaching their goal and finding themselves in the north of France, many were so exhausted by their ordeal that they collapsed where they stood. Others thrust banknotes at those fortunate enough to have cars, offering small fortunes to be allowed to join them. Sam and his friends felt relieved, but their optimism soon turned to bewilderment as they saw some of the refugees were turning back to Belgium.

"What is going on?" Sam called out.

Someone shouted an answer. "The Germans have arrived and the French coast is completely blocked."

There was no other option: they too had to return to Koksijde. Together with a few families, they rented a villa near the sea for several nights. Different items of information about the war situation had come filtering through to the would-be refugees: the news that the Allied soldiers were stranded on the shoreline at Dunkirk, that the Germans were advancing on them rapidly, and that a huge evacuation was under way. Dunkirk was only about 15 kilometers away from Koksijde – just over the French border to the south. It was becoming evident that it was Sam's fate to be caught up in some of the most significant events of this supreme conflict, to find himself in places that afterwards attained almost mythical significance as symbolizing the heights and depths of the war.

Over in England, the British people had become aware of the perilous situation in which their soldiers were trapped. At that dark moment, King George VI called for a national day of prayer, and in Westminster Abbey and in churches and synagogues throughout the land petitioners gathered in huge numbers. Meanwhile, an urgent request went out for boats of all description to cross the English

Channel to help in rescuing the besieged army, and Churchill ordered Operation Dynamo to begin.

Yet even before the prayers had been offered up, a strange and inexplicable development took place. On May 24, just as a crushing force of nine panzer divisions was beginning to cross the canal defense line close to Dunkirk, Hitler made a decision that still confounds historians – he ordered his army to halt. The British attack on the Germans at Arras had been so fierce that Rommel formed the impression that he had encountered a force of hundreds of heavily armored tanks. Fearing it might be a harbinger of further assaults, Hitler insisted that the German forces should pause in their offensive against Dunkirk, take time to regroup, and make plans to deal with this potential new threat.

This surprising halt of the German armies bought vital time for the Allied forces, the narrowest of windows of opportunity. Covered by rear-guard actions by British and French units, the exhausted troops converged on the port, where they found themselves with their backs to the sea and hemmed in by their enemies. It was a stunning replay of the original biblical Exodus situation. Threatened with imminent annihilation, the men looked out over the barrier – the English Channel – that separated them from their desired haven – just as the Children of Israel had gazed over the Red Sea while Pharaoh's armies were in hot pursuit. Could a whole army be saved? The military leadership in England did not dare hope for more than a fraction of the troops to make it to safety.

On May 27, the first full day of the evacuation, the British Admiralty had arranged for eight destroyers to rescue as many troops as could be taken, but the same day the Luftwaffe launched a deadly campaign against Dunkirk, bombing the town and the docks, destroying the oil tanks, wrecking the harbor and killing a thousand civilians, while the Allied troops sheltered from the explosions in cellars or in the dunes behind the beaches. Thick black smoke coming from the burning oil tanks blanketed the town, and as the water supply had been taken out it was impossible to extinguish the raging fires.

The ruin of the docks meant that the men had to be evacuated from the beaches and long breakwaters. The first members of the hastily assembled fleet of merchant and civilian ships and boats began arriving on the morning of May 28, lifting men off the beaches and ferrying them to larger vessels waiting offshore. Together with the Royal Navy's fighting ships – over 900 vessels in all – they plied the dangerous waters to and from Dunkirk loading more and more troops under frequent and intense German attacks from land, sea and air, as shipping losses began to soar. British, French and Belgian troops defended Dunkirk, while the RAF fought a courageous battle to keep the Luftwaffe from gaining control of the skies.

Sam and his friends had arrived in Koksijde as the evacuation was proceeding. On their first evening in the villa, the violent bombardments taking place around Dunkirk began shaking the windows continuously so that they rattled in their frames, and the air around them seemed to boil with the intensity of the combat taking place between British and German aircraft. All the house occupants trooped down to the cellar where they spent a miserable night, like a deathbed vigil that seemed it would never end. One of the women shouted an unrelenting oracle of doom: "We'll all get killed, we'll all get killed." Finally her hysteria dissolved into diminuendo and she began sobbing. But little sleep was had by any.

When they arose in the morning, bleary eyed, Sam talked with his friends. "Let's go to Dunkirk," he said. "We have to get on a ship to England. That's our last chance."

They rode the 15 kilometers to Dunkirk but as they drew close found scenes reminiscent of the *Inferno* section of Dante's *Divine Comedy*. The port was on fire where the German planes had hit a petrol tank, and angry red flames shot heavenward; vast billowing clouds of gray smoke filled the air and made it difficult for Sam to breathe. A line from the Italian masterpiece echoed in his mind:

There is a place within the depths of hell

Call'd Malebolge.

He and his companions made their way on foot, pushing their bikes through the deserted side streets of the town until they reached a line of low sandhills. "Wait here," said Sam to his friends. "I'm going to see what's happening."

He scrambled over the last of the dunes, and then stood still, amazed at the scene which unfolded before him. Vast sandy beaches stretched into an endless distance, mile upon mile of them, and they were covered with countless numbers of uniformed soldiers of the British army. Many had formed queues, endless queues, and were standing in line, waiting with the patience and weariness of Job for their rescue. The skies overhead were bleak and gray, but the sea itself lay with a sheen like pearl, calm and still as a millpond – and it was alive with craft. Over the Channel was moving a myriad of boats – some small, others larger, of every class and description – one of the strangest armadas of all time.

Sam knew some English as a legacy of the cosmopolitan atmosphere at the Art Academy, and he moved forward over the flat sands, hoping to engage some of the soldiers in conversation and learn more about what was happening. But they shook their heads when Sam asked about passage in the boats.

"Sorry, son – only Allied soldiers."

With dispirited hearts, Sam and his friends returned to Koksijde. At 6 o'clock the next morning the German conquerors arrived in the town, but he and his group were able to make their way back to Antwerp in the covered container of a truck. All the way on that return journey, Sam pondered the incredible sight he had seen on the desolate beaches of Dunkirk – the vast numbers of patiently waiting troops, and the sheer heroism and resourcefulness of the motley fleet which had come on its mission of mercy, resolved to rescue their soldiers and lift them out of hell.

27

JUNE 1940 – OCTOBER 1940: INTO FRANCE

By June 4, close to 350,000 British and Allied troops – including French, Polish and Canadian soldiers – had been landed in England, making it possible for the Allies to regroup and fight on. That same day, Churchill made a speech admitting that wars were not won by evacuations, but making a stirring declaration of the British resolve:

"We shall go on to the end ... whatever the cost may be, we shall fight on the beaches, we shall fight on the landing grounds, we shall fight in the fields and in the streets, we shall fight in the hills; we shall never surrender."

But Luxembourg, the Netherlands and Belgium had fallen, and France was to be next. Even before the last of the Allied troops had left Dunkirk, a thousand Luftwaffe aircraft swept over France, launching a devastating aerial bombardment, and the German army moved to initiate Case Red, striking southward from their positions on the Somme into the heart of France. On June 9, Rommel's tanks were over the Seine; the French government fled to Bordeaux, and on June 14 the Germans marched into a deserted Paris – dealing the coup de grace to whatever French morale remained. Meanwhile, the victorious panzers fanned out across the land, exerting everywhere their fearful hegemony: France had fallen, a disaster of unimaginable magnitude.

On June 22, the French signed an armistice with the Germans, the terms of which divided the nation. Germany was to occupy northern France and all of France's Atlantic coastline down to the border with Spain; the southern half of France was permitted to remain under French civil administration. The new French government established in the town of Vichy under Marshall Henri Petain declared neutrality in the war between Germany and Britain, but was committed by the armistice provisions to cooperation with Germany. In London, de Gaulle announced his refusal to recognize the Vichy regime, and instead established a new government, "the Free French."

The campaign against the Low Countries and France had lasted less than six weeks. By the summer of 1940, with almost all Western Europe under German control, the Nazis seemed unstoppable, and Hitler was at the height of his popularity in Germany. At that point only England was still free, but it seemed inconceivable that the British would be able to liberate Europe from the forces engulfing it.

Sam was back in Antwerp, and glad to be reunited with Hennie as life proceeded under the German occupation of Belgium. There was at first no difference made between Jews and non-Jews, but that began insidiously to change, and, in October 1940, the military government adopted anti-Jewish legislation modeled on the Nuremberg Laws. A curfew was installed, study prohibited, Jews were forced from certain professions, and businesses were seized. The 18:00 hour curfew was applied to the letter, and Jews caught outside after that time were arrested and brought to Fort Breendonck near Mechelen, requisitioned by the Germans as a prison camp for detaining political prisoners, Resistance members and Jews. Grim details of the torture and executions taking place at the Fort soon began leaking out, and Sam determined once more that he must escape from Belgium. But where could he go? For the thousandth time, he pored over the reports reaching Antwerp. The news was not good.

It was clear that the war was only increasing in intensity as more nations were being swept up in the conflict. Germany, Italy and Japan had signed the Tripartite Pact; soon Slovakia, Hungary, and Romania would throw in their lot with the Axis powers. The war had spread to North Africa and the Pacific, and the Battle of the Atlantic had also begun, the struggle for control of the waters separating North America and Europe. It was vital for the Allies that supply lines between the two continents should be kept open, but German U-boats were everywhere prowling the ocean, taking a murderous toll on Allied shipping. And the Battle of Britain was raging in the skies over England.

After the Dunkirk evacuation, Hitler was determined to invade the British Isles, and from July 1940 the planes of the Luftwaffe launched a series of massive air assaults against the airfields of England. The pilots of the RAF, flying a new generation of fighters including the Hurricane and Spitfire, and aided by technological innovations such as radar, had prevented the Luftwaffe from gaining the air superiority needed for invasion. However, since September bombs had been directed toward London and other large provincial cities: it was the beginning of the Blitz. In the capital, the citizens huddling in the Underground for protection endured the onslaught with notable stoicism, but the bombing raids caused enormous destruction and heavy casualties. By the time the Blitz came to an effective close the following year, when Hitler decided to concentrate on the Eastern Front, thousands of British civilians had perished.

And of course Sam was deeply concerned about the situation in Poland: he had not heard from his parents or any family members since the 1939 conquest, and the news that was coming through was disturbing in the extreme. From the first days of the war, violence against civilians had been a feature of the German occupation, and persecution of Polish Jews was growing in intensity also. The Germans were establishing ghettos and forced labor camps on a vast scale, all Jews had to wear yellow stars, and Jewish businesses were being seized. Meanwhile, hundreds of thousands of Jewish and non-Jewish refugees had fled the advancing German army into eastern Poland, only to be trapped when the Soviets annexed the region.

Many of these refugees were then arrested and deported by the Soviet secret police to the depths of Siberia.

Reading about what was happening in Poland and other nations taken over by the Nazis filled Sam with dread. Escape he must, and eventually he decided that his best bet would lie in making his way through France to try and reach Spain, a neutral country. He had some meager savings and thought of acquiring a forged French passport, but when he checked the price realized there was no way he could afford it. But he did have one thing in his favor. A friend from the Academy named Jules Glatt lived in a place called Bagnères-de-Bigorre in the High Pyrenees, almost on the Spanish border, and he thought it might be possible to make his way there before attempting a crossing. He went to Hennie and consulted with her.

"Sam," she said to him, her eyes wide and glistening with unshed tears, "You have to leave. You are without papers – they can arrest you any minute. Don't worry, darling. The war will soon be over." She kissed him and gently pushed him outside.

Being on the run always ... would it ever end, he wondered mutinously. The burdens he was carrying, not just concern for his own safety but also for Hennie's wellbeing, were weighing heavily on the young man. He loved Antwerp and he loved Hennie, who was so sweet, but he had little choice. Two of his friends were also hoping to make their way into non-occupied France; one was Leonard, with whom Sam had unsuccessfully tried to escape into France from Koksijde; the other was a man named Jean, who had some experience working for the Resistance. They met together and Sam suggested an initial strategy: "Let's take the 6 o'clock train to Brussels. At such an early hour they will presume we're workers."

His idea was accepted, and from Brussels the three young men took the train to Lille in France, located just over the border. They had brought only a few belongings with them and kept silent so as not to draw attention to themselves. When they arrived in Lille, the three walked out of the town, continuing until they came to a large forest. Jean explained what they should do.

"You need to cross this wood, and on the other side you'll find a village. There won't be any military guard there, and you'll be able to get on a train to Toulouse in the south. But right now we should split up. We look more suspicious if we stay together."

The three men took different paths into the forest. Sam was then alone; he took a deep breath and strode on. Finally he reached the village, but could see no sign of Jean or Leonard. The night train for Toulouse arrived at the small platform and he clambered aboard. The journey seemed endless. They eventually reached Toulouse but Sam remained on board; his destination was the town of Tarbes, a little further on. From there he planned to take a connecting train to his destination, Bagnères-de-Bigorre, in the foothills of the Pyrenees.

At 5 o'clock in the morning he arrived at Tarbes, happy that the journey had so far proved without incident, but as soon as he stepped out of the train two gendarmes approached.

"Papers, please," came the oh-so-familiar request.

"I don't have any."

"Where do you come from?"

"Belgium."

"Come with us, lad."

Just as so many times before, Sam was pushed into a car and taken to a prison. The interrogations began, a report was written, and he was condemned to six weeks in prison. The jail in Tarbes was very cold, the food was bad and it was very dirty, with rats swarming everywhere. There were two prisoners in each cell; many had been jailed for "Gaullism" – supporting General de Gaulle and the Free French Forces, who sought to put France back in the war on the Allied side. On the walls former prisoners had scribbled, "Long live the RAF."

The days passed slowly. Sam shared his cell with a Frenchman who had been arrested for fraud; he had a melancholy nature and confided in Sam that he found some respite from his nagging wife while in prison. Finally the six weeks was over, and Sam was looking forward to his freedom.

As soon as he walked outside he was dazzled by the sunlight. He felt his arm being seized, and two men in uniform hustled him into a car.

"Where are you taking me? I'm free now!"

The men laughed at his French accent. "Don't be so curious – you'll soon find out."

Sam fell asleep ... in difficult moments this often happened. What was this incredible coping mechanism he possessed, that gave him such a courage to endure? Was it in his mind – his *psyche*? Was it part of his nervous system, or an unconscious reflex of self-preservation? In any event, it was about to be tested again, to the limit.

28

NOVEMBER 1940 – MAY 1941: GURS

"Hey, wake up." He was prodded. "We've arrived."

Sam stared. They had drawn up before a gate where a large sign proclaimed, "Welcome Center." He had been brought to the infamous concentration camp of Gurs, located in an isolated area of Southwestern France. Here, in the foothills of the Pyrenees and surrounded by high snow-capped mountain peaks, the scenery was beautiful. Apart from that it was impossible to find anything good to say about it.

The French government had established the Gurs camp in 1939, before the war with Germany began, to serve as a detention center for Spanish Republicans and members of the International Brigade fleeing Spain after the Spanish Civil War. After the armistice it fell under the authority of the Vichy regime, and the character of the camp changed as the French started sending "undesirables" there, including refugees, political activists – and, of course, Jews. There were approximately 350,000 Jews in France as war broke out, more than half of whom were refugees from Germany who had arrived during the 1930s. After the Vichy government promulgated the *Statut des Juifs* they were excluded from public life and subject to large-scale internment.

By late 1940, there were 15,000 inmates in the Gurs camp, enduring extremely primitive living conditions, and Sam now joined their numbers. He was ushered through the gate and gazed about at his new living quarters, where row after row of bleak-looking huts might cause an anchorite to shudder. They were assembled from thin planks of wood which offered no protection from the cold, and in the overcrowded cabins the detainees slept on the floor on sacks of straw. The food was scarce and poor in quality; there was no sanitation or running water. Illness was rife, and hundreds died of contagious diseases, including typhoid and dysentery. But there was another feature of the camp which caught Sam's eye instantly. The perimeter was enclosed by a double barbed wire fence, only two meters in height, and it was not electrified, nor were there any lookout towers or armed guards.

Sam's stay at Gurs was to prove as demoralizing and dehumanizing as any of his other prison experiences. In his first weeks there he began to sort out the different people groups and the power structure operating in the camp. It was supervised by demobilized French soldiers, but some of the Spaniards who had fought in the Civil War also acted as if they were in charge. They carried clubs and used them regularly. However, it was a huge Alsatian who dominated the pecking order; he was pro-German, bullied everyone and was called the Chief.

For some weeks Sam and some other inmates were made to sleep outside without blankets, but when temperatures dropped below freezing each night they were shown to a filthy, mud-filled barrack. There was a canteen, but only those who had managed to secrete some money could buy food there. As soon as Sam arrived almost all his savings had been taken, but he was able to send a letter to Jules Glatt, who sent him packages with bread and sugar. Otherwise there was almost nothing to eat, and Sam's heart was wrung with pity as he saw children and old people dying daily for lack of nutrition. There were two other young Belgians in Sam's barrack. The Belgians were especially regarded with suspicion because they had a reputation for trying to escape. Of course, Sam was instantly attracted to them, and they decided to run away together.

It was a clear night as the three young men made their way stealthily to the extreme perimeter of the camp. Sam kept guard while his friends scrambled over the barbed wire. When they were safely over, he turned to follow but felt a powerful hand grabbing his collar from behind. It was the Chief.

"You dirty thug," he snarled, "you were planning on fleeing, weren't you?"

With the back of his hand he hit Sam on the mouth and blood began flowing from his lips. The Alsatian immediately realized that the other two Belgians were missing.

"Where are they?" he shouted.

"I don't know."

"Oh, no?" He punched Sam violently in the face. "I am going to do everything in my power to make sure that you stay here until the end of your days," he threatened viciously.

Sam answered, "That means that you too will rot here."

This made the giant so angry that he punched Sam several times in the solar plexus. The young man collapsed and fell in the mud. When the Alsatian left, other inmates took him and put him on a pallet.

The next day Sam dragged himself to the doctor, who was himself a prisoner. Sam asked him to write a certificate that his numerous bruises were the result of being punched, but the medic was afraid and refused. The Alsatian saw to it that Sam was locked up in a hangar alone, a sort of prison within the prison. There was a terrible stench and it was very dirty. Sam was under permanent surveillance and only allowed outside in order to go to the primitive sanitation; water and stale bread were his rations. After a week of this punishment he was allowed back in his more salubrious quarters – the ancient barrack.

He decided to make another attempt to escape. His companions this time were an Austrian refugee and a German Jew who had been a soldier with the German army during the First World War and had become deaf. Sam was the only one who knew some French. Their first attempt didn't succeed. They had chosen a misty night for the breakout, but when the haze dissipated rapidly and the stars appeared, illuminating the camp, they returned crestfallen to the barracks.

They tried again some months later. This time the night was dark; the heavens had opened, and the sound of heavy raindrops falling to earth masked the sound of their footfalls as they stole to the fence. They managed to climb over the barbed wire, with bleeding hands and torn clothes their only casualty. Now they found themselves in the depths of a forest, and with no map to guide them decided to try and make their way in the direction of Spain. They struggled through the dense trees, hampered by the cold and damp, but when dawn eventually came were shocked at what they saw. They were right in front of the camp – they had been walking around in circles.

At this point, hungry, thirsty and exhausted, they hid among the trees, staying in one place until night fell. They tried drinking from a puddle but felt sick afterwards, and their thirst became intolerable. Scouting a little further afield, they found a dilapidated house and in desperation broke into it. Here, in a long-disused kitchen cabinet, they found a treasure – a bottle of wine. They were disappointed when they opened it; it tasted like vinegar. Nevertheless they drained it to the last drop, then lay down on the dirty floor and were able to sleep for a few hours. They were beginning to feel their meager reserves of strength draining away. So many escapees from the camp had been captured at this point.

Emerging from the hovel and continuing to walk, the three came across a prosperous-looking farmhouse.

"Let's go there," said Sam.

The Austrian demurred. "They might denounce us."

"We don't have any choice," Sam pointed out.

They approached and knocked at the door. It opened, and a large peasant woman stood there, looking suspiciously at them with arms akimbo. A divine smell wafted from the interior of the house, and the three men nearly fainted with longing.

"What do you want?" she asked.

The German gestured to show that they wanted to come inside. Sam said in French, "We are on our way to the border."

"Come inside." She opened the door and invited them in. It was a Sunday and her family was in church; meanwhile, she was busy preparing a cassoulet – the slow-cooked casserole which is a specialty of southern France – for their midday meal. The aroma was even more exquisite now they were inside the house, and the woman saw the hunger that spoke so eloquently in their eyes.

She laughed. "I'll give you some of my cassoulet," she said.

It was delicious, but the chicken and beans were swimming in fat. The three men, starved of nutrition for so long, were able to eat only a little, and drank a lot of water.

"Can you show us how to get to the border?" asked Sam, after thanking her.

She accompanied them outside. "It's very simple," she said. "Go straight ahead along this path until you see the windmill; the road leading to the border with Spain is just behind it."

They started walking, but when they suddenly saw a German patrol marching ahead they scattered and hid in the forest. After a while Sam decided it was safe to leave his hiding place, but didn't dare to call his friends. With a heavy heart he continued alone.

Once again he ran into another patrol, but this time when he caught sight of the soldiers it was too late to try and hide. He quickly picked up a large beam of wood that was lying beside the path, slung it over his shoulder and continued walking with his head bowed. In his blue overalls and with the log on his back he resembled one of the local peasants, and the Germans ignored him. When the sound of their jackboots diminished, Sam took to the cover of the trees again, seated himself on a log, and wiped the cold sweat from his forehead.

He sat there, immobile, for some time, drained of energy. Above him was a dark green canopy of leaves, with shafts of sunlight piercing it in places as if through a rent curtain. A bird chirped and fell silent, all the small rustling noises of the woods ceased, and it became very still. The deep peace of the forest gradually stole over him, and he became conscious that the tension that had so cruelly assaulted his nervous system was draining away. A fragment of the prophet Isaiah came knocking at the doors of his mind: *And there shall be a tabernacle for a shadow in the daytime from the heat, and for a place of refuge ...*[1] The tall trees around him seemed a kind of defense – a succah – protecting him in his own journey through the wilderness. He knew it was time for some serious thinking about the next steps he should take, and opened himself up to what the trees would say to him.

Sam had had enough time in the camp to converse with the Spanish inmates and learn about the various trails that led from France into northern Spain. These escape routes over the central Pyrenees would eventually be taken by hundreds of Frenchmen and Jews fleeing their German oppressors, and also by many RAF and American airmen who had either crash-landed or parachuted to safety after being shot down over Nazi-occupied Europe. Sam realized that it was not an easy hike over the high mountain route, that there were rushing rivers, steep climbs, hindrances of snowdrifts and freezing weather, as well as guard posts to evade. He was aware that his physical strength had been sorely depleted in the Gurs camp, but it was not only the perils of the journey that were weighing on his mind.

Once the escapees arrived on Spanish soil, this did not mean the danger was over. The Franco regime had constructed almost 200 concentration camps throughout Spain to incarcerate thousands of Republican prisoners. The largest camp of all was at Maranda de Ebro and used to detain non-Spanish nationals trying to escape from Occupied Europe. Sam had heard of the notorious Maranda camp and knew that the Nazi regime was involved in advising the Spanish how to run the camp. The thought that, after having managed to escape from Gurs, and enduring the hardships involved in trekking over the Pyrenees, he might still be captured and sent there after arriving in Spain was suddenly too much for him to contemplate.

Crumbling a leaf in his hand and watching it fall to the ground, Sam coolly set himself to consider his other alternatives. He felt that life in France, as a Jew in hiding with no papers, would be extremely difficult. Poland was out of the question, as was Palestine. That left only Belgium. At least there he had some status, and some influential friends. Besides, he missed Hennie. She was like a magnet drawing him back.

It was too late to try and find his way out of the forest, so he found a small copse, piled some foliage on himself for a covering and lay down to sleep. He was cold, but through the tangled branches overhead the stars seemed to blaze down upon him with a special intensity; they made him think of van Gogh's *Starry Night* and the whirling splendor of that celestial canopy. Then there came to him the memory of the sun burning on the gentle waves of the Vistula, his encounter there with "the prophet" and the words he had spoken: "You will become exactly what you want to be."

A deep conviction was borne in on Sam during that lonely night in the forest accompanied only by the small bush animals – that it was the province of the artist to portray a dimension of transcendence in all its fullness and meaning; in the words of the English Romantic poet William Blake, to see "not with, but through the eye."[2] Somehow, also, he knew that all his suffering could be transmuted through his art; and that, when a man made in the image of God became stripped to the barest essence of his humanity, it was then that he might also become clothed with a new, mystical power.

The dawn came and the sun rose, lighting the woods with fire. Sam also rose, strengthened in his soul, and began to make his way out of the forest on winged feet. He was not to know that there were still further depths into which he must plunge.

---

1. Taken from Isaiah 4:6.
2. From William Blake's "Auguries of Innocence":
   This Lifes dim Windows of the Soul
   Distorts the Heavens from Pole to Pole
   And leads you to Believe a Lie
   When you see with not thro the Eye
   That was born in a night to perish in a night
   When the Soul slept in the beams of Light.
   According to literary critic Northrop Frye, Blake is suggesting in these lines that we must see *through* the vision to the transcendent reality lying beyond it, which has both provided the vision as well as the means of apprehending it.

29

MAY 1941 – JUNE 1941: A WEDDING

Sam had succeeded in hiding a little money in his clothes, and took a train for Paris where he arrived dirty and hungry. There were German soldiers everywhere, bearing themselves with the air of conquerors. But that same mysterious power that had protected him thus far seemed to render him invisible to their gaze. He passed through the streets and paused in front of – incongruously enough – a souvenir shop. The temptation was too much to resist. He went in and bought a postcard of the Eiffel Tower, then sent it to his Alsatian tormentor with the words, "*Best wishes from Paris, from Sam.*"

Food was rationed and the only thing he was able to buy was a fruit yogurt, but it was too much for his neglected stomach and gave him terrible diarrhea. From Paris he traveled to Amiens where he met a couple of Belgian Jews also leaving France, and together they took a ferry that brought them to the other bank of the River Somme. From there they went to the train station and took the train to Brussels, arriving late at night. Sam spent the night with relatives of Hennie, and the next morning he went on to Antwerp.

When he saw Hennie his first thought was, "Oh God, I'm so grateful I didn't succeed in making it to Spain."

The Teichteils gave Sam permission to sleep at their home. There was no employment to be had in the fur trade and he found work with a baker, delivering loaves of bread in the early morning. He soon found that Antwerp had changed a great deal since his departure.

The German military government assessed the costs of their occupation at staggering levels: about two-thirds of the national income of Belgium. Many thousands of citizens were also forced to serve in labor programs within Germany. Food rationing was introduced, and each individual was allotted only 1,300 calories per day; there were also serious shortages in basic goods. Daily life under occupation was far from easy, and indeed galling for many of the citizens. The press was censored, Nazi flags bearing the hated black swastikas festooned public buildings, and German posters warned the population that any resistance would be swiftly repressed. Meanwhile, the anti-Jewish measures were increasing.

Belgium is a largely Catholic country, and the Jewish population was comparatively small. Most lived in the major cities of Brussels, Charleroi and Liège, but the biggest concentration of Jews was in Antwerp. On April 14, 1941, Easter Monday, a pogrom took place in Antwerp instigated by paramilitaries from the VNV, the Flemish nationalist political party, which early in the war began to collaborate with the Germans. Armed with iron bars, the mob burned two synagogues, destroyed Jewish shops, then proceeded to attack the home of the city's Chief Rabbi; the German authorities turned a blind eye. It seemed that the plight of Jews in Antwerp was becoming worse than in other large cities in Belgium, and Hennie's father was deeply concerned about Sam's situation.

"It would be safer for you in Brussels," he urged.

But Sam was deeply in love with Hennie. "If I go to Brussels, it will be with your daughter," he replied.

Their wedding date was set for June 22, 1941; Sam was 23, while Hennie, the bride, was 18. The ceremony took place at the home of Esther Polarski, with only a few close friends in attendance. Bride and groom stood together beneath the small flower-strewn chuppah which had been set up in Esther's living room. And, as Sam stood beneath the canopy, it seemed to him that past, present and future were dovetailing in his life.

His mind flew back to the carpenter's shed in Zawiercie, and the succah where his family had gathered each year to celebrate the feast with such warmth and simplicity. He remembered also the many friends who had opened their homes to him in his journey, and provided him with shelter and encouragement as he sought to find his way toward his life's purpose. Another image came crowding in: that time of peril in the forests of southern France, when the trees had seemed to bend their branches over him with a protective power, and he had felt certain he should return to Belgium. And here now, with Hennie, he had found a bower and refuge, had experienced a sense of homecoming and belonging, and knew that their wedding was an affirmation of the goodness and continuity of the life they would share.

Sam looked at the kindness and goodwill which shone out of the faces surrounding them, then drew Hennie's veil over her face, a memory of the way in which the biblical Rebekah had covered her face before she was wed to Isaac. The Rabbi uttered the prayers which bound them together in matrimony, and Hennie lifted her veil to sip the cup of wine Sam handed to her. Her face was radiant, and he slipped the gold ring on her finger, making his vow:

"Behold, thou art consecrated to me with this ring, according to the laws of Moses and Israel."

The Rabbi uttered the traditional final prayers:

"Blessed art thou, O Lord our God, King of the universe, who hath created joy and gladness, bridegroom and bride, mirth and exultation, pleasure and delight, love and brotherhood, peace and friendship. May there soon be heard in the cities of Judah, and in the streets of Jerusalem, the voice of joy and gladness, the voice of the bridegroom and the voice of the bride, the

jubilant voice of bridegrooms from the wedding canopy, and of youths from their feasts of song. Blessed art thou, O Lord, who gives the bridegroom joy in his bride ..."

Sam lifted his foot, his heel came crashing down on the glass, and he and Hennie were united as husband and wife. He wished desperately that his own parents were there to witness the ceremony, but his heart was filled with a great joy which stayed with him, not just during the small feast in Esther's apartment, but also in the difficult days that lay ahead.

The same day that they were married, Germany invaded Russia in Operation Barbarossa.

30

JULY 1941 – DECEMBER 1941: IN HIDING

The newlyweds settled down to life in the Teichteils' apartment. Sam bought two old sewing machines and used them to work at home for the fur shops of Antwerp. But the situation in the city continued to cause them concern.

"Sam," said Hennie finally, "it's getting too dangerous here. We have to look for another apartment. We might be better off in Brussels."

"You're right, Hennie." Sam could not bear the thought that harm might come to his new bride as a result of his own precarious situation.

"If you don't mind," she said, "I'd rather go alone to look for a place. After all," she laughed, "I look like a *shikse* with my blonde hair ... while you, with your black curls, might get caught." She ruffled his hair as she spoke. "And it wouldn't be the first time!" she added with a teasing smile.

Hennie found a two-room furnished apartment in Kino Street; the owner, the widowed Madame Meeuws, was an intelligent and gracious woman, who made a living with her clothes store at the front of their building. The young couple confided in Mme Meeuws that they were Jewish, and thus their landlady became one of many non-Jewish citizens of Belgium – "righteous Gentiles" – who aided the beleaguered Jews in their midst. Sam began working for a furrier in the north of Brussels, but only from home; he also bought astrakhan paws, and after he sewed them together Hennie would try to sell them. It was now too dangerous for him to go out during the day; sometimes he would venture out at night to get some fresh air but even that soon became perilous. Hennie brought him drawing materials and books from the library and these helped him endure the isolation.

Sam was to spend the next three years in this hidden life. As he persevered in this twilight existence, as the days and months of confinement threatened to press heavily upon him, he consciously endeavored to train his mind to cope with the situation without giving way to despair or depression. He poured out his soul in his canvases, just as King David had done in the psalms of Israel when he also had lived an undercover life, on the run from Saul in the years before he came to the throne. Sam's rich, accumulated store of memories – his early life in the village as part of the Jewish community in Poland, the Passover feasts and other festivals "at their appointed times" that had shaped his upbringing, the devout faith of his parents – these all became invested in his mind with a new clarity and significance.

Sam clung also to the assurance that the artistic calling on his life came from a place that was beyond him, and involved a transcendent force that had carried him through many challenges already. He was coming steadily to realize that the great creative works he had so far encountered sprang out of a breadth of soul and perception that infused any mere technical ability with the power of their vision, and the certainty that

"Beauty is truth, truth beauty, – that is all

Ye know on earth, and all ye need to know." [1]

At the same time, though, the searing prison experiences that had begun in Russia and continued haunting his steps even into Western Europe, like a dog that has hold of his coat tails and just will not let go, meant that he had been brought to the awareness of a fathomless abyss that could exist within the human psyche. Into its fearful depths he did not at this point dare peer too closely; it threatened the revelation of a power of evil so dark that it was beyond human comprehension, and for which even the negative circumstances he had endured left him unprepared.

Memories both light-filled and painful now began to co-exist within his soul in a deep creative tension. Some of the dominant themes of his later art began to emerge and take formative shape as the experiences were processed during those long months in hiding. He had the sensation that the events through which he had passed themselves had a tangible life force, and were able to pour themselves into his hands with a power all their own, that was independently able to shape his art.

Another way Sam coped with the situation was through following, with a fierce concentration, the events of the war as they unfolded both at home and abroad. In Belgium, as in all the occupied countries, the press was strictly controlled by the German overlords, but he and Hennie had access to underground newspapers. They also listened daily to the BBC on the radio, as the life and death battle between the Allied and Axis powers increased in unbelievable scope and intensity, and the dogs of war snarled their way far beyond the borders of Europe.

———

The year 1941 was one of escalation of armed conflict all around the world. By the time the Germans launched their campaign against Russia, the Nazi hegemony over Europe seemed well-nigh complete. The swastika flew in the north over Norway and Denmark, in the west over France and the Low Countries, and as far south as the desert sands of Africa. Smoldering ruins in great cities such as London, Coventry and Rotterdam bore mute testimony to the power of the Luftwaffe, while German U-boats were stalking their prey in every ocean. The Nazi war machine, which had just overrun Greece and Yugoslavia, had reached a zenith of military power and gave a terrifying impression of invincibility. But the firestorm which burst upon Russian territory on that fateful June day, as Hennie and Sam prepared for their wedding, was unparalleled in ferocity.

Operation Barbarossa commenced with the Axis powers smashing through the frontier Stalin and Hitler had drawn across Poland, and moving into the territory of their erstwhile treaty partner with a massive force of over four million troops. The invasion covered a front from the North Cape to the Black Sea, a distance of over 3,000 kilometers. The Nazis were supremely confident of victory; in their minds, this was not a war against the civilized nations of the West but a fight to the death against their Judeo-Bolshevik enemies. Hitler was convinced that the Soviet state was ready to fall under the Wehrmacht hammer blows and that the war would be over by the onset of the Russian winter, thus providing the Reich with the Lebensraum that would ensure its thousand-year reign.

The spectacular German advances during the first weeks of the invasion seemed proof of the Führer's calculation. In Barbarossa's opening month, the German armies overran the Baltic states and pressed deeply into Soviet territory, capturing huge swathes of land and taking hundreds of thousands of prisoners. The German battle strategy encompassed a far-reaching plan of separate attacks on three major Soviet targets: Leningrad in the north, Moscow in the center, and Ukraine in the south. By early November, Leningrad was almost completely encircled; in the south, the Germans were in control of Ukraine, and the capital, Moscow, seemed to lie open to their advance. To Sam and other anxious observers in the West, the fall of the communist state seemed inevitable. And the news was no more encouraging in other arenas of the war.

After the Germans had defeated France in 1940, Mussolini entered the war, making Libya hostile territory, and the battle for North Africa began to unfold. At stake was control of the Suez Canal, which provided access to oil from the Middle East and raw materials from Asia, crucial to sustaining the

Allied war effort. In March 1941 Rommel was summoned to the aid of the Italians with his Afrika Korps, and the British and German armies faced each other in the Western Desert, an inhospitable region where the soldiers endured freezing nights and searing daytime temperatures. By April the British had been swept back over the Egyptian frontier – but the Germans failed to take the strategically important garrison of Tobruk. Its defenders – including 14,000 Australians from the 9th and 7th Divisions known as the "rats" of Tobruk – prevented Rommel's advance to Egypt and the Suez.

The tiny island of Malta, the key stronghold from which the Allies sustained their North African campaign, had become center stage in the theater of war in the Mediterranean, and the stones of its ancient port were being pounded with savage intensity by the Germans. The battle in the Med had also reached beyond Gibraltar into the wide waters of the Atlantic. Britain's naval power was formidable, but she had been stretched by the loss of French support, while the German acquisition of bases on the Atlantic coast facilitated their attempts to cut off Britain's supply lines. After the Royal Navy sank their state-of-the-art battleship Bismarck the Germans launched a full-scale U-boat campaign in the Atlantic and developed hunting techniques such as "wolfpacks" to attack convoys. In 1941, more than 800 Allied merchant ships went down, and the central area of the ocean where the heaviest convoy losses occurred was becoming known as the "Black Pit."

Still further afield, another war front had opened in the Pacific, where the Japanese, having long nursed an ambition to become rulers of all Asia, had signed an agreement with the Axis powers pledging mutual aid, a move intended to deter the United States from entering the conflict. Japan had the most advanced armed forces in the Far East, and in 1937 captured Nanking, the Kuomintang capital, where they signaled their intentions toward the nation by carrying out a horrific massacre. The islands of the South Pacific, scattered like a string of pearls across the sapphire waters, were beckoning them, even as the colonial powers were in no position to come to the aid of their Eastern possessions. Only the United States Navy was a formidable threat, but Pearl Harbor, the main base for its Pacific Fleet, was some 6,000 kilometers away from the Japanese mainland.

As winter began to set in during that calamitous year, Sam and Hennie were sharing the doubts and fears of millions on the Allied side. However, in November, some better news reached them from Russia: the German drive on Moscow had met with severe setbacks. The Russian skies had opened, sending heavy rains that hampered the movement of German troops and tanks. The soldiers struggled on, and by the end of November advance units could see the towers of Moscow through the snowflakes. But the thermometer kept dropping, and on December 6 the Soviets launched a massive counteroffensive, having brought in Siberian divisions especially trained for operating in harsh winter conditions. The shivering and debilitated German soldiers were forced to conduct a slow retreat in appalling conditions, evoking echoes of the disastrous defeat suffered by Napoleon's Grand Army in 1812.

The all-powerful Wehrmacht had failed to take Moscow or Leningrad before winter set in; Hitler's plans for a quick defeat of the Soviet Union had not been realized. And the Soviets had been driven into the arms of the Allies.

Then came another day in early December, the 7th. Sam was listening to the radio, leaning forward, his face intent, and as he listened his eyes blazed.

"Hennie," he called, and she came to his side.

"What is it?" she asked.

"The Japanese have bombed Pearl Harbor," he answered.

She shook her head uncomprehendingly. "Where is that?" she asked. "What does that mean for us here?"

"Pearl Harbor is in Hawaii, it's the American naval base in the Pacific," he answered. "This changes everything. It has to be one of the major miscalculations of the war so far. This means for sure that the US will enter the war."

Although, he thought somberly to himself, *it might still be too late for the Jews of Europe.*

---

1. From English Romantic poet John Keats' "Ode on a Grecian Urn."

31

JANUARY 1942 – DECEMBER 1943: CATACLYSM

The war was now a global conflict, as the ancient gods of bloodletting and violence threw a heavy pall over the nations, encompassing the proud and beautiful cities of Europe, the deserts of Africa, the once-dreaming shores of the Mediterranean, the islands of the Pacific and the gray swells of the Atlantic: occident and orient alike swathed under a blanket of carnage and fear – a situation which would only intensify in 1942.

As Sam had foreseen, the US Congress declared war on Japan the day after the attack on Pearl Harbor. At first, however, the raid seemed to be a coup for the Japanese forces, which went on to capture a string of Western colonial possessions – including Burma, Hong Kong, Indonesia and the Philippines. Singapore also fell, a military disaster of the first magnitude. In fact, throughout much of the year an ultimate Axis victory still seemed possible in both theaters of war.

The German army began a renewed offensive in the Soviet Union in the spring, taking Crimea and advancing toward the oilfields of the Caucasus, reaching Stalingrad on the River Volga by August. This city had a symbolic significance as well as a strategic one, and the stage was set for a titanic struggle. The Germans first sent in the Luftwaffe with the intention of bombing the city into submission; their tanks and troops followed, and by the end of September occupied most of the shattered city.

Further south, the picture for the Allies was no less dire. In North Africa, Rommel's soldiers captured the fortress of Tobruk; then, as they forced the Allies back into Egypt, looked poised to take Cairo and advance on Suez. In the Atlantic, also, the situation remained severe. But from the beginning of 1942, the Americans began pouring massive resources into the conflict, adding to the arms production of the British Empire and Russia, even as the Nazis were beginning to struggle to obtain the raw materials and goods needed for their war effort. Above all, the Germans were short of fuel with which to supply the voracious needs of the Wehrmacht's tanks and fighter planes.

The Nazis also had to contend with the fact that the war had come home to their own soil. A new Allied objective was the destruction of Germany's industrial might, and heavy bombers such as the Avro Lancaster made their entrance into the conflict, attacking Germany's airbases and manufacturing complexes with their huge payloads. Bomber crews with the RAF and USAAF came from across the globe. As they hurtled in their winged metallic chariots each night to the heart of occupied Europe, they faced unimaginable dangers: crosswinds, anti-aircraft fire and ferocious aerial combat, so that bomber command crews suffered incredibly high casualty rates. Nevertheless, Churchill emphasized the supreme importance of gaining mastery in the air: "The bombers alone," he averred, "can provide the means to victory."

Meanwhile, on the other side of the world, the Americans regrouped after Pearl Harbor, and as 1942 unfolded went on to win stunning victories against the Japanese: at the Coral Sea in May, then the epic Battle of Midway in June, and Guadalcanal in November. It was the turning point of the war in the Pacific, and there was another kairos moment in North Africa. Lieutenant-General Montgomery took command of the Eighth Army, and British troops won a decisive victory in the Second Battle of El Alamein, waged from October through November, dispatching the Axis forces in chaotic retreat across Libya to Tunisia. And yet another crucial development would soon take place in Russia.

The battle for Stalingrad dragged on for three months; the Germans had once again been mistaken in their expectation of a swift victory. A new generation of skilled officers had emerged to take command of Soviet forces, and gleaming tanks and aircraft bore witness to the largesse of Britain and the US. A huge Soviet army gathered in the devastated city to fiercely contest the Germans, launching a counterattack in November which soon trapped the Sixth Army commanded by General Paulus. Starvation and the bitter Russian winter took their grim toll, and finally, in January 1943, Paulus surrendered with his remaining men. Only a few thousand of that vast army returned to Germany at the end of the war; most died from illness, hunger or exhaustion. The hitherto invincible German Wehrmacht had been rendered powerless as the Russians made their agonizing, phoenix-like resurgence.

Stalingrad was one of Germany's greatest defeats, and the ignominious failure marked the end of Hitler's dreams of an empire in the east. He had ignored such unpalatable military truths as the vast distances of Russia and the cruel winters – but his greatest failure was ideological: to underestimate the stoicism, endurance and patriotism of the defenders of Mother Russia. The failure of Barbarossa meant that Germany now must continue to fight a two-front war against a coalition possessing immensely superior resources – and a determination never to come under the heel of the Nazi jackboot.

As 1943 dawned, Montgomery and his troops had been tracking the Desert Fox and his Korps across the coast of Northern Africa for some months. Rommel reached Tunisia at the end of January, but to his chagrin discovered another Allied force waiting for him there. Operation Torch had landed thousands of British and American forces at three points across French Morocco and Algeria in the first major Anglo-American operation of the war. Together with various Free French factions, they helped compel the surrender of all remaining Axis troops in Tunisia by May, and end the campaign for North Africa.

In the Mediterranean, by the same month, the Allies sank a staggering number of Axis ships, and Malta became a launch pad for the invasion of Sicily. The island had been a stepping-stone into mainland Europe as far back as the Punic Wars between Carthage and Rome, and the British and American troops now followed that same road. After a month of fighting they drove the Germans from Sicily, Mussolini was toppled, and in

September the Italian government surrendered unconditionally. The Allied armies advanced steadily northwards toward Rome and Nazi Germany, through many bitter and costly battles, which burned the names Anzio, Salerno and Monte Cassino into the annals of war.

But nothing could disguise the fact that Germany's principal ally had now been defeated and the Fascist regime overthrown. Meanwhile, the Battle of the Atlantic had also drawn to a close. The improved equipment and tactics of the Allies meant that the U-boat fleet began to suffer heavy losses, and for the rest of the war the Allies exercised unchallenged control of Atlantic sealanes.

All these events, most especially the catastrophe of Stalingrad, had a devastating effect on the morale of German citizens at home – but worse was to come. Meeting at Casablanca in January 1943, Churchill and Roosevelt decided on a sustained campaign of bombing German cities, as well as a series of massive raids on the industrial heartland of Germany. In May that year, the 617 Squadron of the RAF pulled off a stunning piece of precision bombing, destroying three dams in the Ruhr Valley in the raid known as Dambusters. British and American bombers began levelling large areas of many German cities, causing severe shortages of food, clothing, and housing, and sending refugees pouring out over the land. By the end of 1943, German forces were retreating all along the line in the east, the Reich had lost command of the skies and the seas, and ordinary Germans knew that the war was lost.

In occupied Belgium, the Allied planes were also targeting factories, ports and other strategic sites used by the Germans in their war offensive. Sam and Hennie were conscious of the frequent shaking and muffled booms which indicated that a target had been hit. The air would quiver with the intensity of the aerial bombardment, and Sam would put down the astrakhan paws, Hennie would lower her book, and her lips would move in silent prayer.

They knew also of several armed resistance groups operating in the land, the members of which risked capture, torture and execution as they waged their campaign of espionage and sabotage. A series of safe houses called the Comet Line had been set up to shelter downed Allied airmen and enable them to make the perilous journey to Spain, while other groups were devoted to finding safe hiding places for Jews and providing them with food and forged papers. In 1942, the persecution of Belgian Jews had intensified and the first roundups started; by November, some 15,000 Jews were deported from the Mechelen transit camp to Auschwitz. The Belgian Resistance had learned a great deal about the fate of the deported Jews: they knew of murders on a large scale through machine gun fire – and through gas.

In late 1943, Sam gazed out the window, and stared in horror at what he was witnessing. He saw a Jewish family in Collignon Place, just across the street from where he and Hennie were living, arrested and brutally taken away. He sensed how close the remorseless reach of the Gestapo was coming.

32

DECEMBER 1943 – MAY 1944: CAPTURE

Sam and Hennie's landlady, Mme Meeuws, had an exquisite tact as well as a deep concern for her young Jewish protégés, and after she closed her store in the evening would frequently call in on them to see how they were faring. She had a daughter, Marie, who lived on the first floor with her husband, and they too came often, bringing their little gray cat with them. Together they would listen to the latest war news on the English radio as the cat lay on their laps, kneading its paws and purring softly.

As the months of war stretched into years, the privations Sam and Hennie were enduring became even more exacting. They had a ration card for food (under a different address) but the provisions permitted to Belgian citizens were among the least in occupied Europe, so that they, like many Belgians, were tightening their belts. Their supply of funds also dwindled alarmingly and they sold first a golden watch, then a ring. As the winter of 1943 approached, they didn't have enough money to buy coal to heat the rooms; yet although circumstances were harsh they were happy, for they had each other. But by the time 1944 arrived the stock of Astrakhan pieces was gone, and there was no other money coming in. Hennie decided she would find work.

Sam was very mature for his age, but Hennie was still something of a child, always trustful and smiling. She had been given the address of an elderly widow called Madame Borisofla who belonged to the Russian nobility, and was also a member of the Resistance. Her house had become a transit place for English pilots; she would provide them with forged identification papers, and it was Hennie's task to bring the documents to her house three or four times a week. Hennie would then eat her meals with those in the house, for food was getting scarce, and this was a way to cut down on expenses. One cold morning in late spring, as the sky was covered with heavy clouds, she was called upon to carry out her assignment, and arrived at the house of Mme Borisofla with the papers securely tucked in her bag.

Sam waited for his wife to return home, but the minutes turned into hours, and still she did not come. He paced up and down in their small living room as the suspense became unendurable. It was impossible for him to go out, and he tried to comfort himself by imagining a possible scenario that had delayed her at the house of Mme Borislova. Evening drew on, but there was no sign of her, and no word from her. As the night hours ticked away, Sam lay rigid and unmoving in their bed, unable to push away a terrible dread. At 4 o'clock in the morning there was a banging on the front door of the building, and he leapt to his feet. Mme Meeuws came to the room, her face tense with fear. "It's the Gestapo," she whispered.

Sam thought desperately of jumping out the window of the back room, but it was too late – the soldiers were at the door, shouting, "Come out, or we shoot."

The door was flung open and three uniformed Germans burst into the room, dominating the space with their arrogant, intimidating presence. One of them immediately punched Sam in the face. "You're coming with us," he barked.

Sam fumbled for some clothes, then began looking for a bag.

"You won't need that," he was told harshly.

All the while, the men were moving about the room, picking up whatever seemed to have any value – clothes, money, books. They stumbled upon some newspaper cuttings.

"Aha," sneered one of the Germans. "You're an Anglophile."

"I'm not a file," Sam answered.

They didn't understand the pun, but all three punched him for his audacity, and his face became covered with blood. They hustled him outside and pushed him into one of the black vehicles used by the Gestapo.

Hennie was inside the car. She was pale and started crying when she saw Sam's face covered in blood. "Oh Sam, what have they done to you?" she whispered.

"I'm so happy to see you," said Sam, taking her small hands in his and caressing them gently. She pulled out a handkerchief and began wiping the crimson stains from his face.

They were taken to the Brussels headquarters of the Gestapo in the Avenue Louise and led to the cellar. Here there were about 20 people locked in small cells, and into one of these Sam and Hennie were now thrust. For the first time they were able to speak with one another at length, and Sam discovered what had happened to his wife. The Germans had discovered an English pilot and followed him to the house of Mme Borisofla; as soon as he entered the dwelling, they had swooped in and arrested everyone, Hennie included. The remaining hours of their cold, uncomfortable and fear-filled night passed, with Sam endeavoring to console and encourage his wife as best he could. They passed some of the time by reading the inscriptions on the walls, carved by former victims of the Gestapo.

The following morning they were led out of the cell and taken to the infamous transit camp of Dossin in Mechelen, where they were lined up with other men and women waiting to be inspected by the SS. Their money was taken and they were ordered to remove their wedding rings and hand them over, but that was not the end of the inspection. The women were taken to a separate room, then forced to undress and endure a brutal examination of anus and vagina as the SS men checked for hidden valuables. One of the Nazi soldiers, who had the nickname Horse, was a sadist who took immense pleasure in humiliating and inflicting pain upon the women during this procedure.

Sam and Hennie stayed for a week in the transit camp, then were pushed into a truck packed with men, women and children. The SS endeavored to make everyone stay calm, but threatened them at the same time.

"The sick people will be taken to hospital," they said soothingly. They gave one man a whistle. "Hey, you! You're responsible for blowing the whistle if someone tries to escape. If you fail to do so, we'll shoot you on the spot."

"Where are they taking us?" Hennie whispered.

"To a labor camp," Sam answered, although he didn't believe it. He didn't want to upset Hennie – but the reality of their destination would surpass his worst nightmares.

The truck arrived at a railway station, where a train consisting of many long boxcars stood idling at the platform. Heavily armed SS guards, brandishing their weapons and shouting in strident tones, herded them aboard. The doors were slammed shut and a whistle sounded, the wheels began slowly to turn, and the engine, at first lumbering and groaning, began to gather speed.

33

JOURNEY TO AUSCHWITZ

If there were a special award given for ruthless efficiency of the highest order, it would surely be given to the plan devised by the Nazis in order to transport Jews from all over Europe to the concentration camps in occupied Poland. The camps were deliberately situated along major rail lines, and hence it was the railway system of Europe which became a key element in their plan and made this mass transference possible. Crucial to this operation was the participation of the German State Railway, which was paid to transport Jews from thousands of towns and cities throughout the continent; trains carrying Jews to the camps were even given priority over other transports needed for the war effort. And Adolf Eichmann, the consummate organizer of the Third Reich, kept the trains running to their schedules with such preternatural precision that by 1944 millions had been carried by rail to their final destination in the camps.

The Germans used both freight and passenger cars for the deportations; if placed in the latter, the Jews were frequently forced to pay for their own conveyance. A more ignominious, cruel and shameful method of transportation than the freight or cattle cars could not be devised. They were routinely loaded to 200 percent of capacity, and those locked in them endured a tortuous journey, suffering from intense heat in summer, freezing temperatures in winter, and extreme hunger and thirst. No provision was made for sanitation aside from a single bucket in each car, and the nauseating odor of urine and excrement would soon permeate the air. The heavily loaded trains traveled slowly, greatly prolonging the ordeal, and many of those deported, especially elderly people and young children, died during the journey.

Sam and Hennie were now trapped in one of these terrible wagons, and a fear greater than any they had known suddenly possessed them. There was only one vent for air in the roof, and the two minuscule barred windows were sealed tightly, preventing the air from circulating. Because people were pushed so tightly together in the overcrowded space, this meant that the effect of suffocation was compounded. In the middle of the compartment was a bucket which became filled to overflowing with human waste within a day, and then tumbled over with the movement of the train, creating a horrific stench. Sam had managed to hide a pair of scissors, and used them to carve out a small hole in the side of the compartment. He and Hennie took turns in putting their mouths against it to breathe a little fresh air.

The journey lasted four days, during which no sustenance was given, while the minimal amount of water provided gave no relief to those who were crazed with thirst. Following behind the train was a truck filled with SS soldiers and armed guards, who were there to prevent anyone escaping. On the first day some of the Nazis climbed onto the roof of the train and shot randomly into the crowd – just for sport. They never missed a target, and the compartment became filled with the dead and wounded. Sam felt an overwhelming sense of helplessness, unable to tend to those injured, or even show compassion for those racked with pain and drawing their final breaths. The foul air became even more unbearable, and people were also dying through asphyxiation.

The train reached the central station of Berlin. The platforms were packed with people, but nobody cared about the fate of 1,500 Jews who were half dead in the train. Those who were still able to walk tried to go to the exits, but the doors of the train remained closed and the engine started to move again. Slowly, stopping often, they reached a scarred landscape of open mine pits, chimneys, smoke and lowering skies. There were more and more deaths. The children didn't have the strength to cry any more, nor did the badly wounded moan any more ... they were too far gone in their suffering. Finally the train stopped; they had arrived at their destination. But the doors remained closed and they were forced to stay inside for another day.

Time had ceased to have any meaning for Sam by this stage. He cared only to somehow impart strength and endurance to Hennie, as she languished at his side, prostrated by the nightmare they were living through. He gazed out the small window at the scene in front of them, and the hair on the back of his neck prickled. He knew a place of incarceration when he saw it and this one evoked an almost visceral reaction. A forbidding dark tower loomed over the railway tracks like some formidable beast with an open maw; Sam had been in many prisons but never one that struck his heart with so much foreboding. Another movement crossed his line of vision: three trains similarly packed with Jews had stopped by a large ramp constructed near the tower.

Sam was arriving at Auschwitz just as events were transpiring which would turn the camp into the site of the largest mass murder in history. The wrath of the Nazi executioners was about to fall on the defenseless heads of the Jews from one particular country – Hungary – who were now, in the spring of 1944, beginning to arrive in mass numbers. The Jews of Hungary until that time had remained relatively unscathed by the events of the war. At the beginning of the conflict, the Fascist-leaning government had concluded an alliance with Nazi Germany, then sent troops to aid the Nazis in their invasion of the Soviet Union. But as the promised conquest failed to materialize, and as the Germans began to lose ground in the war, the

Hungarian government tried to negotiate a separate armistice with the Allies.

In retaliation for this fickleness the *Wehrmacht* drove into Hungary in March 1944, meeting no resistance. The subsequent German occupation proved disastrous to the Jews of the kingdom. They numbered three quarters of a million and their communities were still largely untouched, but Eichmann had followed the German army, charged with the task of expropriating everything possible from them, and then deporting them. At Auschwitz special arrangements were made to receive this vast influx. Forty-four parallel tracks already led to the camp, but a new railroad spur was completed, running directly into the heart of Birkenau, as well as a new ramp. Hundreds of thousands of Hungarian Jews were then forced to board the trains to Auschwitz; they had no idea of the horror that awaited them.

Neither did Sam and Hennie, waiting sick at heart inside their boxcar. Finally, in the late afternoon, the doors were opened, and an SS man shouted, "Quickly! Everyone out." He began hitting the poor creatures with a club as they fell or staggered from the train. Sam and Hennie climbed down and gazed with consternation as they took in the heart-chilling scene before them: neither had suspected that such a place could exist.

This, then, was their first glimpse of Auschwitz-Birkenau. Iron tracks, hissing locomotives, barbed wire and smokestacks stood out against a uniformly gray landscape, under a leaden sky where motes of ash were drifting and the clouds themselves seemed lachrymose. On the vast floodlit platform milled hundreds of weak, bewildered people, men, women and children, many well dressed, but all wearing a yellow star, with fear etched plainly on their faces. German officers wearing peaked caps and imposing uniforms flourished their weapons and shouted commands, while the dogs at their heels strained at their leashes and barked. In the distance, beyond formidable barricades, were some wilting trees, the birches for which the camp was named, but there were no birds, nor any glimpse of a blue heaven.

And then, Sam listened in disbelief. Through the hellish cacophony he heard the strains of Mozart and Bach floating eerily over the arrival ramp: it was a performance by members of the camp orchestra, who were playing in obedience to the Nazi strategy devised to give a false sense of assurance to the newcomers. But, for Sam, the airy beauty of Strauss waltzes and other pieces of classical music juxtaposed with the infernal landscape they were witnessing only compounded the surreal nature of the scene. The fragile musical notes hanging in the atmosphere could make no assault against its harsh reality. It would be as if a butterfly, fluttering on gauzy wings, were to dash itself against the immovable granite of a mountain.

Despite Sam's exhaustion and fear, a visionary arrow seemed to pierce the depths of his soul, filling it with a prescient light. In his mind's eye he saw a faraway stony peak with two solitary figures ascending, heard the searing question of Genesis, the mystified words Isaac addressed to his father Abraham, the query which had echoed down through the centuries:

"Father, here is the fire and the wood, but where is the lamb for a burnt offering?" [1]

He took Hennie by the hand, sustaining her. "Breathe deeply," he said to her.

The SS men were rapping out orders as the dogs continued to growl and bare their teeth. And now the women, many with young children clinging to their skirts, were being forcibly separated from their menfolk. Anguish ravaged their faces as they were torn away from husbands, fathers and sons, their arms stretched out toward them in yearning. Then came the turn of Sam and Hennie. He also was directed one way, Hennie another. He watched helplessly as she was pushed remorselessly further and further away from him. Her blonde hair and pale face stood out luminously in the bleak light, and as the distance between them increased he shouted to her with all his strength. "Don't worry. We'll meet after the war at my parents' place. They live just 50 kilometers from here."

Those were his last words to his young wife. He would never see her again.

---

1. From Genesis 22:7.

PART III

AUSCHWITZ AND
MAUTHAUSEN

34

FROM PERSECUTION TO GENOCIDE

The concentration camp system birthed in Germany during the 1930s did not at first bear any significant relation to Nazi policy toward the Jews. It was designed primarily to silence Hitler's political enemies, entrenching the violence and hatred the Nazis felt toward those who opposed them.

In the years leading up to the war, the Nazis were concerned about the image they presented both at home in Germany as well as abroad, and the extreme antisemitism of the Third Reich was cloaked to some extent. The favored solution to the Nazis' self-created "Jewish problem" was that of encouraging emigration through a newly created Department of Jewish Affairs under Adolf Eichmann. Offices were established in Vienna, Prague and Berlin where Jews desiring to leave would be granted safe passage – after parting with the bulk of their worldly possessions. But because the pace of antisemitic policy was so gradual, many Jews tragically elected to remain. Who could have dreamed of what was to come?

The illusion that Jews could continue existing under a Nazi regime was shattered, quite literally, by Kristallnacht in November 1938. And shortly thereafter, in January 1939, Hitler showed his hand openly, declaring in the Reichstag that "I want today to be a prophet again: if international finance Jewry inside and outside Europe should succeed in plunging the nations once more into a world war, the result will be ... the annihilation of the

Jewish race in Europe." This was the same conflict which he himself was, at that moment, planning to unleash. In the immediate aftermath of the outbreak of war Poland found herself once again carved up by her conquerors; to the west were the districts incorporated into Germany itself, and the Soviets seized territories in the east. The large central area known as the General Government was administered by Hans Frank, "the Butcher of Krakow," who set up headquarters in the Wawel Castle.

The Germans saw their task as creating a new ethnographic order in the areas they now ruled. Poland as a nation was to be intellectually and politically destroyed: the Poles were to receive no education higher than elementary school and function as illiterate slaves for the Nazis. From the first days of their occupation, the Nazis launched a campaign of terror and violence aimed at wiping out Poland's elites: intellectuals, scholars, nobility, clergy, teachers, and political activists. It was code-named Operation Tannenberg, after a medieval battle in which the Poles had broken the power of the Teutonic Knights.[1]

And as for the Jews? According to Frank, "We have now approximately 2,500,000 of them in the General Government, and we shall be able to take measures, which will lead, somehow, to their annihilation, and this in connection with the gigantic measures to be determined in discussions from the Reich." At this stage, however, Eichmann suggested that the Jews be rounded up and forced into ghettos and labor camps, the locations of which were chosen for their proximity to railway junctions, pending those future "gigantic measures."

In April 1940, SS Hauptsturmführer (Captain) Rudolf Höss was given the task of creating a model concentration camp in Southwest Poland, in one of the territories transferred to the new Reich. The name of the town in Polish was Oświęcim, in German, Auschwitz. The first two letters of Oświęcim, "Os," mean "axis" and the town is located almost exactly in the middle of the continent.

The camp was originally intended as a detention center for the many Polish citizens arrested by the Nazis, including Resistance members, priests or the intelligentsia. Twenty thousand were sent initially, and given the task of building the camp with their bare hands on the site of a former Polish army barracks located on the edge of the town – but the first actual prisoners to arrive, in June 1940, were 30 German criminals who would become the first Kapos, agents of control between the SS and the Polish prisoners. The SS had taken their first steps in implementing their regime of murderous brutality. And Höss affixed over the entrance gate to the camp a metal sign, the idea of which he had brought from Dachau, bearing a slogan unmatched for hypocrisy: "Arbeit Macht Frei" (Work Makes Free).

In 1941, a radical change took place in the Nazis' policy toward the Jews, precipitated by their invasion of Russia. During the summer, as the Wehrmacht was making good progress against the Red Army and flush with victory, Himmler, who viewed the Soviet Union as the home of a Jewish-Bolshevik conspiracy, decided to send in the Einsatzgruppen behind the army, reinforced with units of SS cavalry and police battalions. They were charged with killing communists and any male Jews who were in the service of the party or state, but the decision marked a turning point. The Nazis decided to also gather women and children, line them up next to open pits, make them strip, and shoot them, such as occurred when a large proportion of the Jewish population of Kiev was massacred at Babi Yar, a ravine northwest of the city. The Führer had expressed his desire for a German Garden of Eden in the East, but this was a paradise where Jews were clearly "verboten."

In the first months of the war against Russia the Germans took more than three million Red Army prisoners, and soon began sending thousands of Soviet POWs to Auschwitz. At first, many of them were executed by a firing squad in the gravel pits near the camp. But plans were under way for a massive new camp to be built a short distance away from the existing one on an area of ground dotted with birch trees, which gave it the name Brzezink in Polish and Birkenau in German. The task of constructing this huge complex fell to the Soviet POWs, but the harsh labor meant that the death rate among them was very high. Thousands were also killed in the walled-off yard of Block 11 in the main camp in front of a specially built Death Wall. And the Soviet prisoners had the distinction of being used for the first tests of the new poison the Nazis were considering, Zyklon B.

According to the Nazis' tenebrous racial theory, certain individuals by their very existence violated the ideal of Aryan supremacy; prominent among these were the intellectually or physically disabled, who were also thought to be a liability to a country at war. Accordingly, in 1939, the Germans initiated the T4 program to do away with those termed "life unworthy of life." Parents of children with disabilities were encouraged to admit their offspring to pediatric clinics where specially recruited staff murdered their young charges with lethal overdoses or by starvation. Beginning in January 1940, T4 functionaries also began to remove adults thought to be a genetic or financial burden from their institutions; they were transported to special killing centers, mostly former mental hospitals, where gas chambers designed to look like shower rooms had been built. Within hours of their arrival at such centers, they had perished, their bodies were burned in crematoria, and their families received an urn with a death certificate listing a false cause of death.

The program reached Auschwitz in July 1941, when about 500 sick inmates were transferred to a mental hospital near Danzig to be euthanized. But the gravel pits and expulsions began to seem ponderous to the Nazi elite in the camp, who began searching for a more effective method of murder. In late summer, Fritzsch, the deputy commandant, took note of a chemical used to remove infestations of insects around the camp, crystallized prussic acid or cyanide, commonly known as Zyklon B. It was then that he conceived an idea of colossal evil. A group of about 600 Soviet POWs was taken to the cellars of Block 11 into which SS men wearing gas masks dumped Zyklon B; the prisoners died after two days, and it was decided that the dose should be made stronger. Höss attended the next experiment, protected by a gas mask; the poisonous crystals were thrown in, and in the crowded cells death came instantaneously.

The gassing experiments continued in early 1942 in the camp crematorium, but this was a more exposed site, and, although the SS revved two motorcycles so no one would hear the cries, it was impossible to hide the murders from the other inmates. As a result, a cottage known as the Little Red House or Bunker 1 was used for the first time at Birkenau in the spring of that year. Around 800 people could be murdered there at a time, crammed tightly into the gas chambers, with no disturbance to the camp.

Soon another killing installation with a capacity for 1,200 people was built, called the Little White House or Bunker 2. The gassings took place at night and a special unit buried the bodies the following day, covering them with powdered lime and soil. Eventually, however, it was necessary to disinter the bodies and put them into giant burning pits, a kind of makeshift crematorium. The Nazis had not yet streamlined their system to the degree of efficiency they were seeking.

As the SS was engaged in increasing the killing capacity of Auschwitz, and the destruction of Soviet Jewry by the shooting of men, women and children proceeded apace, the Jews of Western Europe and the Reich remained relatively untouched. However, in September 1941, Hitler decided that the German Jews should be deported to the Lodz ghetto in Poland, where 165,000 Jews were already forced into an area of four-square kilometers. The influx of large numbers of German Jews would clearly be a logistical nightmare, but according to the perverse logic of the Nazi administrators there was an obvious solution. In Chelmno, a small village 80 kilometers northwest of Lodz, a country house named the Schloss was prepared to become the first location for the killing of selected Jews from the ghetto. The murders were to take place in stationary gas chambers linked to engines producing carbon monoxide.

This already horrific state of affairs was about to take a turn for the worse through events which then transpired on the other side of the world. When the Japanese bombed Pearl Harbor in December and the Americans entered the war, this was, to Hitler, proof that the Jews had engineered a world conflict. His anger toward them, compounded by the rage he felt over the lack of progress in the war against Russia, became infused with an even darker malignancy.

In January 1942 a meeting of top SS officials was held at a villa on the shores of the Wannsee, a lake outside Berlin. It was called by Reinhard Heydrich, chief of Reich Security and a main architect of the Holocaust, to discuss the Final Solution of the Jewish question. A formal change in Nazi policy was announced: instead of the emigration of Jews to countries outside Nazi control, there would now be "evacuation to the east." This was meant to include Jews in countries such as Ireland, Sweden and Britain, not yet under Nazi control. According to Heydrich, "just as with the Russian Jews in Kiev, the death sentence has been pronounced on all the Jews of Europe."

Participants at the Conference understood "evacuation to the east" as a veiled statement, the true meaning of which was deportation to centers of annihilation. It was at this point that the leap from persecution to genocide formally took place. The Nazis had long believed that the entire human race was engaged in a struggle for supremacy, and that the Jews, who they saw as biologically and racially distinct, had acquired vast power. It was this, according to the grotesque Nazi vision, which had led to the Bolshevik revolution and brought down Imperial Germany. Armed with their idea of an international Jewish conspiracy to attain world dominance, the Nazis now managed to legitimatize the creation of their Final Solution. It was directed toward the elimination of an entire people and their culture from the earth.

Just a few months later Himmler announced that the "resettlement" of the entire Jewish population of the General Government would take place. Again, it was another euphemism for annihilation. The majority of the murders would be carried out at three new camps which were to be established in the forests of Poland, the killing centers of Belzec, Sobibor and Treblinka. This secret plan to destroy the Polish Jews was given the codename Operation Reinhard, after the SS leader who had chaired the Wannsee Conference, who had been assassinated shortly thereafter. The victims were taken to the Reinhard camps by train, often in cattle cars, and the majority of those who arrived there were immediately murdered in the gas chambers. In these factories of death the SS and police would slaughter close to two million Jewish men, women and children within a matter of months.

At the same time, the death camp Auschwitz-Birkenau was evolving in a different direction – consequence of the fact that, as the war progressed, economic considerations were growing in importance for the Nazi leaders. It was thought that the concentration camps would provide the raw material for the new Germany; as Albert Speer, Hitler's favorite architect, put it, "After all, the Jews were already making bricks under the Pharaohs."[2]

Auschwitz eventually became the center of a huge, semi-industrial complex with up to 45 subcamps in operation as well as a plant belonging to the giant conglomerate IG Farben. As a result, a unique procedure was developed at the camp, terrifying in its cold-bloodedness. Prisoners arriving at Auschwitz were subjected to a selection process by which they would be separated by SS men into two groups: those useful for work would be admitted to one of the barracks, and those thought to be unfit would be gassed immediately.

Once Auschwitz developed this role of selection on arrival, the first Jews from outside Poland arrived in the spring of 1942, on trains from Slovakia, and by summer that year Auschwitz was receiving transports from all over Europe. Then, in 1943, another turn of events convinced Himmler even more firmly that the key to future management of the Final Solution lay in Auschwitz.

The Warsaw ghetto represented one of the largest concentrations of Jews in the Nazi state, and Himmler had ordered it should be liquidated at Treblinka. About 300,000 were deported, but the remaining Jews, knowing they were going to be murdered, decided to face their Nazi captors with armed resistance. The Germans, at first stunned by this action, decided on a simple and brutal retaliation – they set fire to the ghetto. But then, in autumn, a similar act of resistance occurred at the death camp of Sobibor in eastern Poland. And in dozens of other ghettos, including Vilna, Kovno, Będzin and Częstochowa, Jews took up arms against their persecutors. It was becoming clear that the ghetto system in Poland could no longer be maintained.

In March 1943, just before the Warsaw ghetto uprising took place, the killing machinery at Auschwitz was augmented in Cyclopean measure. The first of four combined Badeanstalten (bathhouses) and Einäscherungsöfen (cremating ovens) opened at the Birkenau camp. It consisted of two underground rooms, one of which provided a large undressing area, while the second was a gas chamber. The Zyklon B was to be poured in through hatches on the roof, while peepholes in the doors allowed the SS to check that the prisoners had perished. Using a small lift, the bodies were then to be transferred to the ground floor, where the large crematorium had three mufflers, each capable of burning five corpses. By *summer 1943, the SS had the capacity to murder about 4,400 people every day, and also efficiently dispose of the bodies – murder on an industrial scale.*

By winter of the same year, it was also clear the Nazis were losing the war. But even as the dream of the new Nazi Order in the East was collapsing around them, the leaders of the Third Reich began prosecuting their murderous goals with ever more obsessive hatred and determination.

---

1. The name was chosen as a deliberate allusion to Germany's centuries-old rivalry with Poland. The original Battle of Tannenberg (1409-1411), one of the great battles of medieval Europe, saw the Teutonic Knights decisively defeated by the rising Polish-Lithuanian empire. The 20th century Operation Tannenberg was planned by Hitler, Himmler and Heydrich before Germany invaded Poland, as part of the *Generalplan Ost* for the colonization of the East. It was conducted with the use of top secret lists which identified more than 60,000 members of the Polish elite, who were to be interned or shot. From the first days of occupation, *Einsatzgruppe* units along with regular army formations carried out this systematic campaign of slaughter, rounding up and shooting thousands of Poles. The staggering acts of violence that took place in these initial weeks of the war demonstrated that Nazi aspirations extended well beyond territorial conquest. They served as an overture of things to come, paving the way for the descent of Nazi Germany into a morass of unparalleled mass murder and genocide.

2. Quoted in Rees, L. (2005) *Auschwitz: A New History*, p 24.

35

MAY 1944 – JUNE 1944: PRISONER A-2649

As he stumbled out of the train at the platform, Sam had recognized that he and Hennie were in Auschwitz in Southwest Poland, not far from his hometown of Zawiercie. He had made his final desperate call to his wife as the women and children were forcibly separated from the men and she was torn away from him. Then, together with hundreds of other male prisoners, he found himself undergoing another selection process. The faces of those around him on the ramp were woebegone in the unearthly light. As he waited his turn, he saw the men ahead of him directed one way or the other, and a visionary awareness continued to grip his soul. The words from the Succot prayer, the *Unetaneh Tokef,* drummed in his ears:

Who will live and who will die?

Who in their time, and who not their time?

Who by fire and who by water? ....

Soon he was standing in front of a group of SS officers, one of whom stood out for his good looks and aura of crisp authority. His gray uniform, with twin lightning bolts on the collar representing the SS insignia, was immaculately tailored, and his boots were polished to a high sheen. This was Doctor Mengele, who was making the final decisions concerning the newly arrived prisoners.

The hand lifted, pointed, and Sam was hustled into a group to the right.

He and those selected with him were forced to run some distance to the main camp bathhouse, The Sauna, urged on by SS men with dogs and flashlights, and herded so closely together that their feet intersected and some stumbled. Sam threw away his scissors as they went; he was afraid that if they were found it might cost him his life. They arrived at a low-set wooden building and were lined up in a large courtyard. Some brawny Poles were waiting there to brand them with tattoos, and one of them looked over the group dispassionately.

"You guys are coming from Belgium, right? It's pretty rich there," he guffawed. "Those who offer gold or diamonds will get a painless treatment."

When Sam's turn came to be pushed forward to the tattooists, he had nothing to offer as a bribe, and the Pole took his revenge, digging the needle in viciously. After he finished his work, Sam stared at the digits tattooed on his left arm. His number was A-2649. He realized with a stab of outrage that he was considered by his captors to be less than human.

But the SS guards were shouting at his group again, and they were moved toward a large shower room with bench seating along the walls. Here, it seemed, Jews from every nation in Europe were gathered. They were ordered to strip, remove their glasses, and leave everything on the benches. The men pulled off their filthy clothes, divested themselves of belongings, and were pushed into the showers. Sam shivered as the freezing water cascaded over his shoulders, but was relieved to wash away the sweat and grime of the journey.

The men were soon hauled out and taken back to the courtyard. Now the Poles were brandishing razor blades, and once again the men waited in line, this time to have all the hair shaved from their bodies. After Sam succumbed to their less-than-tender ministrations, he looked ruefully at the black locks that Hennie had loved to caress, now strewn over the floor.

He was shoved back into line, and another announcement was made, with a smirk: "We are bringing you some special outfits. You will just have to wait a little."

The men were forced to remain standing there, naked and vulnerable, for the rest of the night. To Sam, the scene was becoming more and more like a surrealistic painting of hell. In his utter exhaustion of mind and body, he found himself passing into a realm in which the physical surroundings began to vanish from sight, the strident noises ceased dinning in his ears, even the harsh lighting of the courtyard dimmed into a soft opacity. He had the strangest sensation as if the bright wings of his spirit, which had formerly borne him aloft to artistic vision, were now folded, drooping, and he was beginning to plummet to a depth and darkness he had never before fathomed. He sensed it was an abode of the dead.

The morning came and the men were tossed some tattered garments. They dressed, trudged through muddy lanes between block-like buildings and arrived at the quarantine barracks, BIIa, a wooden structure originally designed as a horse stable, into which about a hundred people were packed. Sam was given a sleeping space in the attic, in a hutch that he would be sharing with two others.

The quarantine period for the prisoners was a baptism of fire, intended to plunge them ruthlessly into the reality of concentration life in "Planet Auschwitz,"[1] to make them aware of the great gulf fixed between their old life and the new, between the world outside and that inside. Very shortly the prisoners became aware of their new and shattering reality. The maniacal daily regime began as soon as they were driven from their straw pallets in the morning, and continued with prolonged exercise drills, lessons in basic German, and instruction in the draconian camp rules, all accompanied by insults, vicious punishments for imaginary infractions of rules, and buckets of ice-cold water.

From the outset of their stay in the concentration camp, the prisoners were made to endure a relentless onslaught of planned humiliation, and the primitive facilities and overcrowding combined with rampant terror immediately had a disastrous psychological effect. They had been thrust into a world which no longer recognized the values of human life and dignity, which robbed a person of individuality, and made him merely an object to be exterminated. The struggle for each prisoner was to somehow hold on to his sense of personal self-worth, the knowledge that he was a human being with a mind and inner freedom, and to guard against the disintegration of his personality. At the same time he needed to cope with a pervasive sense of unreality, the disbelief that such things could really be occurring to him. Many of the inductees took refuge in suicide. Those that clung grimly to life and sanity during the first weeks hoped against hope that, when they were released to their work units, things would improve.

On his first day in quarantine, Sam learned about the camp hierarchy. There were around 3,000 SS men in Auschwitz-Birkenau and the subcamps, but most were rank and file; only a small percentage were officers. But the evil genius of the SS had found a way to manage the large prison population with very little energy expenditure on their part. This was through the appointment of prisoner functionaries, who formed an elite group within the camp, and were given the tasks of controlling the other inmates and supervising forced labor. The system inevitably turned victim against victim, as the functionaries heavily oppressed their fellow prisoners to maintain the favor of their SS overseers. Many were recruited from the ranks of criminals known for their brutality, and frequently became more cruel than the SS themselves, with the result that terror and violence were instilled as the bedrock of the camp ethos.

The first functionary Sam encountered was the *Blockältester* (block leader), who was responsible for the prisoners in the individual barracks. In Sam's case this person was a *Volksdeutsche* (ethnic

German). He regarded the new group with beady, malevolent eyes that stared at them through fleshy cheeks. With a pompous air, he let them know they would be under his authority for the next three weeks, then his voice rose in a crescendo.

"The good time for the Jews is over," he screamed at them. "From now on Jews will not suck the blood of the Aryans. Those who won't work will disappear in the chimney."

"What do you mean? We don't understand!" someone protested.

"This ... is ... my ... translation," he said, stressing each word and laughing.

He displayed a heavy club and started to hit the prisoners indiscriminately while they tried to shield their heads and bodies. Then he began to kick and beat those who could no longer stand up straight at his command. Later on, there was another variation on this cruelty: he would make the prisoners kneel for two hours while lifting a stool in the air. If the wretched creatures moved he would hit them until they collapsed on the ground. In fact, whenever he spoke to the prisoners, he would strike them in order to bring home his point.

Another official was the *Stube-ältester* (room leader) who was responsible for hygiene, delousing and orderliness; he also wielded a club. As it was terribly hot in the room many men fainted but were reanimated with heavy blows; they were treated by him as if they were dangerous wild animals. There was no toilet in the room, which was a horror for all of them. A *Stube-dienst* (room attendant) would shout at them, "Clean the mess." Then, pointing at a few men, he would command, "Quickly, damn it! All on one side." They would stumble and fall over one another trying to comply with the order, and as they did so he would hit them and blood would flow. When one part of the room had been cleaned, the hallucinatory spectacle would start again. Sam wasn't spared and he was petrified. All this was too incredible.

On their first day in quarantine, nobody had eaten anything. They had been given a disgusting liquid labelled with the name of soup that had been cooked with rotting leftovers.

"Eat," an SS soldier commanded them contemptuously. "There's nothing else. There will come a time when you will beg for meals like these."

Sam stared at the unappetizing mess in his bowl; that later they would fight over a soup like this seemed unimaginable. But when he finally reached his crowded, bone-breaking bed that night sleep eluded him: hunger twisted his stomach in knots. As he lay there, the image of Hennie's face appeared before his eyes, her last imploring look as she was led away from him. Eventually, mercifully, he was submerged by utter emotional and physical exhaustion.

The interminable days followed one after another, and the prisoners counted them off, thankful for each one that passed. It didn't take long until all were swallowing the dirty slop they were given, simply because there wasn't anything else. Meanwhile, they hoped desperately that after the quarantine period deliverance would come. That is what kept them alive.

As the three weeks' quarantine drew to a close, the *Oberführer* had a pile of wooden shoes tossed into the attic, with all the sizes mixed together, some not even in pairs. The camp officials had taken away their shoes as well as their clothes, and the prisoners threw themselves onto the footwear, each seizing whatever he could. There weren't enough to go around, but the fortunate ones tried on their shoes, then traded them for different sizes.

At that point an SS soldier intervened, and ordered that the shoes be returned. "Tomorrow you'll get them back." He laughed.

Next morning the prisoners were woken at 5 o'clock as the wooden clubs landed on their supine forms.

"Here are the shoes," it was announced. "Get them."

Once again everyone threw themselves on the clogs, but this time there was no opportunity to exchange them. Those who missed out in the mad race to obtain the new footwear were forced to remain barefoot as they all stumbled outside and the first day of work began. But they were to find that it was not the liberty they had hoped for.

A functionary approached their new work detail, and began reeling off a series of numbers. After a moment of nervous confusion, the prisoners realized that the numbers related to the tattoos on their left arms. Standing by was an SS man with an air of aloof disdain, slapping his thigh with his riding crop, and when the rollcall was finished he addressed the group in German.

"Prisoners! You are fortunate to have been chosen to work in this camp and assist in the war effort for the Fatherland." He gestured to the functionary beside him. "This is your *Kapo* and you belong to his *Kommando*. Obey his orders and you will see another sunrise tomorrow. Heil Hitler!"

Work crews outside the camp, the *Kommandos*, were supervised by a *Vorarbeiter* (foreman), a *Kapo*, or *Oberkapo* (chief *Kapo*). It was the *Kapos'* job to ensure that the prisoners carried out the assigned labor, no matter how weak and starving they might be. They possessed absolute power and could hit, beat and even kill their fellow prisoners with impunity.

The SS officer strode off and the *Kapo* surveyed his group coldly. "As you heard," he said in thickly accented German, "I am your boss and you are to do as I say. And I warn you – there are penalties for laziness." He slapped a fist into a meaty palm. "Follow me," he snapped.

They marched out of the camp for quite a long distance, with strains of music from the camp orchestra floating about them as they went, a macabre accompaniment. The men could walk only with difficulty in their wooden shoes, and most took them off because if they didn't go quickly they were beaten. It was the month of June and very hot. Sam's shirt was torn and the sun began burning his back.

Eventually the prisoners arrived at a wide piece of ground with large piles of loose earth at the perimeter, where they worked all day without being permitted to rest; those who lagged behind were beaten. Nor were they given anything to drink. There were puddles on the ground, but it was known that one could get dysentery from drinking the water. Sam found a small empty bottle of mineral water; he waited for the *Kapo* to look the other way and filled the bottle at a faucet. He hid it in his pants and regularly took a sip.

And what was the labor at which the prisoners were forced to toil all day in these appalling conditions? Their task was to bring loads of earth and form a mound; when it was completed they were made to flatten it again. The work was intended for their sheer humiliation; and this, for Sam, was beyond comprehension. He knew that to dwell upon it would lead to madness, and even in his weakness and weariness the resolve formed in his mind that he would not succumb, that the Nazi beast would not have its way with him.

At the end of their 11-hour day the work detail took another road; they were being sent to the main camp at Auschwitz. All of them were half dead with exhaustion and had open wounds on their feet. On the way, Sam slipped the little bottle from his pocket surreptitiously and let it fall to the ground so it would not be found on him. They entered the camp through an iron gate upon which the words *Arbeit Macht Frei* were emblazoned in large metal letters.

As Sam caught sight of the sign, he thought immediately of another inscription which he felt would be far more appropriate, the words which Dante described in his *Divine Comedy* as marking the entrance to Hell: "*Abandon all hope, ye who enter here*".[2]

Through me you pass into the city of woe:

Through me you pass into eternal pain:

Through me among the people lost for aye.

But even the vivid imagination of the Italian poet would have failed to envisage the horrors befalling the innocent sufferers inside Auschwitz.

1. The phrase comes from a Holocaust survivor named Yehiel De-Nur (*De-Nur* means "of the fire" in Aramaic), who testified at the Adolf Eichmann trial in June 1961. Originally from Sosnowiec, Poland, De-Nur spent two years as a prisoner in Auschwitz. After migrating to Mandatory Palestine in 1945 he wrote several works about his experiences in the camp, using the pen name Ka-Tzetnik 135633 (Ka-Tzetnik is Yiddish for "Concentration Camper" and the number was that which was tattooed on his arm as his camp identification). In May 1960, Eichmann was captured by Mossad and Shin Bet in Buenos Aires, where he had been living under a false name since 1952. He was smuggled back to Israel and put on trial for genocide as a leading architect of the Final Solution. The decision was made to film the trial for a TV audience and viewers around the world became transfixed by the unfolding revelations. Speaking at the trial, De-Nur gave an electrifying testimony, presenting the Holocaust as a *sui generis* event, not comparable to anything else in this world, saying: *"I do not see myself as a writer who writes literature. This is a chronicle from the **planet Auschwitz**. I was there for about two years. The time there is not the same as it is here, on Earth. (...) And the inhabitants of this planet had no names. They had no parents and no children. They did not wear [clothes] the way they wear here. They were not born there and did not give birth... They did not live according to the laws of the world here and did not die. Their name was the number K. Tzetnik."* After speaking these words, De-Nur collapsed and fainted, and gave no further testimony. It was the most dramatic moment of the trial, and helped begin change perceptions of the Holocaust, both in Israel and around the world.

2. One of the most famous lines from the *Divine Comedy*, the medieval masterpiece by the Italian poet, Dante. The work is divided into major three sections: *Inferno, Purgatorio* and *Paradiso*. The first of these describes Dante's journey through Hell, accompanied by the ancient Roman poet Virgil. He depicts the region as consisting of nine concentric circles of torment within the earth, and at the entrance finds that this is the inscription over the gate. Canto III, 1–3, 9.

36

DAILY LIFE IN PLANET AUSCHWITZ

Sam's life in the main Auschwitz camp had begun. He and his fellow prisoners were taken to another two-storied barracks which, he thought, resembled nothing so much as a chicken coop. There was nothing but a mud floor, a leaking roof, and wooden pallets covered with scraps of straw. The men were so weary that they climbed on the woeful beds, and, packed so closely together that it was impossible to turn over, fell asleep.

The next morning, they were woken as the clubs began descending in their prescribed arcs. "Get up, get up!" came the cry that intruded upon their troubled slumber. Between 4:00 and 4.30 am there was a rush to use the desperately inadequate latrines and washrooms, then they dressed again in their striped garments, worn day and night, made their "beds" and cleaned the barracks, all tasks to be completed in an impossible time frame.

Once the sun rose, the prisoners set off for work. This labor could be based in Auschwitz itself, but inmates were also employed in projects outside the camp, in coal mines, rock quarries, or construction projects. They were, in addition, hired out by the SS to factories that produced weapons and other goods that supported the German war effort, fulfilling Himmler's dream of harnessing prisoner labor for economic advantage. The company that manufactured Zyklon B and came to be known as "the devil's chemist," IG Farben, exploited more than 35,000 slave laborers, many of them from Auschwitz. Other large German companies desiring to benefit from this huge army of cheap and expendable labor established plants in the Upper Silesia area: mining, cement and steelworks, oil refineries and textile manufacturing.

The number of prisoners assigned to work in the various German industries had been constantly on the rise throughout the war years, so that by the middle of 1944 when Sam arrived at the camp there were around 42,000 inmates involved in the forced labor. The sign over the entrance to the camp might have read *Arbeit Macht Frei*, but this was a cynical euphemism disguising the real purpose of the crushing toil to which the inmates were subjected daily. The Sisyphean labor assigned to each one was another measure aimed at the ultimate annihilation of the Jewish people, just as much as were the mass shootings and gassings. But this method, that the Nazis called "extermination through work," had an added advantage: it was also profitable to the economy of the Third Reich.

When Sam learned to which *Kommando* he was assigned he stifled a silent groan; it was one of the harshest. He was sent to the *Bahnhof* (train station) situated a mile outside the camp, where the work involved unloading materials – tiles, wood, iron, bricks – from the trains as they arrived. It was Sam's job to catch the heavy loads as they were thrown from the train, and after half an hour on the first day his hands were bleeding. On his way back to the camp he found some dirty rags, which he used the next day to cover his hands, softening the impact as each unwieldy burden came crashing into his grasp. He was distressed that his artist's hands were being subjected to this trauma, but knew he had to endure the work without complaining. Other inmates who had been longer in the camp warned him: "Don't go to the *Krankenblock* (sick quarters)." Men unable to handle the loads often had their fingers chopped off.

Prisoners were usually forced to march to each place of work on foot, sometimes a distance of several miles. They trudged with leaden feet and sullen gloom in their hearts, as the prospect of the long day of burdensome toil weighed heavily upon them. On the way they were often made to sing belittling songs about themselves or others in the camps for the amusement of the SS officers. One day a group of Jews from Holland surprised the men in Sam's work detail. They seemed unaware of the true nature of the situation in which they were caught up, and on their way to work broke spontaneously into a Dutch folk song: "*Ouwe taaie-ouwe taaie*" (Old Strong Man). Sam wondered how long their blithe spirits would last ... the singing soon stopped.

Once work had finished, around 5 or 6 pm, prisoners trudged back to the camp to participate in evening rollcall on the *Appellplatz*. This was a vast rectangular area of packed earth, where the exhausted men were forced to remain standing as they were counted and sometimes recounted many times. During these proceedings, they were required to keep completely still, under threat of sudden violence by SS men or *Kapos*. The rollcall would take place even in extreme weather, so the prisoners were exposed to all the elements: rain, snow, burning heat; any who collapsed or were found missing faced beatings or torture. After the rollcall was completed they were sent back to their barracks, where they had "free time" and at 9 pm lights were switched off.

So extreme a daily routine necessarily required huge reserves of strength and energy, yet the food provided for the prisoners would not even have nourished an invalid. It was certainly woefully insufficient to sustain people working long hours at backbreaking labor, and in such harsh conditions. In the mornings there was an unsweetened coffee substitute, at lunch a watery soup made with rotten vegetables, and at dinner a hunk of bread which was often dry and moldy. Sometimes the prisoners would beg for spoons because they had nothing with which to eat these pitiful rations. In 1944, the German war economy was beginning to fail and the portions for camp inmates were cut still further.

This meant that hunger was the most terrible ordeal of life in the camps. It gnawed at the prisoners day and night, with a powerful demoralizing force all of its own. Food was their continuous preoccupation, and the most precious possession in the camp was the daily bread allotment. Because of the conditions of continuous starvation, it required an effort of great self-control to save part of the ration from one day to another. The food was even more scanty on Sundays, and Sam did try to hide part of his portion to eat that day – but stopped doing so after the morsel was stolen. The inmates in his block also made some sort of scale to weigh the bread slices before they were distributed, but this led to fights because many felt discriminated against.

Yet Sam knew of a number of Jews who exercised a remarkable degree of magnanimity, even in the midst of the famine-like conditions. They would fast on Mondays and Thursdays in order to give their meager scraps to those who were weak or ill, and would pause before eating in order to give thanks: *"Blessed art Thou Eternal, our God, King of the Universe, who brings forth bread from the earth."* It was a reminder of a spiritual realm which could break through into the grim reality of life in the camp, bringing a remembrance of the values they had once cherished: kindness, devotion, self-giving love. It was these small acts of courage that gave Sam hope that it might be possible to survive.

It was not just the starvation rations and cruel labor which created huge physical demands upon the prisoners; life in the camp required them to manifest enormous psychological strength. They were subjected to unimaginable pressures from the moment they arrived: forcibly separated from family members and uncertain of their fate, exposed to constant abuse and beatings, with the threat of death always hanging over their heads. All their physical and psychical energy had to be directed toward trying to cope with the hellish environment into which they found themselves thrust, through no fault of their own, save that they were Jewish.

Few of the prisoners at Auschwitz could make that titanic effort and retain their will to live. Most survived only a few weeks or months. Some committed suicide by throwing themselves against the electric wires. Others resembled ghostly skeletons, drifting about the camp like walking corpses. Weakened by dehydration and hunger, they succumbed quickly to the contagious diseases that spread through the barracks. When they were too ill or weak to work any longer they were condemned to death in the gas chambers.

Yet, other inmates wanted against all the odds to stay alive. Sam was among them. As he sat on the hard wooden bunks in his hut, with his thin striped garment covering him, he would often hear the soft chant of Hebrew melodies coming from another corner of the room. The knowledge that some of his fellow prisoners clung to their life of faith and worship would once again instill a measure of strength in his soul. It was a desperate time, the worst of times, a time when a way out appeared unimaginable. But he was determined to survive.

37

JUXTAPOSING BEAUTY AND HORROR

Escape from Auschwitz seemed unthinkable. Encircling the camp was a double row of electric fences, studded at intervals by watchtowers, like knuckledusters on a leather glove. Upon them stood guards equipped with lethal weaponry, their cold bleak eyes staring down unceasingly over their small domain. If a prisoner actually had the temerity to attempt an escape, the Nazi wrath descended in the most terrible way. Once the person was discovered missing at rollcall the SS men would start searching with trained dogs, and if the reprobate was caught he was sent immediately to the gallows. When someone was found to have actually escaped there were shocking reprisals for the remaining prisoners. The officers would select hostages from the escapee's block or labor detail, take them to dark cells in Block II, and let them starve to death.[1]

Another petrifying event sometimes took place on Sundays: an extra rollcall. The camp director, Rudolf Höss, would be present, his uniform impeccable, buttons polished and shining. As the prisoners ran on their wooden clogs to fall in he would shout at them: "Come on, quickly." Once in line, those who did not stand sufficiently straight were taken out of their rows and punished. The SS also examined the pockets of the shabby clothes the prisoners wore. Some had secretly sewed pockets into their uniforms, and if the smallest object was found there, even a rag, they were taken to the double row of electric fences and made to stand between them. The space here was so narrow that at the slightest movement the prisoner would be electrocuted, which meant that most of them died – it was almost impossible to keep from moving for any great length of time under the burning sun. The SS men could watch this spectacle for hours.

It was on Sunday also, in the *Appellplatz*, that the Nazi soldiers would gather to attend the hangings. The victims were those poor wretches whom the SS had found guilty of some paltry misdemeanor – perhaps not working hard enough, or speaking in a way deemed insulting. The inmates were compelled to watch these appalling scenes – it was part of the camp culture of brutal intimidation, reminding them that the SS held the power of life and death, and that their lives too could be forfeit at any moment. The orchestra was forced to play at these occasions: heavy, lugubrious music which served as a suitable background for the terrible tableaux. But to Sam, the air seemed to throb with the cries of the innocents who perished there on the gallows, tried in the shifting sands of Nazi justice, and condemned to die for no crime other than that of belonging to the "Chosen People."

It seems incredible that the scene of such misery and horror could sometimes also be the stage for more light-hearted affairs – or even for experiences of sheer beauty. On some other Sundays, the camp administration would organize concerts, and Sam and his fellow prisoners would be called to the *Appellplatz* where they would be made to sit on the ground. They would see in front of them, arranged in a semicircle, a group, sometimes of men, sometimes of women, all wearing dirty prison uniforms, and emaciated from hunger. They came from all over Europe, and each would be holding a violin, a cello, or some other musical instrument. This was one of the motley camp orchestras.

There would be a moment of silence, a hush ... but then! The music that flowed from the fingers of this bunch of ragged scarecrows seemed to come from another sphere, a transcendent realm of time and place that existed far beyond Auschwitz. Starving, desperately unhappy as the players undoubtedly were, forced to perform through suffering and humiliation, yet their music was the music of heaven. Something of their sorrow communicated itself as an undercurrent in those bright flowing melodies, the waltzes made for days of happiness beside the sparkling waves of the Danube, or nights of love under a star-studded sky. It evoked the world that had been lost, and all its brightness and charm – the world to which the prisoners could never again aspire to belong.

As the SS men danced in the square to the music, the juxtaposition of beauty and horror would once again prove unnerving for Sam. He listened to the compositions of Schubert, Bach and Beethoven, whose sublime creations had been intended for the glory of God and spiritual exaltation, who could have never imagined such players, nor such an audience. As the musicians drew their bows over the strings, and the violin sobbed its melody, as the deep sonorous bass of the cello echoed about them, and the flute sent forth notes of immaculate purity, the hearts of the prisoners were pierced. The music expressed what they could not articulate, bringing forth a cry *de profundis*.

As if the bow was drawn across his own soul, Sam heard the voices of the dying, the voices of those whose loved ones, whose wives and children, more precious to them than life itself, had been cast into the flames. They were uttering their grievous complaints, but there was no prayer, no liturgy that was equal to the crime: *What shall I cry? the voice asked – Mercy*, they cried, *Vengeance*, they cried.[2]

To Sam, the countenance of every Jewish inmate in the camp represented a vivid picture of his people, a race set apart, enduring the greatest spiritual and physical onslaught in the history of humanity. It seemed to him that their trials carved new lineaments on their faces, that could arrest the gaze with an intense, unspoken eloquence. There in the depths of hell, as their strength and life burned away, they appeared to him transfigured, as though the flesh had become transparent to his gaze, and he could see through their wasted frames to the radiant spark within where the embers of life yet glowed. The images that imprinted themselves on his mind and heart were endowed with a mystic quality, evoking the fires of suffering his people had passed through, and he would carry them forever.

During his work Sam sometimes saw women, with their thin bodies covered in rags and their heads shaved. These glimpses wrung his heart with pity. He felt they had a special aura of beauty in their suffering and humiliation, and when he gazed into their haunted eyes he was forced to look away. If an SS man saw a man and woman interacting in any way they would be beaten. But Sam would scan their faces covertly, longing that he might catch a glimpse of Hennie and know that she was still alive. The thought of her fate was a constant torture to him.

He learned also of the indomitable strength and tenacity of his people, and began to understand a new kind of heroism. Somehow, in the midst of this unparalleled misery and degradation, there remained those individuals who seemed able, despite their utmost physical weakness, to maintain a freedom of the spirit.[3] Many of the prisoners in Sam's block were from Eastern Europe, where the majority of the Jews were of the Orthodox faith. A little *Beit Midrash* was formed on the highest tier of the bed bunks by a group of Hasidim who would secretly assemble there, scorning the risk of discovery. With prayer books smuggled into the camp, even managing to don tefillin, they would pray together and study, discussing the mysteries of suffering and redemption, remembering the God who had given His name to Moses, "*I Am Who I Am*,"[4] and who had promised, "*I will be with you in trouble and deliver you.*"[5]

On Friday nights when they gathered on the upper bunks, they would speak together about the Sabbath, honoring it as God had ordained, a day of rest and joy. They were all hungry and suffering, they knew they would be forced to work on the morrow as on any other day, but for a few brief hours seemed able to forget their state. On wings of prayer they were transported to the Sabbaths and holy days of the past, when they had gathered around the laden tables in their fathers' houses, when the candles illuminated the rooms with their soft luster. For a time, they would even forget the most pressing question that lay heavily on their souls: the mystery of God's silence. Sam noted that the faces of these Jews, as they met in secret, often became illumined by an unearthly radiance.

Young people would often gather there as well, take their *siddur* from its hiding place and read chapters from the Book of Psalms, especially the verses of consolation. And for a few fleeting minutes, their quiet utterance would weave a spell of peace and solace over the crushed hearts of the inmates as they lay listening in their bunks:

Whither shall I go from thy spirit? or whither shall I flee from thy presence?

If I ascend up into heaven, thou art there: if I make my bed in hell, behold, thou art there.

If I take the wings of the morning, and dwell in the uttermost parts of the sea;

Even there shall thy hand lead me, and thy right hand shall hold me.

If I say, Surely the darkness shall cover me; even the night shall be light about me.

Yea, the darkness hideth not from thee; but the night shineth as the day:

The darkness and the light are both alike to thee ...[6]

---

1. This was the fate that befell Franciscan priest Maximilian Kolbe who died as prisoner 16770 in Auschwitz on August 14, 1941. He offered his own life to save a fellow prisoner, Franciszek Gajowniczek, condemned to death by the camp authorities after a successful escape by a fellow prisoner.
2. Alluding to Isaiah 40:6, Hosea 2:1, Revelation 6:9–10.
3. Austrian psychiatrist Viktor Frankl, who was also imprisoned in Auschwitz, noticed the same phenomenon and described it in his famous book, *Man's Search for Meaning*. "We who lived in concentration camps can remember the

men who walked through the huts comforting others, giving away their last piece of bread. They may have been few in number, but they offer sufficient proof that everything can be taken from a man but one thing: the last of the human freedoms – to choose one's attitude in any given set of circumstances, to choose one's own way."

4. Quoting from Exodus 3:14, the scene where God encounters Moses in the desert at the Burning Bush, and charges him with bringing the Children of Israel out of Egypt. Moses was understandably fearful and reluctant, and asked how he should identify the God who had sent him. "What shall I say to them?" he asked, and God's answer came: "I AM WHO I AM. Thus you shall say to the Children of Israel: I AM has sent me to you." The Hebrew version of the name God disclosed is more properly understood as being in a future tense: "I will be what I will be." According to the medieval Jewish commentator, Rashi, God is therefore saying in these words: "I shall be with them in this anguish as I shall be with them in future crises." God, who alone knows the future, saw that nations and individuals throughout the course of history would face many devastating situations, but His power would be present to respond to the need and answer the cry for help.

5. Quoting from Psalm 50:15, Psalm 91:15.

6. Quoting from Psalm 139:7–12, KJV.

38

THE ULTIMATE CONFLICT

Open your eyes visitor,

And gather your inner strength;

What you will see here

May put your mental sanity

And moral quest in peril.[1]

Time and again it seemed Sam's destiny to have his life caught up with the most dramatic events of the era during which he lived. His arrival at Auschwitz in the early summer of 1944 coincided with the supremely tragic period in which the mass killing reached its peak.

Between May and July, nearly 440,000 Jews were crammed into freight cars and deported from Hungary. *Clackety-clack* went the train wheels, spelling out the doom which awaited them. Arriving at Auschwitz-Birkenau they underwent a rapid process of selection, and the vast majority were sent to the heart of darkness within the camp – the gas chambers. The SS worked 48-hour shifts to keep up with the pace of unloading, herding, gassing and burning, and day and night smoke ascended from all chimneys of the crematoria. Adding to the stupefying total were Sinti and Roma – the gypsies. By 1944, over a quarter of a million had been brought to Auschwitz, about half of them children and young people, and in May that year Himmler ordered their murder.

To deal with the volume of the arriving transports the Nazis also increased the number of *Sonderkommandos* working in the four crematoria; these labor details were composed of prisoners, usually Jews, who had been forced on threat of their own lives to aid with the disposal of gas chamber victims. They had no way to refuse other than by committing suicide, and hence were given an assignment requiring an ethical decision as cruel as any human being would ever have to face. But *Sonderkommando* members did not participate directly in killing; that responsibility was reserved for the Nazi officials alone.

In fact, it was the SS doctors, many of them high-ranking physicians, who were involved at every level of the genocidal agenda. It was they who made the fundamental decision during the initial selection at the ramp: who should live and who should die. Without compunction these white-coated professionals – including the "Angel of Death," Doctor Mengele – selected camp inmates for their unspeakable medical experiments. Finally, at the crematoria, they arranged to have the Zyklon B transported in a pseudo-ambulance marked with a red cross, and as it arrived they themselves dropped the crystals into the gas chambers.

It would seem utterly impossible to reconcile the actions of these doctors with the Hippocratic oath they had sworn, that they would do all within their power to alleviate suffering and heal the sick. But, in the crazy looking-glass world of Auschwitz, where values were smashed to smithereens, where "nothing is, but what is not,"[2] this behavior had a certain logical symmetry. They were able without a qualm of conscience to

> ... *call evil good, and good evil; put darkness for light, and light for darkness; put bitter for sweet, and sweet for bitter!*[3]

All the Nazi officers conspired together to veil the true nature of their new killing mechanism. Crucial to its success was the creation of a specious atmosphere of peace and calm among the new arrivals. They were taken to the large hall of the crematorium, given coffee, and required to undress under the pretext that they were to take a bath. Lulled into a false sense of security, they would go like lambs to the slaughter; they undressed, folded their clothes neatly and tied the laces of their shoes together.

Then they went into the gas chambers, the doors were locked, and the powder was dropped in. Countless numbers went to their deaths in this way, and as they did the terrible distinction of becoming the largest site of mass murder in the world was conferred upon Auschwitz-Birkenau. And *Obersturmbannführer* Höss was awarded the War Merit Cross for fulfilling his mission.

Many generations of Jews had suffered martyrdom for their faith before Auschwitz loomed on the horizon. The tale is a familiar one from the Hebrew Scriptures: it began in Egypt with Pharaoh's genocidal program, and continued through Nebuchadnezzar, Haman and Antiochus, up to the commencement of the present era. Since then, exiled from their land for nearly 2,000 years, the Jews have been forced to drain constantly proffered cups of bitter suffering[4] – persecution, pogroms, crusades, inquisitions – all fueled by the ineradicable phenomenon known as antisemitism.

Manifold, indeed, are the evils that have befallen the Chosen People through the centuries, but at the same time they have given rise to a catalogue of deeds which in themselves merit the name "immortal." And when they were faced with the supreme test, as happened so often, thousands of Jews went to meet their deaths with unshakeable, shining courage. Plunged into an abyss of suffering, they used their last moments on earth to declare their faith in the Almighty, in the majestic simplicity of the words which form the centerpiece of Jewish prayer: "*Hear, O Israel: the Lord our God, the LORD is one.*" During the years of Nazi hegemony, a vast company went to the gas chambers with the *Shema* on their lips, or singing *Ani Ma'amin* (I believe) in quiet dignity.

Yes, affirmation of the goodness of life was the fundamental message of the Torah, but these Jewish martyrs understood in the depths of their souls that if required to give up their lives this itself could be a form of worship. As their faith rose on wings of fire to meet their challenges, as they went forward to their destiny while bearing witness to steadfast trust in the Creator, this was, they believed, the supreme expression of *Kiddush HaShem*: of sanctifying the name of God. In the world of Judaism, it was thought that even those who went involuntarily to their death, who had no knowledge of the suffering about to confront them, also merited the title "*Kadosh*" (Holy).

For that reason, it is as if the whole of Auschwitz were metamorphosed into one gigantic altar, lying open to heaven. This sacrificial dimension transfigured the landscape into a new holy of holies, as all the prayers, sighs, tears of anguish, cries of perplexity and despair blazed their way into heaven in a white flame of infinite purity. But the offering upon that altar was made by men who by their actions forfeited the title of human beings, the offering of Cain the murderer, the fratricide, who did not know that in that murder he signaled his own doom. And why did Cain slay his brother? *Because his own works were evil, and his brother's righteous.*[5] The hatred of Nazism for the Jewish people is explicable only on this basis.

It is a striking fact that, after the tide of war turned against the Germans, and all their energies should have been devoted to salvaging victory on the military front, this did not occur. Instead, a new measure of virulence began to infuse their efforts to carry out the Final Solution concerning the Jewish people to its fullest extent. This mystifying development suggests that the war in which they were engaged was not simply for *Lebensraum* and political supremacy. Rather, it was an absolute conflict taking place in a spiritual realm between two opposing principles, between the people of Israel and all they represented on the one hand, and Nazified Germany and its motivating powers on the other.

The Jews exist on a supernatural level as the Chosen Race through whom the revelation of God's light and truth were to be mediated to the world. According to the scriptures, God set His love upon them not because they possessed any inherent greatness, for in fact they were *"the least of all peoples"* (Deuteronomy 7:7). Nevertheless, He chose them as a "special treasure" for Himself because He loved them, and wished to keep His promise to their forefathers, Abraham, Isaac and Jacob. The New Testament regards the nation of Israel as receiving unparalleled gifts – *the adoption, and the glory, and the covenants, and the giving of the law, and the service of God, and the promises*[6] – and their destiny ultimately as providing streams of blessing from Zion to all the peoples of the earth.

What is undoubted is that the Jews have had a beneficial influence upon the world sublimely disproportionate to their numbers, a distinction which is evident throughout history. From the national literature of the Jewish people, the Bible, have flowed the ideals which have shaped the course and direction of Western civilization and permeated its political, legal and cultural institutions. The monumental impact of the Hebrew Scriptures has ensured the word given to Israel concerning the Oneness of God and the divine-human encounter, the great principles of righteousness, justice and mercy it sets forth, have blazoned their way to the ends of the earth.

This is all the more astonishing when it is considered that the revelation given to the Jewish people came to a little-known and politically insignificant nation. But Israel's understanding of the word was gained at great cost to herself: through many centuries of steadfast devotion, endurance and trial, as well as times of bitter failure and repentance. It was only in this way that the "boundless waves" of the scriptures could provide the source:

From which the tortured brethren drew

In evil days their strength of soul

To meet their doom: stretch out their necks

To each uplifted knife and axe,

In flames, on stakes to die with joy,

And with a whisper, "God is one"

To close their lips ...[7]

The Nazi ideology could not be more diametrically opposed. Hitler had risen to power on the wings of such political factors as Germany's shameful defeat in the First World War and resulting economic chaos, but occult elements clearly played their part. Despite their assertions of scientific enlightenment, the Nazi leadership still recognized the advantages to be gained through appealing to the longing for myth and significance existing in the post-war nation. The darkest elements of the past were recalibrated, and German history divided into three momentous stages suggesting a high and mysterious destiny for her people. Charlemagne's First Reich and Bismarck's Second of "blood and iron" were to be followed by the final act, the Third Reich, in which their chimerical visions would come to pass, and dominate the world for the next thousand years.

In the final analysis, the Nazi ideology was not essentially a political one; it was birthed through engagement with the ancient Teutonic gods of bloodletting and violence, and focused on achieving the goal of conquering the earth through use of unrestrained force and demonic powers. A creed such as that of the Nazis, which tramples upon the idea of a spiritual realm of goodness and truth, insists there are really no values in the world except for the stark reality of racial struggle, a combat in which stronger races must inevitably prevail over weaker. Accordingly, to prepare the German state for world mastery was to prepare it as an instrument for destroying other states, and it was to this end that the SS and the concentration camps were created. Thus, when German power began to reach out it invariably brought destruction, as it did to Austria in 1938, then

Czechoslovakia and Poland, and as it attempted with the Soviet Union.

Beyond all else, the regime was intent upon the destruction of the Jews, for the deeper the antipathy toward the realm of the spirit, the greater the hatred against the people of Israel. It is they who represent in history the affirmation of values that have survived independently of military might and the structures of earthly power. There is an awesome, baffling truth about the Jewish people: however many times the attempt has been made to "destroy, kill and annihilate"[8] them, they continue to exist. That they have come through so many catastrophes as have toppled mighty empires in the past is testimony, not just to the Jewish spirit, but to an inexplicable power which has guarded and kept them in all their trials.

Hence, the Final Solution was intended not only to eliminate the Jewish people, but to vanquish the mysterious spiritual force which had sheltered and favored them. Implicit in the Nazi program was the thwarting of the biblical plan for redemption of the earth, the overturning of transcendent values, and the eradication of the divine image in man.

The Nazis sensed the ultimate nature of the conflict they were waging, and that an unseen spiritual dimension was operative in human history, directing the course of events. Their intimation that if they did not succeed in overcoming the Jewish people they would also fail in their plans for world conquest was also correct. Already, in fact, their downfall was being manifested. Hitler's notion of his own mystical destiny had caused him to make fatal errors in military leadership: "This mania for ordering distant troops to stand fast no matter what their peril was to lead to Stalingrad and other disasters and to help seal his fate."[9]

It seemed as if the actions of the Nazis could only reach a certain pinnacle before the whole rotten superstructure, built over a dark and malignant abyss, must collapse in on itself. Things were reaching a dramatic crisis at Auschwitz; events were also gathering pace in the world outside.[10]

1. From a message by Elie Wiesel, upon the opening of a new exhibition, SHOAH, at the Auschwitz-Birkenau State Museum, Block 27, in June 2013.

2. Macbeth's moral compass begins to go awry as his sense of truth and reality becomes overturned in Shakespeare's play, Act I, Scene 3.

3. Isaiah 5:20.

4. Psalm 73:10

5. I John 3:12.

6. Romans 9:4.

7. From Haim Nachman Bialik's "The Source of Strength," quoted in Feinberg, C. (1980) *Israel: At the Center of History & Revelation*, Portland: Multnomah Press, p 180.

8. From Esther 3:13. This passage details Haman's genocidal plan to bring about the destruction of the Jewish people who lived in the Persian empire following the Babylonian exile.

9. Shirer, W. (1959) *The Rise and Fall of the Third Reich, A History of Nazi Germany*, Fiftieth Anniversary Edition. New York: Simon & Schuster. Concurring with Shirer is Ron Rosenbaum in the introduction to the new edition: "...few ideas were more stupid and evil than Hitler's notion of his own divine destiny, forbidding, for instance, even tactical retreats."

10. Many of the understandings expressed in this chapter were deepened through engagement with the writings of Holocaust theologian Eliezer Berkovits, including *Faith After the Holocaust* (1973). I am also indebted to the writings of Abraham Joshua Heschel for my comments on the impact of the Bible.

39

D-DAY

"You are about to embark upon the Great Crusade, toward which we have striven these many months. The eyes of the world are upon you. The hopes and prayers of liberty-loving people everywhere march with you. In company with our brave Allies and brothers-in-arms on other Fronts, you will bring about the destruction of the German war machine, the elimination of Nazi tyranny over the oppressed peoples of Europe, and security for ourselves in a free world."[1]

In these words, General Dwight Eisenhower addressed the Allied forces on the eve of D-Day, June 6, 1944. For months the Allies had been amassing troops and equipment in Britain in preparation for the invasion of Northwest Europe, code-named Overlord. Eisenhower's Supreme Headquarters Allied Expeditionary Force (SHAEF) had authority over all the branches of the armed units of the countries taking part – the largest number ever committed to one operation on the Western Front. Over a million Americans had poured into the UK by May, and they, together with British and Canadian troops, underwent months of special training to ensure faultless timing and cooperation between ground, sea and air forces as they crossed the English Channel and advanced into the Continent.

Hitler had anticipated an Allied invasion along the French coast, and charged Rommel with completing the Atlantic Wall, Germany's 4,000-kilometer line of fortifications along the coastline of continental Europe. The colossal guns and batteries, landmines, beach and water obstacles, as well as the thousands of German troops stationed in its defenses, made the task of breaching the Wall a formidable one. The D-Day invasion was planned for Normandy, but the Allies had carried out a massive program of deception, utilizing fake equipment, a phantom army commanded by George Patton, double agents and fraudulent radio transmissions, intended to make the Germans think the main target was Pas-de-Calais, the narrowest point between Britain and France.

The epic invasion began at dawn on June 6, as some 156,000 Allied forces were brought across the English Channel by 6,500 vessels and landed on five Normandy beaches – a massive reversal of Dunkirk, and one of the largest amphibious military assaults in history. Stormy seas made the landings incredibly arduous, with many regiments coming ashore far from their target destinations. On the western half, the First United States Army landed on the beaches Utah and Omaha. Eastward the Second British Army assaulted the beaches of Gold, Juno and Sword. The Canadians were responsible for Juno in the center of the British front.

Although the Wehrmacht had been misled into thinking the Allied invasion would take place at Pas de Calais, the landing forces were met with around 50,000 German troops. The British and Canadians overcame comparatively light opposition to capture their beaches, as did the Americans at Utah. But US forces faced heavy resistance at Omaha, where the first waves of fighters were drastically pummeled by machine gun fire as they scrambled across the mine-littered beach. They persisted in pushing forward to the fortified seawall and then up steep bluffs to take out the Nazi artillery posts by nightfall – but with over 2,000 casualties. More than 4,000 Allied troops lost their lives that day, and thousands more were wounded or missing.

Nevertheless, the Atlantic Wall had been breached, a magnificent accomplishment, and supplies and men were pouring ashore to continue the fight: the Allies were back in Europe. Less than a week later, the beaches were fully secured and the troops immediately began installing two massive temporary harbors prefabricated in England. On June 19, however, a massive gale descended upon the English Channel, and when it finally blew out to sea the American harbor had been destroyed and the British piers were badly damaged; more than 140,000 tons of supplies were destroyed, and 800 ships lost or beached. A replacement harbor was urgently needed, and the nearest one was Cherbourg. Despite fierce German resistance, US troops seized the city by the end of June, and rebuilt the harbor and piers.

The Allies, now provided with vital material to sustain their war effort, were poised to continue their march across France. In the ensuing weeks they fought their way across the Normandy countryside, their progress hampered by the narrow lanes and thick hedgerows of the French landscape. By the end of August, the Allies reached the Seine, and supported the Free French forces as they entered the capital. Paris was liberated, and the Germans were removed from Northwestern France.

Since the breakout from Normandy the Allied front line had moved forward at an astonishing pace, and once again a large port was desperately needed to serve as a landing area for supplies. The clear choice was Antwerp: it was Europe's second-largest port, with 50 kilometers of docks, and British forces had captured the city. However, German forces still controlled the River Scheldt which connected Antwerp to the North Sea, and as long as they commanded the sea approaches Allied shipping to the port would be impossible.

The task of liberating the Scheldt was entrusted to the First Canadian Army; their assignment was incredibly daunting. The unique geography of the area as well as the fact that the Germans had flooded land areas in the estuary made it one of the most dangerous battlegrounds of the war. But, after five weeks of grueling fighting, numerous amphibious assaults and many casualties, the Canadians carried the day. Their victory in the Battle of the Scheldt enabled the approaches to Antwerp to be freed and the crucial supply line secured, and, on November 28, the first convoy entered the port, led by the Canadian-built freighter Fort Cataraqui.

In the east, also, time was running out for the Germans. To coincide with D-Day, Soviet forces had launched a massive offensive in Belarus which resulted in huge casualties for the German troops and destroyed their front line. The Germans were now fighting a defensive war on both the Eastern and Western Fronts, and the rollback of Wehrmacht forces continued relentlessly. In Germany itself, the long-simmering opposition to Hitler from within German military and civilian ranks erupted on July 20 in an attempted assassination. A bomb planted by Count von Stauffenberg exploded at Hitler's Wolfsschanze (Wolf's Lair) headquarters in the Prussian forest. The Führer managed to escape, but thenceforth stayed largely confined to his bunker under the Reich Chancellery in Berlin.

As the Soviet troops marched into South Poland they liberated the camp of Madjanek, and when they crossed the Vistula were only a short distance away from Auschwitz. It was at this point that the SS began the systematic dissolution of the camp. About half of the 155,000 prisoners were sent to concentration camps in the West, including Buchenwald, Ravensbrück, Mauthausen and Bergen-Belsen, where many died. But nothing changed in the daily routine in Auschwitz, even while the camp was being broken up. Prisoners still had to turn up for forced labor, new buildings were being constructed, and the massive amounts of material taken from the Hungarian Jews had to be sorted.

The deportees who had come from all over Europe to Auschwitz were each allowed to bring with them three travel bags: a suitcase, a piece of hand luggage and a rucksack, which together could not exceed 50 kilograms. The provision of luggage helped them feel connected to their old world, and gave them hope there was a promise of life at their destination. Invariably they packed their most valuable and sentimental possessions, as well as personal documents, medicines, and of course food for the journey. Observant Jews brought their religious artefacts: kippahs, tallits and tefillin, as well as prayer books and candlesticks, while children clung to their favorite belongings – perhaps a teddy bear or doll, a book or diary.

This luggage was confiscated immediately upon arrival, and as many as 2,000 prisoners were assigned to collect and sort the bundles of household goods, clothes, even furniture and carpets, which ended up in the camp. The garments of the deceased were also searched for the diamonds, gold and jewelry which had been hidden in seams and linings, where an enormous *range of currencies also turned up. One day there would be French francs, another Czech korunas, Polish zlotys, or Hungarian forint – and always American dollars. Better than gold was the array of liquor and food items. When the guards weren't looking, the starving prisoners often hid some of these treasures, risking death to do so.*

All these personal effects were processed and stored in barracks guarded with barbed wire, warehouses which were nicknamed "Kanada," a land thought to be a magical place of boundless wealth. A staggering number of barracks were needed for the mountain of plunder, no less than 30, and all valuables taken were thought to be the property of the Reich. The Nazis were determined to obtain the greatest possible economic benefit from those whom they were destroying, and after the Hungarian influx hundreds of fully laden railway trucks left the camp headed for Berlin, filled with the stolen goods.

Working in "Kanada" was considered one of the more desirable *Kommandos* but was a job which went most often to women, and Sam knew it was out of bounds for him. During those critical months in late summer 1944, he got promoted and became an iron bender. The work involved screwing iron bars with huge keys, and the overseer was a muscle-bound German criminal. But for Sam it seemed like more hard labor; he still had enough strength to do the job but realized that in order to survive he needed to find work that was less physically strenuous.

There was a *Kapo* where he worked, a *Volksdeutscher* who was not such a bad guy. Sam decided to approach him and ask if there was another work detail he might join.

The man looked at him appraisingly. "I need a strong guy who speaks Polish for the inmates' canteen," he said. "What languages do you speak?"

"Polish, German, Russian, French, English ... and Yiddish," Sam answered.

"Hmm ... just don't think it's an easy job there. You'll have to work hard!"

"I'm your man," Sam said.

Through the cacophony of clanging metal, shouting of guards and barking dogs, the *Kapo* leaned forward and gazed into Sam's eyes. "What makes you keep going?" he asked.

Sam met his gaze levelly. "I'm a survivor," he said.

---

1. Eisenhower's speech was intended to impress upon the Allied troops the seriousness and magnitude of the mission upon which they were embarking; it was distributed as a printed leaflet to all the forces. It was also widely disseminated outside their ranks, being read to 50,00 people in Central Park, New York on the evening of June 6. Later it influenced the title of Eisenhower's 1948 book about the war, *Crusade in Europe*.

40

THE WARSAW UPRISING

The demigods in the disordered hierarchy existing at Auschwitz were the prisoners known as "privileged," who had been granted a special status within the system. Their number included young boys known as "piepels," usually 15 to 16 years of age, who were taken by the *Kapos* and other prominent prisoners as personal servants to clean their rooms and perform other tasks. But everyone knew what their duties really were. There was a prevalence of homosexuality in the camp and the boys were used to service all their patron's needs – including sexual ones. It was the only chance of survival for these youngsters who would otherwise have been gassed.[1]

To be one of the "privileged" prisoners carried other benefits as well. They were able to "shop" in the canteens located in the main parts of Auschwitz and the subcamps, provided they had money with them when they were registered, or when their families sent it to them. The canteens opened several days a week and sold foodstuffs such as marinated beets, snails in a salty sauce and mineral water, as well as cigarettes, shaving equipment, toothpaste, and stamps – items which helped to make life in the camp more endurable. The Nazi administration was very cynical when it came to canteens; they included a notice in every letter sent by prisoners to their families which said, "You must not send parcels to the prisoners; there is a canteen in Auschwitz and prisoners can buy anything they want there."

The canteen where Sam began working was in a former theater outside the camp; his task was to unload heavy boxes of mineral water that arrived in truckloads from Czechoslovakia. But for him, like the other famished prisoners, there was no possibility of access to any of the goods sold in the canteen. Sam did sometimes succeed in keeping a bottle of mineral water for himself. The foreman was an SS man from Dresden; he was not a sadist, although he did keep strictly to the letter of the law. Once he even shared with Sam a cake his wife had sent him for his birthday. There was another guard who was drunk most of the day; he was eventually transferred to the front.

Fall started and it rained continuously; everything was covered in mud, and the clothes of the inmates could never get dry. Sam felt his forces diminish and feared that death was approaching; he knew he must again try to find a different job. In his work at the canteen he had got to know one of the privileged prisoners, a Greek kid named Gino who spoke some French and German. The Greek Jews were the first to arrive at Auschwitz, and many spoke only their native tongue. The sentence "Me Greek – don't understand" often signed their death warrant. Those who survived learned to speak German or Polish.

"Gino," Sam asked one day, "can you help me to get a better job?"

"Don't bother. Auschwitz will soon be evacuated," the boy told him. "Don't tell anyone," he cautioned. "Here, take a bar of soap."

It was an incredible luxury. Sam washed himself and his rags and felt a little more human. But he still needed to find another job, and after a couple of weeks he spoke again to the child. Gino didn't appear enthusiastic, but he liked Sam.

"Perhaps I can find something for you. I'll look tomorrow," he said.

He kept his word. "I've found another place for you," he told Sam, a brief smile lighting his face. "It's in a laundry, outside the camp."

"Thank you, thank you." Sam put his hand on Gino's shoulder. They looked at each other – the child with the look of an old man, and Sam with a look of compassion and understanding.

The laundry was located in an ancient tannery bearing the inscription *Lederfabrik*; inside were a number of large basins in which SS uniforms and other items were washed. Sam was able to stay in the laundry both day and night, and the morning after he arrived he looked about carefully. There were as yet no *Kapos* around. He climbed into one of the large basins and sank into the hot water, immersing himself fully, luxuriating in the sensation as the water caressed his whole weary body. He closed his eyes, experiencing the sheer bliss of the moment, and for one fleeting instant even thought he was at home hearing Hennie's sweet laughter. His work at the laundry meant that he was finally able to have clean clothes, and at night he slept in pajamas; he almost forgot he was in so infernal a place. A number of women from Birkenau were also employed in the laundry; whenever Sam saw them his heart gave a jolt – but he never saw Hennie.

A febrile atmosphere was beginning to envelop the camp. Rumors that the Russians were advancing were swirling about, and on a few occasions the IG Farben plant was the target of Allied attacks. Distant explosions could be heard and the alarm sounded frequently. In early October, some of the *Sonderkommando* staged a revolt; sadly it was a failure and there were terrible repercussions – but it did leave one crematorium in ruins. They also managed to take photographs and smuggle the film out of the camp to reach the Resistance in Krakow. On another occasion, English planes bombed an SS barracks and the prisoners saw the Germans running around like madmen. Many were killed, and the inmates were filled with savage joy. They could feel the front approaching.

Alas, it was not coming as quickly as the prisoners desired.

On July 27, Soviet forces had appeared on the east bank of the Vistula, so close that the citizens of Warsaw could hear the thud of their guns. Columns of retreating German soldiers began streaming through the city, fleeing westwards, and leaving behind a garrison of only 2,000 soldiers. A day or two later Moscow Radio broadcast a message from Molotov to the inhabitants of the city, calling on them to rise against the remaining Germans and promising them aid.

The demand put a great deal of pressure on the Polish Home Army or AK (Armia Krajowa), which was perhaps the largest resistance organization operating during the war. Their members were loyal to the Polish government-in-exile in London, and they were wary of Russian intentions. The Soviet Union had already assumed direct control in eastern Poland, and the AK feared that unless they liberated Warsaw the Red Army would sweep in and forcibly set up a communist regime. It also seemed to them that it would take only a few days for the AK to overwhelm the depleted numbers of Germans and liberate the city. Accordingly, units of the Home Army went into action on August 1 as part of Operation Tempest and established initial control over most of central Warsaw.

However, when news of the Uprising reached Hitler, he ordered Himmler to send in his most battle-hardened troops, kill every Polish man, woman and child, and destroy the whole city as a warning to the rest of Occupied Europe. The SS and Wehrmacht soldiers stormed in, equipped with artillery and tanks, while the Luftwaffe dive-bombed Polish-held areas. The air filled with smoke, fire and sulfur as the German troops gradually recaptured the city, surrounded the Old Town and other areas, and pushed the AK back house by house, slaughtering the civilians as they went. Between August 5 and 7, in the district of Wola, 40,000 to 50,000 inhabitants were massacred, most of them in one terrible day known as Black Saturday.

Desperately short of equipment and weaponry, the Poles fought on fiercely, begging the nearby Russian forces to launch an immediate attack. The Western allies dropped ammunition and supplies, but these were insufficient for the critical impasse, and the Soviets on the other side of the Vistula ignored the Polish attempts to make radio contact. Moscow Radio denounced the uprising as a conspiracy against the Soviet Union, and the Red Army soldiers facing Warsaw stood idly by as the fighting raged on. The Soviet betrayal was deliberate. Stalin was supremely content to wait while the Germans liquidated the fighters who would have resisted his intention to turn Poland into a Soviet satellite.

After 63 days of staunch resistance the remnants of the AK group defending the Old Town decided to evacuate. On the night of September 1, 4,000 men climbed out through the city sewers carrying their wounded with them, while the Germans dropped grenades and burning gasoline down the manholes. Other pockets of resistance were reduced one by one, and eventually the Poles, having run out of arms, supplies, food and water, were forced to capitulate.

The Warsaw Uprising was the single largest military effort taken by any European resistance movement during the war. It is estimated that about 16,000 members of the Polish Resistance were killed, and between 150,000 and 200,000 Polish civilians died, mostly in mass executions. The remaining civilian population were herded into cattle trucks and sent to concentration camps or forced labor in Germany; as soon as they were removed the next phase of the Nazi plan swung into operation: this was to make the city "completely disappear from the surface of the earth" and "raze it to its foundation."[2] Squads of German engineers were dispatched to burn and demolish every structure that remained standing, using flamethrowers and dynamite, and taking special care to erase Polish national monuments.

By January 1945, when the Soviets marched in after the retreating German army, there was nothing left to liberate; 85 percent of the buildings had been destroyed. Over the remains of the once proud and beautiful city a pale winter sun filtered its cold light. In this wilderness of ruins, all the splendid palaces, squares, museums, all the dignified neighborhoods, had been reduced to chunks of debris, and mountains of rubble littered the former parks and gardens. Street after surreal street were lined with tottering ruins, and only stray dogs and cats roamed within the ghostly shells of former stately buildings and homes. Their eyeless windows gazed down on the indescribable scene, and over the city that had suffered more than any other during the war a mournful silence prevailed:

How lonely sits the city

That was full of people![3]

After this unparalleled destruction, there were certainly no Poles left who could organize resistance to Soviet plans for establishing political dominance over the country.

Back in the camp, Sam did not know of the further disasters befalling the country of his birth. Winter started and with it came the snow, but in the laundry it was warm. Looking through the windows he saw Germans coming from the front using sledges as means of transportation. The Auschwitz inmates understood that the Nazis were losing the war, and the hope that they would be liberated filled them with joy.

Sam too held on to this glimmer of hope. He stayed for three months in the laundry; it certainly saved his life.

---

1. The "piepels" were not the only ones who endured sexual slavery. Himmler had ordered brothels to be set up across the camp network; he believed that if male prisoners – excluding Jews – were offered a "bonus" for working hard their productivity would be increased. The brothel at Auschwitz was set up in Block 24, just behind the infamous *Work Makes Free* gate, and opened every evening after rollcall. Most of the women who worked there were selected from the inmates of Birkenau and forced to have sex with approximately six men each day. They received extra rations of food and were given a warm place to live, as well as luxurious clothes and underwear coming from the Kanada warehouse. That, of course, made surviving the camp easier – but their suffering was as acute as that of any of the other inmates, the destruction of their self-worth just as ruthless. These women also knew that this daily humiliation meant the difference between living and dying.

2. According to Himmler, Warsaw was to "completely disappear from the surface of the earth and serve only as a transport station for the *Wehrmacht*. No stone can remain standing. Every building must be razed to its foundation." The destruction of the city had first been planned as part of the Nazi's program for Germanization of Central Europe under their *Generalplan Ost*. But at this point, in late 1944, the war was clearly lost, and the destruction of Warsaw could no

longer serve any military purpose. It was undertaken purely as an act of revenge. The Nazi plans for the city were reminiscent of the Babylonian intention to destroy Jerusalem, described in the great psalm of lament, Psalm 137:7: *Remember, O Lord, against the sons of Edom, the day of Jerusalem, Who said, "Raze it, raze it, to its very foundation!"*

3. From Lamentations 1:1.

41

DEATH MARCH TO MAUTHAUSEN

The weeks continued passing by in seemingly endless procession, according to the time dimension peculiar to Auschwitz, but they did finally bring in 1945. As the Polish winter advanced the days became shorter, and the leaves falling from the birch trees left them as bare, lonely sentinels. Snowflakes also descended, swathing the drab barracks and killing fields of the camp, but the white purity of that blanket could never completely disguise its sinister outlines. Within their closely guarded confines, the inmates waited with dogged hope, seemingly holding a collective breath. The sense that the war was drawing to an end was almost palpable.

As Germany's military might began collapsing, and the Allied armies were closing in on Polish concentration camps, the SS began frantically to evacuate many thousands of prisoners. Hitler had ordered that all camps should be destroyed before the liberators arrived, and the plan upon which the Nazis determined, even as the war was entering its final stages, beggars belief. All surviving prisoners were to be sent to other camps inside Germany – Flossenbürg, Gross-Rosen, Buchenwald, Dachau and Mauthausen – where they would once again be used as forced labor. It was not just that they needed the prisoners as an economic resource; the Nazis also wanted to prevent their stories being told. Some SS leaders even nursed the absurd hope that the Jewish prisoners could be used as hostages to bargain for a peace deal that would guarantee the survival of the Nazi regime.

The manner in which these weak and broken individuals were to be sent to the German camps also strains credulity: they were to make a large part of the journey, in the dead of winter, on foot. In the early part of 1945 altogether 59 different marches from Nazi concentration camps took place, some covering vast distances, with few provisions for food or shelter and little opportunity to rest. For the prisoners, the death marches, as they came to be known, proved an excruciating marathon that tested their endurance and will to live beyond even their other experiences in captivity – more than the selections, the starvation diet, the filthy huts and the backbreaking work. Many died on the way, from starvation, cold and exhaustion. Those who fell behind or who were too weak to continue were killed on the spot, and their bodies left on the side of the road. So, whether it was to hide their crimes or to continue their goal of annihilating European Jewry, the Nazi death marches only furthered the torment experienced by the Jews.

In Auschwitz itself, as the Red Army drew near in early 1945, the Germans began clearing the camp, and between January 17 and 21 sent 65,000 "fit" prisoners to begin the journey west through Upper and Lower Silesia. The main evacuation routes led to Wodzisław Śląski and Gliwice, where the different columns were merged into rail transports.

By January 19, when Sam's turn for evacuation arrived, the camp was nearly emptied of prisoners. He sensed immediately that there was an ordeal ahead which was new and horribly different. Many prisoners tried to hide from the SS roundups, but were found and executed. This did not prevent Sam and a small group of companions from making the attempt to conceal themselves in a cellar – but, as the noise of barking dogs and the shouts of guards drew close, they grew afraid and returned to their block. As they climbed out of the cellar Sam looked back longingly at a new pair of shoes that had been stashed there – but knew that if he took them he might be shot for stealing.

In the evening he and his fellow inmates were ordered outside. Despite the shattering noise of a Soviet bombardment nearby, the SS still insisted on a rollcall and headcount before dividing them into groups of a hundred each. It seemed to Sam an obsession that bordered on madness. A piece of bread and a can of food were thrust into the hand of each prisoner; this was to last them for a week. They were forced out through the gate with its grim sign, but it was not the freedom for which they had longed: it was freezing, snow lay hard on the ground, and the wind whistled through their meager rags. Sam and his closest acquaintances tried to walk together to support one another, but as they stumbled on their way the knots of prisoners kept changing in an unwieldy kaleidoscope. The first bodies began falling.

As they marched along, the local citizens stared incredulously, seeing the rag-and-bone figures with matchstick arms and legs protruding from their scanty garments drifting past them in endless rows. It was another Dante-esque vision from hell: humans who no longer appeared human. There were many Poles among those being evacuated, and some actually passed their own homes, but didn't dare try to make the dash to safety: the guards were all too ready to punish any infraction with instant death. Along the sides of the road lay the corpses of prisoners who had gone before and had incurred their wrath for offenses as minor as bending down to seize a handful of snow to quench their thirst.

The hallucinatory trek proceeded on its terrible way. The SS guards became more jittery with each hour that passed, and started to shoot all who could not keep up with the pace; blood began to stain the snow, blooming in bright red patches, terrible flowers marking the path of their journey. The prisoners were all pushing themselves to walk faster, and some put their hands on the shoulders of those in front to encourage them. Sam walked like an automaton. At one point he encountered a Trotskyist who was carrying on his back a bag filled with books, and asking the other prisoners if they would help him. Of course, they all refused. Despite Sam's stoic concentration on placing one foot in front of another, he was struck by so strange a concern at such a moment. The books must have proved to be fatal, because after a while the Russian wasn't seen any more.

And so they walked day and night without stopping, heading toward the Czech border – and always there were more and more falling. They were all sensing the nearness of death's cold breath. In the morning their column passed through a small town which boasted a football stadium.

"Rest," commanded a guard.

The prisoners dragged themselves to the snowed-in field and lay down. There was no bread or water given, and they put handfuls of snow in their mouths to quench their raging thirst. After an hour the march started again, and by evening the column reached a deserted farm where they would spend the night. In the cellar there were piles of beets, but they were rotten and covered with excrement. Some of the prisoners couldn't resist their hunger and ate them, which certainly would have signed their death warrants through typhus.

Sam left the cellar and found an abandoned chicken coop where others were already sleeping. He lay down, surrounded by chicken droppings, but the cold was piercing through his flesh, his feet were wet, and his shoes were torn. He took them off, but still couldn't sleep. At 5 o'clock in the morning the SS came in, shouting and wielding their sticks. Sam tried to put his shoes on but they were frozen, and one of the guards started to beat him. He tried to breathe on his shoes to make the ice melt a little, and with a superhuman effort managed to force his feet into them.

It was the third day, and the trek still continued. Sam's shoes didn't thaw and the journey became for him a terrifying ordeal; he was pushing himself forward in a desperate fight against death. They arrived at the Czech border as evening fell – for many it was their last night. Some tried to hide in a large farmhouse but were found by the SS and shot. The next day they were again forced onward, without food or water, and around 4 o'clock in the afternoon arrived in Wodzisław Sląski. From there, the surviving prisoners were to be transported by rail through Czechoslovakia to a camp in Austria.

Through the early evening gloom, Sam and his companions caught sight of a platform where open freight cars were waiting; the next stage of their journey was about to begin. The living mass of suffering humanity shuffled toward the wagons and began hauling themselves on board. Sam reached the wagon and tried to get on, but even as he grasped the wooden strut a sharp pain shot through his heart and made him gasp. With his last remaining strength he managed to raise his hands and those already in the wagon grasped hold of them; despite their own weakness they succeeded in hoisting him aboard. Light-headed and dizzy, with a roaring in his ears, he heard the train begin to move. Then someone spoke to him in French, and he recognized the voice.

"Camille?" he whispered. It was his old friend from Belgium, who had joined the Resistance after Sam had left for Spain.

But the pressure in Sam's chest was increasing; it felt as if his whole upper torso was being squeezed and set on fire: he was having a myocardial infarction. The pain moved and spread out toward his lower abdomen, and he was seized with diarrhea. He tried to find a place in a corner but it was impossible to move. With his head bowed he vomited and at the same time was relieving himself. The terrible bout of pain and weakness finally passed and he was left spent.

Eventually he looked about him and located Camille; the two men grasped each other's hands, thankful to have found each other. Camille, Sam learned, had been in Auschwitz for three years, and with him was another political prisoner whose name was Brichart, a pharmacist who was also from Belgium. Brichart had a small bottle of alcohol and gave Sam a sip; the fiery liquid ran down his throat and provided a little warmth to his system.

Riding in the open carriage with the prisoners there were some ten Polish *Kapos*. They began shouting: "All on one side!" and brandishing their clubs, pushing a hundred men into one half of the wagon and keeping the other half for themselves. The prisoners were crammed so tightly together they couldn't move, but the close-packed bodies provided Sam with some heat, and may even have saved his life. Half of the men died during the journey – some frozen to death. The floor of the wagon became littered with corpses.

They rode on the train all night long, and in the morning arrived at a small Czechoslovakian town where the train halted. Some of the Czech prisoners spoke to workers standing on the station platform, who looked with astonishment at the human skeletons in the open wagons. One after another began throwing their food packages onto the train, ignoring the apoplectic screams of the SS guards who threatened to shoot them. Even this humane gesture cost some lives because the inmates rushed to seize the packets and hit one another as they did so – yet still others were undoubtedly saved by the food. Sam, in his corner, felt a deep sense of gratitude. Weakened, emaciated men had hauled him onto the train ... strangers were giving up their food for the prisoners and risking their lives to do so.

That night, they rode through Vienna, and finally in the late afternoon arrived at their destination.

"Out!" shouted the SS guard.

Those still living clambered out of the wagon, leaving behind the comrades who had perished. Sam could barely stand on his feet, but knew he had to walk or be shot. The men gazed with trepidation upon the formidable façade of their new place of incarceration, with its gray granite walls and massive gatehouse.

Mauthausen!

Sam had heard about this camp in Auschwitz, which was known to surpass all others for brutality. It seemed to him as if hell had suddenly opened another circle, where an entirely new chamber of horrors awaited them. But, despite their long and grueling journey, he and the other men were not yet permitted to enter, and were forced to spend another night outside in the snow.

This was Sam's most horrific night. Restless and shivering, he dozed intermittently as the tormenting thoughts and images crowding at the edges of his mind demanded ingress, threatening to shatter the fragile union which held body and soul together. As the hours of darkness wore away, his agonizing vigil finally drew to its close, and he and the other prisoners who woke looked about them.

The morning light crept over the scene and fell with infinite gentleness upon the soft white shrouds of snow beneath which lay the worn and lifeless bodies of many of their comrades. They had endured that infamous odyssey, the six days of the death march, and had now been laid to rest in the dark earth of that inhospitable place, having finally departed the world which had so rejected and turned its back upon them.

42

THE BATTLE OF THE BULGE

The camp at which Sam had arrived was situated high on a hill amidst the magnificent scenery of Upper Austria and close to the famous Danube River. Created at the time of the Anschluss in 1938, Mauthausen had become one of the largest camp complexes in the Nazi empire, with subcamps at Gusen, Ebensee and Melk. Detained within its walls were those considered political enemies of the Reich, whose number included convicted criminals, Spanish Republicans, Soviet prisoners of war, and intellectuals who opposed the Nazi regime. And, of course, Jews, but at first they were only a small minority.

Mauthausen was not classed as a death camp; its main purpose was Vernichtung durch Arbeit: extermination through labor. The site had been chosen because of a nearby granite quarry, with an eye to provision of materials for the grandiose reconstruction of major German towns envisioned by Albert Speer and other Nazi architects. The rock quarry in Mauthausen was located at the base of 186 steps known as the "Stairs of Death," the Todessteige, up which prisoners were forced to carry roughly hewn blocks of stone often weighing more than 50 kilos – a task calculated to break both spirit and body.

The inmates could also be rented out to various national and local businesses as slave labor, ensuring that Mauthausen and its subcamps became one of the most profitable enterprises of Nazi Germany. The fact that prisoner mortality rates soared was of no concern to the German overlords, for no sooner had one group perished than their number was replenished by transports of new detainees. From 1943, however, the focus of the camp changed dramatically as the work switched from quarrying to armaments production.

Germany was in a technological race with the Allies, and the Messerschmitt aircraft was one of its breakthrough designs. Flying without propellers, these jets were faster than anything else in the sky and could be used to devastating effect against Allied bombers. The German scientists were also working on another "secret weapon": the V-rockets. The V2 was especially lethal: each was tall as a four-story building, carried a ton of explosives, and could blast its way to the edge of space before falling back like an avenging Valkyrie, wreaking havoc on target cities. German propaganda hailed it as a Wunderwaffe (wonder weapon) that might enable them to regain ascendancy in the war.

But German plans received a setback in August 1943, when Allied bombers launched punitive strikes on both the Messerschmitt aircraft factory in Bavaria and the base in Peenemünde near the Baltic Sea where the V-weapons were launched. This was the catalyst for the Nazi decision to move war production to underground facilities that would be impenetrable to Allied air raids. At the Mauthausen subcamp of Gusen, prisoners were forced to construct vast tunnels into the surrounding hills for the new factories. The largest of these, at a length of 20 kilometers, was the Bergkristall, intended for the production of fuselages for the Messerschmitts, and other war materials including the V2 rockets.

Secrecy was extremely high, but despite the feverish production lines Germany's strategic situation was disastrous. By June 1944, just after the D-Day landings, Allied armies were marching steadily across France, and from the skies British and American fighter planes were inflicting huge damage on German cities. This prompted Germany to release its Vergeltungswaffen (revenge weapons) and in the early hours of June 13 the first V1 rocket attack was carried out on London. It would eventually be followed by almost 10,000 further strikes, and soon the V2s were also *raining down terror from the skies. The onslaught brought about 18,000 mostly civilian deaths and caused immense suffering to the British, who believed that enemy air attacks had been vanquished by the Blitz. England was bloodied, but unbowed.*

The other main target of the V-rocket bombardment was Belgium, which had been liberated by the Allied troops in September 1944. The end of four years of German occupation brought a period of exuberant rejoicing to the nation – but because Antwerp now functioned as a port of entry for the Allies it became one of the main targets of the German "flying bombs." The first V1 fell on the city in October and was followed by another 7,000 over Belgium – the start of months of fear. The V-weapons became responsible for taking the lives of many thousands of civilians, and when on December 16 a V2 rocket hit a cinema in Antwerp, killing 567, it marked the most lethal total from a single rocket during the entire six years of combat.

This also happened to be the day that one of the last great battles of the war began.

By mid-December 1944, most Allied commanders believed it was "all quiet on the Western Front," and the conflict in Europe was nearing its close. But, with the onset of winter, the Germans were about to launch another Blitzkrieg-like assault aimed at turning the tide of war in their favor. Hitler's plan envisaged an ambitious repeat of the successful invasion of France in 1940. It required his troops to strike once again through the Ardennes, break through Allied lines, then press on to seize the vital port of Antwerp. It was a strategy against which the Führer's own generals advised, but Hitler, reasserting his control of military affairs, had his way. The offensive was code-named Wacht am Rhein (Watch on the Rhine) by the Germans, but the conflict that ensued became better known as the Battle of the Bulge.

Early on the misty morning of December 16, after thick fog and snow had grounded Allied airplanes, more than 200,000 German troops and nearly 1,000 tanks assembled secretly in the dense Ardennes forests, in a section that was only thinly defended by a few battle-worn American divisions. Caught by surprise, the US 101st Airborne Division fought determinedly, but by December 21 was encircled and pinned inside the small Belgian town of Bastogne at a vital road junction. The German troops went on to advance their spearheads toward the Meuse River, creating the bulge in the Allied line that gave the battle its name.

But this was not 1940. The defenders fought on bravely and continued to hold Bastogne through Christmas, and on December 26 General Patton's 3rd Army broke through the German lines and relieved the town. Running short on fuel for their gas-guzzling panzers, the Germans were forced to return to medieval-style warfare, using horses for transport in the thick Ardennes woods through which they had begun the assault. But the battle continued on for six hard weeks. Along with facing enemy gunfire, the American troops had to withstand the rigors of that frigid white world in which they found themselves, forced to endure blizzards and freezing rain, to wade through snowdrifts and chisel their tanks out of ice. But with their obstinate defense of vital crossroads they slowed the Nazi advance, and attacked the sides of the shrinking bulge until the line had been restored.

British Prime Minister Churchill called this "undoubtedly the greatest American battle of the war." It was certainly the costliest ever fought by the US army, which suffered over 100,000 casualties during that harrowing winter of 1944–45. But by January 25 the Battle of the Bulge had been won, and the stage set for the final Allied drive to victory.

Meanwhile, just two days later on the Eastern Front, soldiers of the Red Army entered Auschwitz. They found the camp smoldering; the SS guards had fled, but not before they had set fire to as much evidence as they could, burned the Kanada warehouse, and blown up the crematoria. The Russian soldiers found at least 600 corpses and some 7,000 prisoners who were still living, many so weak they could hardly realize that the deliverance for which they had waited so long had finally arrived.

In Austria, on the same day, Sam arrived at the gates of Mauthausen, but for him the war was not yet over.

43

MELK

Sam and the other survivors of the march were at last admitted through the high granite walls of Mauthausen. As they came into the camp grounds they were given a hot drink egregiously called coffee; it was disgusting but the men forced it down their parched throats. The *Kapos* stood about threateningly with their clubs and Sam groaned within himself; it was Auschwitz all over again. Some of the prisoners, miraculously, were still wearing gold wedding rings, and they gave them to the *Kapos* in exchange for a second glass of the terrible sludge.

Sam and his group were then herded down some narrow steps into the room of a cellar, where they stripped off their rags, showered, and dressed themselves in the long, striped shirts provided. Following that they were pushed into a tiny room where they were so crammed together they could hardly move. Sam's second period of quarantine had begun, and he was soon to discover that the conditions at Mauthausen were unspeakable. Tens of thousands of prisoners had been pouring into the camp since the concentration camps in the east had been evacuated, and adding to their number were the many Polish civilians deported by the Germans after the failure of the Warsaw Uprising. The facilities were catastrophically inadequate to cope with such an influx, leading to massive overcrowding, starvation and rampant disease.

The toilets in Mauthausen were located outside, and prisoners in Sam's quarantine quarters had first to ask permission from the stick-wielding *Stube-dienst* to go there. No one had shoes, which meant braving the slippery snow and sub-zero temperatures barefoot. If granted permission to go outside, it was also necessary to clamber over the bodies of the other prisoners. During the last days of the quarantine period a rotation was enforced: half of the prisoners were made to stand upright at night so the other half could sleep, and then they switched. Some didn't have the strength to remain standing and collapsed.

When the three-week period was over, the prisoners were taken to a large open courtyard, where Jews and non-Jews were immediately separated. It was common knowledge that living conditions were worse for the Jewish prisoners, and they were under the constant watch of Ukrainian guards. Sam and another inmate said they were Belgians and waited with a smaller group to be assigned their living quarters. As they stood in line he was astonished when a cigarette was handed to each of them. He didn't smoke but took the cigarette anyway; it was worth a fortune. But his subterfuge could not last; the *Stube-dienst* recognized him and hauled him out.

"Dirty Jew," he was told. "Get moving."

To add insult to injury, the guard stole Sam's cigarette. He was placed in a section reserved for Jews and assigned to the subcamp called Melk, located about 80 kilometers from Mauthausen. He and his group were immediately forced to begin marching to the new destination, their hearts quailing at the thought of another journey on foot. The SS invented a sadistic game to keep themselves amused on the way, making some of the prisoners advance so quickly that their feet became intertwined and they stumbled. When they thought the prisoners were not walking fast enough, the beatings began.

The nightmarish journey continued for several miles, and those who perished on the way were left where they fell. The remaining prisoners were piled into a wagon which stank of urine and vomit and gave them a presentiment of what Melk would be like. When they entered the camp, they were taken to their barracks; it was evening, their shirts were wet and their feet in a terrible state. They lay down to sleep on wooden planks, with each "bed" assigned to two inmates.

Melk had been established in March 1944, and the overwhelming number of inmates brought there came from Auschwitz. Prisoners within the camp were not equal: their national origin and the category assigned by the SS determined their life in camp – and also their chance of survival. At the top of the hierarchy stood the German and Austrian non-Jewish prisoners, and on the bottom rung were the Jews and gypsies of any nationality. The main purpose for the camp was to provide forced labor for the different tunneling projects in the surrounding hills. The prisoners worked three shifts around the clock, excavating caverns hundreds of meters in length, installing railroad tracks, electrical and water lines, and constructing barracks for equipment and machines.

On his first morning there, Sam and a group of other men were piled into open trucks; when they passed inhabited areas they were forced to lie flat so they could not be seen. They were taken to the underground factory belonging to the firm of Mayreder, Kraus & Co; it was here that Sam would work for the next several weeks. Civilians were in charge of the operations, but he soon found they were sometimes even worse than the SS. Most of the time he was set to work with a cement mixer, or else excavating tunnels further into the interior of the mountain. The terrain was composed of layers of fine sand and quartz, which he and the other prisoners had to remove with pneumatic drills, then shovel onto conveyor belts and lorries. Sam's body, now down to skin and bones, would shake with every vibration of the jackhammer, and there were other aspects of the working conditions which severely tested his strength.

As the prisoners labored in the depths of the earth, they were continually breathing in cement dust, which led to lung problems and asthmatic conditions. There was also a high-water table inside the tunnels, which meant the workers were often standing in water as they carried out their tasks. In order to protect themselves from the cold they placed the paper sacks in which cement was brought under their shirts or wrapped them around their feet, but this raw paper, when stuffed in the wooden clogs, would create sores. A vast number of prisoners were also buried alive through cave-ins, and Melk had its own crematorium.

Sam had to work well into the night, and this meant that when he finally returned to the camp the food (so-called) had almost disappeared. It consisted mainly of moldy crumbs of bread, which were thrown into the inmates' caps; in the morning nothing was given. For a time, Sam forced himself to keep a crumb, the size of a lump of sugar, which he would eat when he woke. He wrapped it in paper and put it in his pants, and while he slept he put the pants under his head. His comrades eyed him speculatively, and after a week his neighbor stole the bread as he lay dozing in a fitful slumber. Sam decided not to keep the morsel again.

The days passed in infernal procession. When the prisoners returned from the work site, damp or even totally wet, they would be unable to dry their clothes. The prison garments gave no warmth in the harsh conditions, hunger created terrible stomach cramps, and the nights seemed endless. The inmates suffered most severely in the housing units during the cold weather of late winter. They would organize firewood at the work sites and smuggle it into camp, always aware of the danger of being caught by SS guards at the camp's main gate.

The day came, however, when Sam was presented with a huge dilemma. One of the German supervisors told him to bring some wood from the factory back to the camp. Sam knew that this was forbidden, and that every little mistake might cost him his life. He believed that the supervisor wanted the wood for himself, to cook something, and was afraid that if he brought it back he would be accused of sabotage.

"Come on, you idiot," snarled the *Kapo*. "It's not for me. These are orders from the *Oberkapo*."

"No, I won't do it," Sam repeated stubbornly.

The *Kapo* had actually told the truth, and once they were back in the camp the guard almost beat Sam to death. He was an ex-convict and a real torturer and it took many days before the pain disappeared.

Sam had survived thus far in the Nazi concentration camp system, not just through his personality, courage and strength of will, but perhaps most of all through his innate wisdom in dealing with those wielding the authority. This time he had misread the situation – but once again his life had mysteriously been spared.

It was now March 1945, and his next camp challenge was about to begin. He was transferred from Melk to the camp of Gusen, to work on production of the Messerschmitt jet aircraft.

44

GUSEN

Sam stood with the other members of his work detail and gazed at the entrance to the Bergkristall tunnel, which had been carved deep into the hillside at Gusen. The mouth of the tunnel yawned menacingly: what new terrors, he wondered, awaited here? The men passed through the concrete portals and trod their way into the gloomy interior, illuminated by strips of electrical lighting, and soon were in the very bowels of the earth. It was a strange underground world where a vast and intricate web of tunnels stretched deep into the heart of the mountain. Sam was astonished at the huge extent of the network, but also angered; he knew the human cost which must have been exacted in its construction.

In these murky depths thousands of prisoners were laboring day and night to produce the parts for the Messerschmitt fighter jets. The project was top secret, and they were supervised by Messerschmitt engineers and technicians who themselves were forbidden to discuss their work with anyone on pain of death. As Sam arrived there in the spring of 1945 production was reaching its height, and the work was proceeding at a frenzied pace. Hundreds of fuselages were built each month, and trainloads of aircraft parts were sent from Bergkristall to the south of Germany, where they were assembled into the completed warplanes.

Sam – with only a smattering of skills – had been designated for work as an electrician on the production lines. There was one marvelous, unexpected bonus of this placement: he discovered his old companion Camille had been assigned to the same section. The friends embraced, but Camille was alarmed by Sam's skeletal frame.

"It will be better for you here," he said. "No jackhammers or cement mixers!"

Sam had actually been given the role of supervising Camille's work, and in other circumstances the two would have laughed about it. The consciousness of his friend's closeness was one bright spark in the unrelieved bleakness of his situation. As he labored there, Sam often felt that he had strayed into one of the darker tales from the Brothers Grimm – captive minions toiling in the gloomy interior of the mountains to provide materials of destruction for their wicked overlords.

The prisoners tried, by working very slowly whenever possible, to hinder the progress of production, and in that way do something to sabotage the German arms efforts. When they were watched they would show diligence at their work to avoid being punished, but when the *Kapos* or SS men had passed by the pace would let up again. Nevertheless, the Messerschmitt personnel were frantically rushing to transfer as many parts of the new aircraft as possible, and Sam and the other prisoners could sense even more strongly that the end of the war was near. The Allies bombed the camp on several occasions and the inmates secretly enjoyed the panic-stricken reaction of the SS guards. They also saw the first Austrian refugees trudging by close to the camp. As Sam caught sight of them, the remembrance of May 1940 flashed into his mind, and the exultant realization came to him that the refugees now belonged to the enemy.

One of the inmates, a Hungarian named Jozef, had succeeded in getting hold of a German newspaper, and proposed to some fellow workers that he would read it to them in return for a crust of bread. Although the men suffered greatly from hunger they were so desperate for information that they agreed. They knew, however, that they would have to keep this activity secret from the guards, and decided they would hide in an aircraft frame in one of the side tunnels. The men gathered and clambered into the long narrow fuselage of the plane; Sam stood guard outside it, and others had an observation point at the tunnel entrance.

The men inside the fuselage were listening avidly to the news when Sam was overcome by a momentary bout of weakness, and swayed, closing his eyes. When he opened them again, with a downward glance, he saw a pair of boots; lifting his eyes slowly, he met the steely gaze of an SS guard. The men inside the plane were hauled out, and the incriminating newspaper was found in a corner. Someone had betrayed them.

Sam decided at this point that the better part of discretion would be to hide in the latrines; he stayed there for a long time but eventually emerged and went to his comrades. They had all received 25 strokes with a wooden club – and soon it was his turn.

"Dog, come here," shouted one of the guards. Sam was dragged into another room, swearing to himself that he wouldn't scream. The first strokes of the club descended; the pain was terrible. The guards were counting the blows ... *one... two ... three*....

Suddenly, the SS men started to laugh. Sam twisted his head around, but couldn't at first see anything that would explain their hilarity ... then he realized what it was. The previous day he had found a tube of dried-up toothpaste which he had put in the pocket of his pants, and the guards were so amused by this pathetic discovery that, although they continued to hit him, they did so with diminished zeal. Nevertheless, it took several weeks before Sam was able to lie on his back, and a long time before the pain was gone.

At midday, Sam and his group had half an hour of rest. Sometimes he and some of the other inmates took a walk along the barbed wire fences which surrounded their camp; it was the only quiet place they could find. Winter was withdrawing, and a weak sun poured some of its life-giving warmth into their worn bodies. Invariably their conversation would turn to one of their main obsessions, food. They would talk about what they would eat when they would be free, and some of the delectable dishes they remembered from their home countries. One day as they walked they saw a bone lying on the ground; it had been gnawed, but some scraps of flesh were still clinging to it. The prisoners stopped and stared at it, experiencing a thrill of hunger and longing. They had to make an effort not to pick it up, and a sense of shame gripped them all. But those who had lost their feeling of shame had only few chances of survival.

On another occasion as they gathered for their lunch break, Jozef from Hungary began sharpening his spoon with one of the production tools. He was trying to turn his spoon into a knife.

"Why do you need that, Jozef?" asked another inmate, laughing. "There is nothing to cut here ... not even bread. We get only crumbs."

The Hungarian didn't answer but continued scraping away at the spoon. As he did so, a *Kapo* came upon their group, caught sight of what Jozef was doing, and started to hit him. The Hungarian lifted the hand which was holding the sharpened spoon to try and protect himself.

"Aha," shouted the *Kapo*. "You tried to attack me!"

His indignation was a ruse. He was reacting that way because he had seen a gold tooth in the Hungarian's mouth.

The *Kapo* began to hit the prisoner harder and harder, as the Hungarian refused to die. Eventually, however, he keeled to the floor, and was dragged by the guard to the room where Sam had been beaten. The door remained open, and Sam saw with horror how the *Kapo* pushed Jozef's head into a large soup tureen. The pot was filled with water, and the death struggles of the Hungarian, at first frantic, gradually subsided. The *Kapo* lifted the Hungarian's head out of the water and pulled the gleaming prize out of his mouth.

Even worse for Sam was that he and another inmate were assigned to bring the body back to the crematorium. The cart was too small to fit Jozef's corpse completely – he had been a red-haired giant of a man in his forties – and part of his body dragged on the ground as they went. When the SS men caught sight of this sad procession they started to laugh, and this laughter was so shocking to Sam that he would remember its sound for the rest of his life.

45

UNCOVERING THE CRIMES

"We're going to hang out the washing on the Siegfried Line..." That was the popular song that boosted the morale of the British troops as they marched across France toward Germany in late 1944.

The Siegfried Line was a chain of fortifications which ran along Germany's western border, corresponding to the French Maginot Line, and German propaganda hailed it as impregnable. After Paris was liberated on August 25, the breaching of this formidable barrier would require some of the most grueling fighting of the war. The Allied soldiers endured a bitter winter and encountered ferocious enemy resistance as they fought agonizing battles at Huertgen Forest, Aachen and Alsace. Their valor and stamina brought eventual victory, and by early spring of 1945, after the Battle of the Bulge, the line was broken along its full length and the way into Nazi Germany lay open.

Even as Hitler was fuming over the failure of his Ardennes offensive, his generals were bringing him disastrous news concerning the Eastern Front, where over two million Red Army troops were massing. When warned that the East was "like a house of cards" the Führer refused to believe it, exclaiming: "It's the biggest imposture since Genghis Khan!" Had he agreed to halt the Ardennes operation while it was losing impetus, troops could have been transferred to the region – but this he refused to do.

The Soviet offensive began on January 12 as Red Army tanks surged across the Vistula and forward over the frozen terrain into southern Poland. As predicted, the front collapsed swiftly. On January 17 Warsaw was captured and on January 31 the first Red Army soldiers crossed the Oder River to form a bridgehead less than 100 kilometers from Berlin. Some Wehrmacht divisions were surrounded; others retreated westward as fast as they could go. Millions of German civilians were fleeing for their lives.

An Allied victory seemed imminent, and in February Churchill, Roosevelt and Stalin gathered at Yalta in Crimea to discuss boundary lines for postwar occupation of Germany and the rebuilding of the shattered European nations. The German capital, Berlin, was located deep within the Soviet zone, but it was agreed that the Allied powers would share control of the city. Much of the discussion turned on the Polish situation as the Western leaders, abandoning their support of the Polish government in London, agreed that the Lublin Committee – sanctioned by the Soviet masters of the country – should form the nucleus of a provisional government. Conflicting visions of Europe's future held by the "Big Three" were becoming evident.

Even as the conference was winding down, some of the largest aerial campaigns of the war began. By now, the Luftwaffe was hampered by a shortage of pilots and fuel as well as a compromised radar system; the Allies were ruling the skies over Europe and dropping thousands of bombs on enemy territory. In mid-February the east German city of Dresden, a major transportation and industrial hub, became the target of a massive Allied air attack. It was one of the most devastating operations of the war and the resulting firestorm almost levelled the city, killing thousands and obliterating many of the cultural landmarks for which it was famous.

In Western Europe, Allied soldiers continued their push into Germany and by March 7 reached the River Rhine, which they crossed at four points, advancing into the heartland of Germany. As the Allies raced toward Berlin, an evil of unfathomable proportions was about to be laid bare, and the shock would pierce through the military preoccupations of the soldiers and reverberate around the world.

On April 4, the US Third Army was passing through the small town of Ohrdruf, near Weimar, where Bach had reputedly composed some of his works. They came across a high barbed wire fence in the midst of a grove of pines; a wooden sign hanging upon the gate read "Arbeit Macht Frei." The soldiers had stumbled upon a concentration camp, part of the Buchenwald system, from which the Nazis had fled after hastily trying to conceal evidence of genocide.

The troops entered the gate, which led to a large square surrounded by wooden barracks. In the center of the compound lay the bodies of dozens of dead prisoners clad in striped clothing; they had been machine gunned the day before because they were too weak to march to another camp. Inside a small shed adjacent to the square the soldiers discovered further piles of bodies, naked and emaciated, stacked upon one another and sprinkled with lime, and other corpses which had been partially incinerated on pyres. A few ghostly inmates, disoriented, were still drifting about this living hell. The American soldiers by this stage were battle-hardened warriors who had witnessed the most terrible sights of war, but they turned pale and became physically ill as they encountered the sights of the camp.

A few days later, General Eisenhower inspected the liberated camp together with General Patton, and was unable to disguise his shock. He ordered that careful documentation of the atrocities perpetrated there should be made, and urged Washington and London to send newspaper editors and members of Congress to visit the camps to see them firsthand. The evidence of what had taken place, he insisted, should be placed before the American and British public "in a fashion to leave no room for cynical doubt." In addition, he required American soldiers to tour the camps as a powerful reassurance of the justice of the cause for which they were laying down their lives.

When Eisenhower left, Patton brought the mayor of Ohrdruf and his wife to the camp to witness what had taken place there, and ordered that they, together with all other able-bodied townsfolk, should dig individual graves for the dead prisoners. The citizens completed most of the burials and undertook to return the next day. That night, the mayor and his wife hanged themselves in their home: the grim retribution had begun. American troops would move on to discover and liberate multiple camps, including Dora-Mittelbau, Dachau and Mauthausen. One of the prisoners set free from Buchenwald was Elie Wiesel, who went on to become one of the most eloquent witnesses to what had taken place during the Holocaust.[1] However, the Allies were too late to prevent the hanging of Dietrich Bonhoeffer[2] in Flossenbürg on April 9, just a few weeks before they arrived. He was the German Lutheran pastor who had so bravely spoken out against the Nazis.

In late January 1945, the Soviet liberation of Auschwitz had made headlines, but these reports didn't seem to prepare the soldiers for what they would find in the camps. They may have expected prisoner-of-war facilities that adhered to the fair treatment laws outlined in the Geneva Conventions, signed by Germany in 1929. When the Allied troops entered the concentration camps, they instead discovered thousands of Jewish and non-Jewish survivors living in the most horrific conditions, suffering from starvation and disease, along with piles of corpses, bones and human ashes – testimony of Nazi mass murder. Confronted with walking skeletons and cadavers piled in bins, many service members were stunned, and tears would spring involuntarily to their eyes.

As more and more camps were uncovered by Allied forces, it became evident to the world that the Third Reich had committed crimes against humanity unprecedented in nature and scope. Some of the Allied actions during the Second World War, such as the bombing of Dresden, are subject to ongoing debate by historians and military analysts, but arguments mounted to compare the Allied bombing of German cities with the Nazi annihilation of the Jews are ludicrously inadequate. There is simply no possibility of moral equivalence.[3] The central truth governing the whole conflict which took place in those catastrophic years is stated most succinctly in the words of the prophet Hosea: the Germans had "sowed the wind and were reaping the whirlwind." It was "the great law of divine retribution,"[4] in the sense that wicked and godless deeds carry within themselves the seeds of their own destruction.

By way of contrast, it was during those tumultuous months in 1945 that the nation of Sweden mounted an astonishing humanitarian endeavor. It sent a number of Red Cross buses, painted white, into Nazi Germany to rescue prisoners from concentration camps and bring them to Sweden. Negotiations for the mission had taken place between Count Folke Bernadotte – a member of the Swedish royal family and vice-president of the Swedish Red Cross – and Himmler, who was operating behind Hitler's back to improve his prospects following the inevitable Nazi defeat. During the "White Buses" expedition, as many as 21,000 prisoners of all nationalities were liberated from the camps and transported to Sweden for medical treatment and recuperation.

On April 12, the news came crackling over the radio that President Roosevelt had suddenly died of a cerebral hemorrhage. FDR's death was mourned by the Allies, but in Berlin Hitler seized upon the news, believing that the event somehow signaled a change in his fortunes. Yet the vast machine of war rolled on. The US armies reached the Elbe River, 100 kilometers from Berlin, while the Red Army, camped on the Oder, had more than a million troops in position to attack. Berlin was caught in an enormous vise, and residents of the city commented sardonically that the optimists among them were learning English, the pessimists Russian.

However, over the objections of Montgomery and Churchill, Eisenhower decided that his troops would not push forward to the capital. The General understood his mandate to be destroying the German armed forces and ending the war in Europe as soon as possible, and although Berlin possessed symbolic value it had little military importance. Eisenhower had no mind to sacrifice the lives of thousands of his soldiers for territory that would be handed to the Soviets at the end of the conflict. On the other hand, the Russian dictator was bent upon the taking of Berlin, both for reasons of prestige, and because he hoped to capture German nuclear secrets.

Cloistered in his lair deep underneath the gardens of the Reich Chancellery, Hitler continued to entertain fantasies of a miraculous last-minute victory over the Allies. For the maniacally determined Führer and his followers, unconditional surrender was not an option, and when Nazi soldiers by the thousands began to discard their uniforms and weapons the SS hunted them down as deserters and hanged them. And so the Nazis prepared for a tenacious last stand in the streets and squares of their beleaguered capital.

The Battle of Berlin was the final large-scale military operation to take place in Europe during the war, and one of the largest battles in human history. It began on April 16 when Stalin unleashed the raw power of four armies against the capital, together with an overwhelming number of tanks and aircraft. The depleted German forces put up a stiff defense, but by April 24 the Soviet army surrounded the city. They began making their way through intense street fighting toward the centrally located Chancellery, and on April 30 seized their ultimate prize, the Reichstag. On the same day, isolated and reduced to despair, Hitler committed suicide together with his mistress, Eva Braun, whom he had just married. Nazi soldiers gave their Führer a final straight-armed salute as they burned his body on a pyre in the Chancellery garden.

Early the next morning, May 1, the Soviet soldiers raised their "Banner of Victory" over the Reichstag, and six days later Germany surrendered. The Third Reich had come to its ignominious and blood-soaked ending.

---

1. Elie Wiesel was born in Romania, in the Carpathian mountains, in 1928, to an Orthodox Jewish family. When the Hungarian authorities began to deport the Jewish community to the death camps in 1944, he and his family were sent to Auschwitz, where his mother and younger sister were murdered. Wiesel and his father were selected to perform labor so long as they remained able-bodied, and eventually were sent on to Buchenwald, where his father also died. After the war, in 1958, he published his first and most famous book, *Night*, a memoir of his experiences in the camps. He went on to pen numerous other works which established him as one of the most eloquent witnesses on behalf of those who perished in the Holocaust, even as he maintained the victory of the human spirit over cruelty and evil, and advocated on behalf of groups suffering persecution because of their religion or race. In 1986 he was awarded the Nobel Peace Prize for his efforts to defend human rights, and remarked in his acceptance speech that: *"Action is the only remedy to indifference: the most insidious danger of all."*

2. Dietrich Bonhoeffer was born in Breslau, Germany in 1906, to a wealthy and influential family, and studied to become a Lutheran pastor and theologian. During the 1930s, as Hitler rose to power, he helped organize the Confessing Church, a movement which opposed the Nazification of the German evangelical church through religious action and moral persuasion. Bonhoeffer's continued objections to Nazi policies, including persecution of the Jews, resulted in his losing his freedom to lecture or publish. He soon joined the German Resistance movement and took part in a plot to overthrow Hitler. In April 1943, after these activities were discovered, Bonhoeffer was arrested by the Gestapo and

imprisoned at Tegel prison, where he pastored fellow prisoners, and reflected on theological issues such as conformity to Christ through personal suffering. Eventually he was transferred to the extermination camp at Flossenbürg. On April 9, 1945, one month before Germany surrendered, he was hanged. The last words of this brilliant and courageous Christian were: "This is the end – for me, the beginning of life." His books, especially *The Cost of Discipleship*, have remained devotional classics in the Christian world.

3. See the lucid discussion in Rees, L. (2005) *Auschwitz: A New History*, pp 292–293. Rees concludes that "any comparison between the pragmatic Allied planners and dedicated Jew-haters like Hitler, Heydrich, or Eichmann, is ludicrous," and that no "legitimate comparison is possible between the Allied bombing of Germany and the extermination of more than a million people at Auschwitz ... the two actions are conceptually different."

4. The phrase is taken from the Old Testament commentary of 18th-century English scholar Charles Ellicott, and is his succinct evaluation of the message of Hosea 8:7.

46

GUNSKIRCHEN

"All Jews – out!" bawled the *Blockältester* in the Gusen camp.

The prisoners formed shaky lines as he prowled up and down between them.

"You are going to be transferred," he announced.

It was the middle of April 1945. The Third Reich was clamped in a deadly embrace with the Allies racing from the west and the Soviet Union charging from the east. During that spring the prisoners of the Mauthausen subcamps wavered alternately between the hope of being soon liberated and fear they would not live to see that day. All the inmates had heard the rumors circulating in the camp that the SS intended to kill the prisoners at the last minute so as not to leave any witnesses of their atrocities. Himmler had, in fact, given orders that the 40,000 prisoners of Gusen should be murdered en masse by trapping them in the tunnels of the underground factories and blowing up the entrances.

But when the *Blockältester* made his announcement to the Jewish inmates they were excited – they had heard about the Swedish White Buses and thought they were about to be rescued. Sam and Camille said goodbye, gripping each other's hands. Few words were exchanged, but Sam's heart was filled with gratitude for the comfort and encouragement his friend had brought. Camille, skeptical of the idea of repatriation to Sweden, thought he would never see Sam again.

The Jewish prisoners had indeed miscalled the situation and it was to be another cruel April for them. The SS were evacuating the camp, and these weakened creatures, some of whom were now hardly recognizable as human beings, were being sent on another march. As the column set out, Sam and his group soon realized that the SS men guarding them were nervous wrecks, and pushing the prisoners with ferocious haste in the direction of the American military positions. The Nazis knew that if they fell into the hands of the Soviets they could expect no mercy for the rape of the Russian homeland by the Germans.

The group reached the Danube and boarded a ferry that took them to the city of Linz, where they disembarked, then continued their trek in a southwesterly direction. As they walked Sam saw a poster announcing that President Roosevelt had died. A horse-drawn cart passed them; inside were youngsters in SS uniform who looked at these walking cadavers in shocked disbelief. Sam pitied them – they were too young to see such horrors. That night they stopped at a farm in Wels where they were given coffee, and the next day the march resumed. Many of the inmates were too weak and sick to keep going, but whoever despaired and fell by the side of the road was lost, for the guards immediately shot them. The sound of gunfire was constant.

After three days, Sam and his group arrived at a subcamp of Mauthausen named Gunskirchen; it was located in a dense patch of pine trees near Salzburg, well-hidden from the main highway. They were led through dark woods where a heavy, dank atmosphere prevailed, directed through the camp gates, and forced into a small hangar which was already crammed with inmates. Immediately it was evident that conditions at the camp were catastrophic. Thousands of prisoners evacuated on death marches from Mauthausen had flooded in, and the German guards had permitted the camp to fall into a state of extreme degradation. The overcrowding meant that diseases such as typhus and dysentery spread rapidly through the weakened population, and bodies were hanging from wooden beams. The stench was nauseating; it hung over the camp like a miasma.

Those who thought they had already seen all the horrors were wrong. Sam said to himself, "My God, what I've seen before looks like child's play compared to this."

That night, he managed to slip outside the hangar, where the SS men were shouting ineffectively at the inmates, and the smell of bodies was insupportable. In the surrounding barracks he noticed women clasping their children, many of whom were in a pitiable state. It was cold, but he piled some branches on himself and dozed fitfully. Dawn came and he looked around. The mud surrounding the hangars was filled with bodies, the pain-racked, skeletal figures jumbled together in death's grotesque postures. Inmates were busy taking clothes from the dead, and Sam noticed that one inmate had a tiny razor. He cut through the shirt of one of the corpses, sliced off some of the flesh and placed it in his mouth. Sam shuddered.

In the evening another group arrived from Auschwitz. "We had to eat human flesh in order to survive. We had no choice," one whispered to Sam. Once again he felt a sense of horror and moved away. The inmates of Gunskirchen were a select group of prisoners – many of them were Hungarian Jews, who for the most part were professional people, with doctors, lawyers and academics among their number. Yet the treatment meted out to these cultured and distinguished people by the Germans – the deliberate prolonged starvation, the indiscriminate murder, the appalling living conditions – gradually brought about a change in even the strongest and reduced them to a state of terrible debasement.

For two days no food whatsoever was provided and a state of

complete anarchy began to descend on the camp. The artillery fire became louder as the battlefront approached and rumors were flying about. It was said that in the nearby forest a plane was hidden in the underbrush, held ready for takeoff, so the SS could escape. Others said the SS had already left the camp. The prisoners gathered in excited knots to discuss what they were hearing; the guards seemed conspicuously absent.

Sam had struck up a friendship with a Frenchman named Volvo, and the two men decided to see if the rumors were true. They made their way toward the entrance of the camp and saw that there was no sentry, and the gate was open. They kept walking toward it, then stopped in amazement. Were they dreaming ... or was this an American jeep they saw making its way into the camp? They stood still in wonder, and then all about them heard a great sound rising, which came from many throats, and soon began swelling until it reached a crescendo ... it was an incredible, unforgettable roar, a clamor of jubilation and ecstasy – the shout of liberty!

The date was May 5, 1945, and Gunskirchen was just about to be liberated by the US 71st Infantry Division, including African-American troops of the 761st Tank Battalion. The SS guards had already fled from the corpse-littered camp and 15,000 prisoners remained. Over the next two days all the remaining subcamps of Mauthausen were freed by American forces, who found the bodies of hundreds of prisoners. Thousands more were so frail that they died in the weeks and months following liberation, despite the medical care provided by the US army medical units. Over 3,000 were buried in cemeteries next to the former camps.

At midnight on May 8, 1945, the war in Europe was officially over. The unconditional surrender of the German forces in Northwestern Europe was signed at Eisenhower's headquarters at Reims in the presence of Soviet, American, British and French delegations. There was unrestrained joy in the streets of Europe as the six years of warfare that had left millions dead and much of the continent in ruins finally ended.

On VE Day, SHAEF's Displaced Persons Executive sent an order to all military units stating that the care of displaced persons was a principal Allied objective. But the journey was not yet over for the concentration camp survivors – nor for Sam.

Once again, he and they would be traversing a new territory of the human spirit.

47

FREEDOM

On that bright May morning when the Americans rolled into Gunskirchen, Sam and his friend Volvo stood at a distance and watched the camp inmates crowding around the jeep. The shouting continued: just the sight of the Americans brought cheers and shrieks from frail chests and lungs that somehow got a new lease of life. The milling crowd pressed forward to touch the Americans, to jump on the jeep, to kiss the hands of their embarrassed saviors – perhaps just to make sure that it was truly happening – and revealing through those suffering eyes the gratitude they were feeling.

The American soldiers were alarmed, petrified even, by the hallucinatory scene they were witnessing. They would have loved to disengage themselves from these human skeletons – so filthy and ravaged were they – but, with a combined mix of pity and horror, none dared push them away. Some of the inmates were even at that moment at the point of expiring, but there was a spark of joy in their eyes as they lay in the ditches and whispered a prayer of thanks with their last breath.

One of the inmates who seemed to have a measure of authority asked the Americans if he could climb on the jeep and speak to the crowd.

They helped him up on the hood and he shouted for order, then spoke in Hungarian as another translated his words into English. He asked the inmates to remain in the camp, to help "the Yanks" by staying off the roads, and assured them that the Americans were bringing food, water and medical help. After every sentence he was interrupted by loud cheers from the crowd; it was almost like a political rally. Everyone was hysterical with happiness at being found by the Americans, yet in a frenzy of hunger, for they had had no food since the Germans left two days earlier. As the jeep moved slowly on it resembled a triumphal procession, with the surging crowd cheering and waving their arms in exultation.

Sam and Volvo, watching from the gate, decided they wouldn't return to the camp. They began heading into the town of Wels, and as they walked along the narrow road were accompanied by a multitude of dazed men, women and children who were also fleeing - for the irresistible impulse after the Americans arrived was to escape and leave that place forever behind them. It was a spectacle of utmost pity. Few could walk upright, some were on carts, others shuffled along leaning on sticks, makeshift crutches and on each other. Their garments were the stuff of comic-horror: ragged wrappings or tattered uniforms that had not been changed or washed for months or years. And so the tragic river of suffering humanity flowed on into the city.

As they reached the cobblestone avenues at the outskirts of Wels, Sam and Volvo came across a food storage depot; the door was sealed but it was possible to get in through the window. A frenzied battle was taking place both inside, where the starving prisoners were crushing one another in their haste to seize something edible, and outside as well, where others were stealing rations from those who managed to exit safely.

Sam was agile; he slid through the window and was able to grab an entire loaf of bread. As he re-emerged, something about his demeanor prevented others from trying to snatch it. One of the

Hungarian Jews had a knife, and Sam traded a piece of bread for it. He cut through the thick crust, and he and Volvo began to devour their first meal in liberty. It gave them strength to continue walking, and to search for an empty house they might use as a temporary shelter. They passed a farm where others had already taken refuge, but these erstwhile prisoners had managed to lay their hands on some weapons and were guarding their hideout with vigilance. Sam and Volvo walked on.

Soon they were treading through a more densely populated area of the city, where prosperous looking villas and houses lined the streets. The two men found themselves entering a city square, and saw it was packed with American soldiers. They were intending to move on but a sergeant stopped them; he had recognized immediately that they were coming from the camps.

"Are you Jewish?" he asked them.

"Yes," they responded.

The soldier called over a sergeant named Max Miller, who spoke some Yiddish mixed with English.

"We're looking for a place to stay," said Sam.

"Come," said Max.

With a hand on the gun at his belt he led them to a villa located across the road; it was occupied by a woman who was living alone.

"Give them a place to stay," the sergeant said, gesturing to Sam and his friends. It was an order.

The woman let them in grudgingly. She was middle-aged and overweight; her appearance formed a strange contrast to Sam and Volvo who were just skin and bones. She looked at them with disgust.

"What do you need?" Miller asked the men.

"A bath," Sam replied unhesitatingly.

The woman said swiftly, "The gas doesn't work."

Her protests were given short shrift by the American. She was ordered to boil water and pour it into a basin in the basement.

It was Sam's first bath in many months. While he and Volvo were reveling in the hot water and soapsuds a group of American soldiers came down to the basement. The troops stared disbelievingly at their fleshless bodies ... at their gaunt faces, with their sharply protruding cheekbones ... at the deep-set eyes where the horrors they had endured were still reflected.

When Sam and Volvo walked back up the stairs, as clean as soap and water could make them but still wearing their filthy rags, they learned that the house had just been requisitioned by the US army. The woman was protesting.

"I already have two from the concentration camp," she said. "If you are going to move in here, then take these two out of my house."

"No," said the soldier, laconically. "You're the one who's leaving – they're staying."

The woman had no choice but to depart.

The American soldiers who settled into the villa were of Italian background, and that evening they prepared a feast, with mounds of pasta, trays of meat in tomato sauce and grilled chicken. Sam and Volvo looked at the food but couldn't bear the thought of eating; the bread still lay heavily on their stomachs. The soldiers dined heartily and drank a toast to Sam and Volvo's health. They prepared beds with fresh linen for them, but the men couldn't sleep; finally they lay down on the floor and drifted into an uneasy slumber. Next morning, they found themselves joined by more survivors, both men and women, for whom Miller began to organize clothes. Sam was provided with a shirt and a coat made of rough linen which floated around his skinny body. He weighed only 35 kilos.

Sam wanted to return to Belgium, Volvo to France; both were hoping to find survivors from their families. Sam was especially longing to know if Hennie might still be alive. And his parents ... his brothers ... his sister – what of them? But in the chaos of the aftermath of war it was hard to find transportation. The two men decided to travel westwards, toward Salzburg, on foot. Once again they set out and as they walked met two Yugoslavian workers, accompanied by a young Austrian woman named Greta, who were also making their way home. They continued on together.

The sides of the road were littered with cars which had been abandoned, and the men examined the vehicles as they passed. After a while they found one which seemed not so badly wrecked; it even had the key still in the ignition. When they turned it, the engine sputtered into life ... but the fuel gauge read empty. Fuel was more valuable – and unattainable - than gold at that point.

"What are we going to do now?" asked one of the Yugoslavians in discouraged tones.

The young woman, Greta, spoke up. "Don't worry about the fuel," she said. "Leave it to me."

There were American troops everywhere and Greta spoke a little English. She struck up an acquaintance with a black soldier, followed him as he led her away, and later returned with a gallon of fuel – she had paid with her body. The four men and Greta clambered into the car; it could barely trundle along, and their hazardous journey continued for only a few miles before they encountered an American patrol.

"Stop!" came the command. The car creaked to a halt. One of the officers sauntered over and looked at the motley group in the battered vehicle. "Show us your driving licenses, please."

The men looked at one another in dismay. None of them had any papers.

The Americans conferred with one another, then the officer made an announcement. "You won't get very far without any documents," he said. "We will take you to a nearby camp and from there you will be repatriated."

Sam was aghast, although the Americans assured them they would be there as free individuals.

Oh my God, he thought, in utter despair, *another camp.*

48

CRISIS POINT

As the war ended, the Allies redrew the boundaries of Germany and divided the country into four zones of occupation: British, American, French and Soviet. However, the administrative problems faced by the various military governments were exacerbated by the presence of millions who had been uprooted from their homes by the fortunes of war; their number included former POWs and released slave laborers, as well as Holocaust survivors. Camps were swiftly set up for these displaced people, often on the site of former concentration camps or military barracks, with the immediate purpose of providing shelter, nutrition and basic health care. Nearly all those interned had serious health conditions as well as psychological difficulties as a result of their experiences.

The interim military governments made every effort to assist these traumatized people, but naturally were not prepared or equipped to understand the special challenges that liberation posed for them. Nor could they be expected to fathom the unique suffering the Jewish survivors had undergone, which meant they required special types of assistance. Initially in the camps all displaced persons were grouped together, which meant that former concentration camp inmates found themselves in the same facility as their Nazi tormentors or those who had been collaborators. The Jewish refugees also lacked the freedom to choose their own destiny. From the army's standpoint, the logical solution to the problems of all the displaced persons was to repatriate them, irrespective of conditions in their countries of origin. For Sam, of course, this would mean being sent to Poland.

Sam and his group were taken to a camp located close to Salzburg in the American zone of occupation. When they arrived, he discovered that the camp was separated into two sections and that a great reversal had taken place: the displaced persons were free, and the SS soldiers were now the prisoners languishing behind the barbed wire. All the struggles and sacrifice on the part of so many over the past years had borne fruit: the captors were now captive and awaited their trial and verdict with due process of law, an intimation of the great truth that "the moral arc of the universe is long, but bends toward justice."[1]

But the camp contained a seething mass of dislocated humanity, and Sam soon discovered that the Nazis were not the only undesirables there. On his journey to freedom, he had acquired some chocolate and packs of cigarettes. He didn't smoke and wasn't able to eat the chocolate, but these were highly coveted items among the camp internees. One of the inmates, a Ukrainian who spoke a little English and German and had a "privileged" position before the liberation, noticed the treasures.

"Give me," he ordered Sam in broken English.

"If you dare to steal from us you'll be behind the barbed wire," said Sam, and Volvo added another threat. Their words achieved the desired impact and the Ukrainian no longer bothered them.

There was another inmate, a Belgian, who declared that he had been in the camps. "I was a *Vorarbeiter*," he said. But he looked so hale and hearty and was so well dressed that nobody believed him. He was also in possession of a gun and when he was drunk would point it randomly at the other inmates. Everybody complained to the administration and his weapon was confiscated.

Most inmates who had been admitted to the camps set up by the Americans were undernourished and seriously ill, and many died only a few days or weeks after achieving freedom. Volvo got typhus and was taken to a US army field hospital. Sam had been sleeping near to him; he didn't contract the illness but was so weak from weight loss and physical strain that after a while he wasn't able to swallow food or stand up. He was left completely alone and felt abandoned, as if he were a flea-bitten mongrel.

Tossing feverishly in his bed, he began to feel that his forces were diminishing and that death was approaching. While he lay there in this critical state, some Ukrainians came in and pilfered his meager possessions, but he didn't have the strength to defend himself; he shouted, but nobody came. Apart from the thieves, not a soul came to his bedside, and he began to experience a sense of utter dereliction.

Oh God, he thought to himself, *am I to die now that I'm free?* He drew a ragged breath. *No*, he addressed himself again, fiercely, *this can't happen!* And the combat with his mortal weakness began.

The life and death contest into which Sam now entered was different from any which he had undergone previously. He had been reduced to a bundle of living nerves covered by skin, a network of sensory cells stretched to an unbearable pitch and thrilling to every psychic vibration. In the extreme reduction of his humanity, as every vital organ was almost extinguished, the memories began to rise and subside in his mind as if they were living chords playing an unfinished symphony. They marched in solemn procession across the banks and shoals of his awareness, as across a formless sea where gray waves were heaving and tossing, alternately precious and horrifying. He was accessing a secret, hidden realm in which the memories had their own separate existence, from where they came to visit him one by one. "Do you remember us?" they seemed to be asking.

There were the images of his early years in Zawiercie, the woods and fields of Poland, and the *szumi* moving among the trees as he embraced them and drew in their scent. There was the meeting in

Krakow with the "prophet" beside the shining Vistula – *"You will become great"* – and after that the recollections came thick and fast. His mind flew on to the river crossing into Russia, the cells and the solitary confinement, interrogation and torture, and his return with his father on the train. Then the danger-filled journey through Germany as war was looming, and that first day in Antwerp, with the vista of the Scheldt and the exquisite paintings in the cathedral. The studies at the Academy, and the eruption of war. Dunkirk, with the black smoke rising above it, and the troops on the vast beaches, Gurs in the Pyrenees and his escape.

And then, his marriage to his sweet Hennie, joy followed so swiftly by the long years of hiding, the discovery by the Gestapo, the train to Auschwitz and the separation at the ramp, watching as his wife was torn away from him. All the hard months of labor, sorrow and loneliness, the death march to Mauthausen, the Bergkristall tunnels and the weapons of destruction ... Gunskirchen and the arrival of the Americans.

Sam knew in some region of his consciousness that all the terrible depths into which he had plunged, all the deathly experiences into which he had been dragged against his will, were intended to snuff out his life:

> *All Your waves and billows have gone over me... out of the depths have I cried unto Thee ...*[2]

Oblivion was beckoning, but other recollections were there, stronger than all the others. All along it had been the passion for art that had propelled him on his journey ... he relived the moments when, looking at a beautiful work, he seemed to access the genius of its creator, or the exultation he felt as he caressed the pure lines of one of his own sculptures ... they seemed to be a key that in turn opened up another realm, transcendent, filled with a glory he could not name, where everything in life that was hard, difficult, excruciating, was expunged, transmuted, resurrected, as the hard skin of a seed will crack open with fructifying warmth and sunshine, and spring into blossoming existence.

The memories were still pressing him, searching for answers ... "Would you do it all again?" they were asking. "Would you choose life?"

There was a force of *Life* that was calling him by name, lifting him irresistibly. After a week the miracle happened and he managed to stand on his feet. He was dizzy and swaying, his limbs were trembling, but the deadly ambush had been routed, and his mind, after the cathartic experience, was clear and calm. He stumbled into an office in the administration block. There were two officers seated behind a table.

"I want to be repatriated to Belgium," he announced.

The officers were sympathetic to his story: his quest to study art, his journey to Belgium, his marriage to Hennie, his longing to seek for her again.

"We can't send you from here to Belgium," he was told, "only to France. Meanwhile, we'll put you in a requisitioned house."

After a couple of days, the first Red Cross cars arrived for those being transported to France. Sam's group was driven first to Salzburg, then through Zurich in Switzerland and across the French border to Strasbourg. It was a journey through some of the most famous scenery of the world, and normally Sam would have delighted in the spectacular views. But he was still very weak, and when they stopped for meals he could eat hardly anything. Eventually they reached the community aid center in Mulhouse; from there another mission would come to fetch the Belgians and take them home.

A car driven by a Belgian soldier duly appeared, and at this point the *Vorarbeiter* who had his gun confiscated showed up wearing a concentration camp shirt to join the convoy. For a time he got treated like a hero. But during the journey they stopped at a roadblock, and when a security patrol checked the passengers it was revealed that this opportunist had never actually been in a concentration camp but had worked as a volunteer in Germany! He got arrested for fraud.

Finally they reached Belgium and the soldier dropped everyone off. Sam was last. He had arrived in Brussels, at his old place of residence. Before entering the store at the front of the building he looked at the second floor where he and Hennie had shared their years in hiding. Then he rang the bell.

Madame Meeuws came to the door. She didn't recognize Sam and looked at him suspiciously. She wondered to herself who this thin, livid man might be.

He whispered, "It's me, Sam."

She recognized his voice and embraced him. "My God," she breathed. "What have they done to you?"

They both cried.

---

1. The phrase originated with Theodore Parker, a 19th-century minister of the American Unitarian church, who used it to declare assurance of the success of the abolitionist cause. Dr. Martin Luther King was inspired by Parker and paraphrased his statement in a number of sermons and speeches.
2. From Psalm 42:7, Psalm 130:1.

PART IV

WANDERINGS

49

NEW CHALLENGES

Summer of 1945, and more than ten million Europeans were on the move: the end of the war sparked the migration of the largest number of people in the shortest period of time the world had ever known. Refugees, fugitives and displaced persons roamed the roads and waterways, crisscrossing the lanes and byways of Europe, making the continent a vast hive of activity. They carried a potent mix of emotions in their hearts as they made their way through the devasted countryside and ruined cities. Some were fleeing, others returning; for some there were jubilant reunions, for others a bitter homecoming.

The Allied project to send all the displaced persons back to their countries of origin as quickly as possible meant that millions were repatriated within weeks of the war's end. But the massive efforts to rebuild the continent had only just begun – and the work of reconstruction would soon be hampered by the competing interests of the democratic Western Allies and the communist Soviet Union. Above all, for the Jewish survivors, the victory had been just too long in coming.

At the start of the war, about nine and a half million Jews had lived in Europe; by the end of the conflict, two thirds of these - six million -

were annihilated. The Jewish community in Poland, the largest in Europe, had been decimated: of the three and a half million Jews living in Poland before 1939, only about 70,000 remained. Entire Jewish communities in Europe had been wiped out, and neither "the king's horses nor the king's men," no mere earthly power, could restore them. This meant that tens of thousands – those who had survived in concentration camps or as partisans, in hiding or posing as Christians with false papers – had no homes, families or synagogues to which they could return. Establishing life as it had been before the Holocaust would prove to be impossible.

Many survivors did make the journey back but swiftly learned of the terrible fate that had befallen their loved ones, in many cases discovering they were the only ones remaining in their entire families. It was at this point that the knowledge of the immensity of their loss was brought home in a very stark way. Up until then, the struggle to survive from moment to moment had consumed all their energy, and deflected attention from the world from which they had been separated. An almost superhuman effort was now needed to face the emptiness and try to reconstruct their shattered lives. The magnitude of the challenge was compounded by the fact that the Jews, having been living in fear and terror for many years, were physically and emotionally exhausted. After years of malnutrition and hard labor they needed to recuperate from illness and fatigue, and regain some sense of mental and social normalcy.

All these different challenges Sam would also meet as he returned to the home in which he had lived in Belgium before the war. He too had survived and returned to civilization, but shared those feelings of simultaneous fear and joy: how *does* one learn to behave again in a "normal" world? He was fortunate that the compassionate Mme Meeuws was able to help him.

"Why don't you take the room in the attic?" she asked him. "You can stay there as long as you wish."

He was thankful to have a place to live, but faced with the immediate problem of money. Mme Meeuws had been able to save one of the two sewing machines he had owned; she had lent it to a friend, asking a small sum of money for its use, and this she gave to Sam. An organization of war veterans also gave 1,000 francs to every survivor, and had donated some clothes and a pair of pajamas. With his financial needs taken care of for the moment, Sam set about trying to discover Hennie's fate, as well as that of his family in Poland.

The Red Cross and Jewish relief organizations had set up tracing services, but inquiries often took a long time because of the chaotic state of communications, the Nazis' erasure of records, and the mass relocations of populations in Eastern Europe. Sam learned that the Germans had taken over Zawiercie as soon as the war began, and that the 9,000 members of the small Jewish community were rounded up into a ghetto. By the end of August 1943, all had been deported to Auschwitz. Sam wrote a letter to the City Hall of Zawiercie to check if any of his family members were alive; the response he got was negative. Nor was there any information available concerning Hennie, nor any record of her fate in Auschwitz.

In desperation, Sam visited Mme Borisofla, the member of the Russian Resistance movement for which Hennie had worked, and at whose apartment Hennie had been arrested by the Gestapo. He learned that Mme Borisofla herself had also been arrested and condemned to death by firing squad, but miraculously survived. She told him that the British pilot whom she had hidden had been sent to a German prison, and after liberation had returned to Belgium and married her granddaughter. *But* - she was unable to give him any news concerning Hennie.

Sam came slowly to understand that Hennie must have perished in Auschwitz, murdered there by the Nazis. Hennie – with all her sweetness, laughter and gaiety. Hennie, his bright angel – now carried away on the waters of the great tide of woe that had engulfed Europe. The reality of her loss suddenly became acute, as if a needle-sharp weapon were being twisted in his heart. He was tormented by not knowing how she had met her death, whether she had immediately perished in the gas chambers, or suffered some of the excruciating toil inflicted on the women of the camp.

There were two sorts of survivors of the camps: those who talked, and those who kept silent. Sam belonged to the second group, and kept deep within his soul the emotions that were too painful to share. He sensed, as did many survivors, that what he had to tell would seem unimaginable. Often the survivors were met with incredulity when they told their stories, which compounded their sense of alienation.

This was brought home to Sam by a conversation he had with some Jewish acquaintances who had spent the war in Switzerland. As they talked together, Sam learned they had very bad memories of the country.

He was curious. "Why?" he asked.

"They rejected a lot of Jews, who because of that met a terrible fate."

"It was a neutral country," said Sam.

"Yes, but the government was pro-German. Those who were not rejected by Switzerland were incarcerated with their children."

"Were there camps in Switzerland?" Sam asked skeptically.

"Of course. There was insufficient food and the abandoned hotels where we were staying were not heated properly. Kids from the age of six were taken from their parents and put in foster homes and from the age of 16 they were put in labor camps."

"Did they have to work hard?"

"No ... actually they didn't do a lot."

"Were they tortured?"

"Of course they were not tortured *physically*. Did you know that couples were not allowed to live together? Men and women were put in separate camps. They saw one another only sporadically and only once a week they could receive letters."

Sam marveled to himself, "And those people thought they had lived through horrible times!" Discussions such as these aggravated those who, like himself, had returned from hell.

He was still feeling sick and disoriented, and his grief over the loss of his loved ones created an overwhelming sensation of hopelessness. He also suffered from ongoing physical problems and his feet were swollen so badly that he could hardly walk. Sleep was eluding him. He would constantly dream of the camp and relive all the events night after night, as if it were a horror movie screening in his mind. He started to smoke.

At this nadir of loneliness and desperation he met a furrier he had known before the war who asked him to work as an associate, and he accepted. The labor was intense and he made almost no money; his partner rarely bothered to exert himself, which meant that Sam was doing most of the work. He didn't care. He also learned that during the war his first employer Moshe had joined the Polish Resistance and was killed by the Germans. He grieved for his merry friend, who had given him his original start in business and enabled all that had followed.

After three months Sam felt he could slowly start living again. With some money coming in he bought a phonograph and records, and started listening to the music he had once loved so much. He realized, though, that he could find respite only in art, and enrolled again in the Art Academy. Because there was no charcoal available for heating, as a result of the strict rationing still in place, this meant that the Academy remained closed during the winter. But in the spring Sam joined the third class, attending in the evenings. Mme Meeuws had also told him he could sculpt in the attic, and he created the first carved pieces he had made since the war began. He threw himself passionately into his new endeavors, and in time-honored fashion the attic soon became the scene of profound artistic creativity. In this he found a measure of peace.

The months passed. In November 1947, two and a half years after VE Day, Mme Meeuws brought him a letter. He turned it over in his hands; it had a Polish stamp and postmark. He ripped open the envelope, drew out a flimsy sheet of paper and looked at the Yiddish words he had not seen for so long.

Mme Meeuws was aware of his intense emotion. "Sam, who is it from?"

"My brother Yehuda ... he is alive! And living in Poland. He has just been repatriated there from Russia, and received my letter ..."

She understood what it must mean to him and hugged him. After she had gone, he sat musing for a long time. For him, it was a moment of almost biblical proportions, as if a light from heaven had shone in his heart. His mind flew to the scene in Genesis where Jacob learned that his son Joseph, whom he had thought devoured by a wild beast, was still alive. Only the grand words of that supreme story could suffice for such a moment:

> And they told him, saying, "Joseph is still alive ..." And Jacob's heart stood still, because he did not believe them. But when they told him all the words which Joseph had said to them, and when he saw the carts which Joseph had sent to carry him, the spirit of Jacob their father revived. Then Israel said, "It is enough. Joseph my son is still alive..."[1]

---

1. From Genesis 45:26-28.

50

YEHUDA

In that same month of November that he had received the letter from Yehuda, on the 29th day of the month, Sam, like millions of Jews around the world, was glued to the radio. An historic vote was taking place at the United Nations to decide whether a Jewish state would be established once again in Palestine. A series of dramatic developments had led to this occasion.

In the initial post-war period, many of the Sh'erit ha-Pletah (surviving remnant) had tried to return to their homes in various European countries, only to find them taken over by strangers, and their former communities in ruins. Many of these survivors, having experienced the horrors of the Holocaust, now desired to leave Europe altogether and rebuild their lives elsewhere, and the majority felt that this new beginning should be in either Palestine or America. But the United States continued with its stringent immigration quotas, and entry to Palestine was still strictly controlled by the British.

Despite the fact that illegal immigration was both difficult and dangerous, many of the survivors were determined to make their way to Palestine. They stole across borders carrying forged documents, traveled over mountain passes through rough territory, or boarded dilapidated vessels to attempt the journey by sea. But the British staged a naval blockade off the coast of Palestine and intercepted the ships, interning the refugees once again in detention camps in Haifa and Cyprus. Britain's policies toward the Jewish refugees who had already suffered so much led to an international outcry, and demands for the establishment of an independent state for the Jewish people. Soon after the scandalous mistreatment of the Jews on the refugee ship Exodus, the United Nations Special Committee on Palestine (UNSCOP) recommended that Britain relinquish control of its Mandate for Palestine, and the area be partitioned into two states: one Arab and one Jewish.

Representatives of the nations gathered on November 29, 1947, at New York City Building, Flushing Meadow, which at the time housed the General Assembly of the United Nations. They had come to cast their votes on the UNSCOP proposal. It proved to be a day of drama and suspense, and many of those present sensed it as a moment of high destiny. Crowds gathered outside, and inside the building an electric excitement gripped the packed galleries. The motion needed a two-thirds majority to pass, and feverish international lobbying had preceded the vote. The nations were called in alphabetical order, and each country's delegate shouted an answer from the floor, either "Yes," "No" or "Abstention." The voting began:

Afghanistan: "No."

Argentina: "Abstention."

Australia: "Yes" – the first positive vote!

Eventually, the president rapped his gavel and read out the tally: 33 in favor, 13 against, 11 abstentions. The motion had passed: Resolution 181 had been adopted by a majority of the sovereign nations of the world, and a Jewish state was to be born anew in its ancient homeland. Jews everywhere around the globe erupted into jubilant celebration and the news brought thousands onto the streets across the future state to dance and rejoice, though it was clear that the Arab states would embark on a relentless war against realization of the plan.

The borders of the proposed state left the Jewish population without key areas of national and religious significance, but the Zionist leaders nevertheless responded positively to the proposal, cognizant of the historic opportunity. It was indeed a moment when the hopes and longings of 2,000 years had come to pass: "If you will it," Herzl had said, "it is no dream." Never before in history had a nation been uprooted from its land, preserved its identity throughout two millennia, and restored to physical nationhood at the end of that time. Undoubtedly, the UN resolution in favor of partition was also a response to the calamity of the Holocaust, a collective act of reparation on the part of the nations of the world, inspired by the horrific images from the concentration camps liberated by the Allies only a few years earlier.

Less than six months later, on May 14, 1948, David Ben-Gurion announced the establishment of the Jewish State, which was to be called – not Judea, not Zion – but Israel. The new political entity was quickly recognized by the rising superpowers, the United States and the USSR. As its first prime minister, Ben Gurion declared that Jewish immigration into Israel would henceforth be unrestricted, and, once the door was flung open, most of the survivors remaining in Europe began flooding in. This was despite the fact that five Arab armies had immediately invaded the fledgling state, seeking its annihilation. Israel prevailed in her War of Independence, but bore a heavy cost.

———————

Sam eagerly followed the developments in Israel and was elated over the creation of the Jewish State. He himself also had plans to travel – but foremost in his heart was the desire to visit Poland and see his brother, Yehuda. In the spring of 1949, four years after VE Day, he finally found the opportunity to make the journey. Few trains were yet running, and in order to purchase a ticket one had to bribe the officials, but by dint of the offer of two American cigarettes he obtained a seat. The train traveled through Germany, where he saw the enormous physical devastation caused by the Allied bombing, but noticed that the Marshall Plan to reconstruct the economies of Western Europe was already prompting rebuilding. Sam was particularly struck by the city of Cologne, where the twin spires of the beautiful Gothic cathedral that had taken 600 years to build were somehow still standing, despite having been pounded by countless air raids.

Soon they were passing over the redrawn borders of Poland into Lower Silesia and coming into the city of Wroclaw, which had been the German city of Breslau before the Allies made it into a Polish city literally overnight. After the war, the Soviet Union had retained control of the Polish territories in the east it had occupied, and as compensation the Allies gave the reestablished Polish state new territories in the west, at the expense of Germany, which meant that the whole country was effectively shifted westward. Wroclaw was the largest city in the newly acquired area; the remainder of the German residents had been expelled and the city repopulated by Poles. Sam gave a wry smile as he remembered his entry into Breslau, through the cemetery and under cover of darkness, all those years ago.

As the train clattered its way further into Poland, Sam's emotions might best be described as mixed – but sadness was uppermost. Poland had been home to the largest pre-war Jewish community in Europe, but fewer than ten percent had remained alive when the war ended. The survivors who returned were confronted with unimaginable loss and destruction, as well as by political turmoil in reconstituted Poland. The country's transformation into a Soviet-sponsored communist state following the liberation from German rule was proceeding apace: businesses were nationalized, Polish political and religious leaders were imprisoned, and rigged elections were held. The full takeover of Poland was complete by 1948, and this had led to a state of civil war. The communists constituted a small minority, and arrayed against them was a wide range of political parties loyal to the Polish government-in-exile.

Sam continued his journey to the city of Lodz, southwest of Warsaw, where Yehuda was living and working. Lodz had been a key industrial center in prewar Poland; after Warsaw, the Jews of the city formed the second largest Jewish community in the land. German troops occupied Lodz from September 1939, and turned the northern part of the city into a ghetto with almost a quarter of a million Jews confined within its walls. Conditions there were horrendous, with starvation and overcrowding as well as hard labor after the Germans established factories inside the ghetto. One of the most shocking incidents of the Holocaust took place in late 1942: all children under ten years of age were taken from their parents in scenes of indescribable anguish and transported to Chelmno. Eventually all the Jews were deported to Nazi death camps.

In the immediate postwar period, as refugees from Warsaw and territories annexed by the Soviet Union returned, the Jewish community in Lodz was rebuilt to become the largest in Poland. When Sam arrived there, late in the evening, he became aware that a strange, somber mood was hanging over the city. He walked down Piotrkowska Street, the long avenue at the city's heart, where the forgotten grandeur of the previous era could still be descried in its buildings and palaces. But the hotel at which he eventually arrived was seedy and not very clean.

The next morning he set out to find his brother, who was working as an accountant in an orphanage for Jewish children, all of whom were survivors of the camps. Sam made his way to the address he had been given, and found Yehuda surrounded by a bevy of small girls and boys. The two men embraced, then searched each other's faces, looking for the changes the years had wrought; they had not seen one another for more than a decade. Sam saw a man in his early forties, with deep lines carved in his face, but with an air of calm and stolid acceptance, and a deep, hard-earned peace lighting a lambent flame in his eyes. Yehuda in his turn looked at Sam with deep, protective affection. He rejoiced that his young brother had grown into such a personable man and could sense the inner power of his artistic gifts, but also that the experiences through which he had passed still left their searing mark on his soul.

Yet Sam was feeling a new spring of happiness in his heart. He was introduced to Yehuda's wife and his two lovely daughters. A whole family group gathered about him and welcomed him; it was balm to his soul. The brothers settled down to speak and reminisce; Yehuda shared a great deal about his stay in Russia. He was one of many thousands of Jews who had been residing in eastern Poland at the time the Soviets and Nazi Germany divided the Polish territories in September 1939. Soon after, the vast majority found themselves deported or imprisoned inside the USSR, then sent to the Urals or Siberia, where they endured forced labor, hunger and disease in the Gulag system. Nonetheless, many managed to hold on despite the extreme conditions, and this meant that the majority of Polish Jews who managed to survive the war did so under Soviet rather than German authority.

Sam listened as Yehuda recounted his experiences, but couldn't bring himself to speak very much about his own war years. His brother continued his story, explaining what it was like to return to Poland.

"Did you notice the young man with arms guarding the orphanage?" he asked.

Sam nodded.

"We had a terrible pogrom in Kielce," Yehuda explained. "A rumor spread that Jews had killed a Polish boy to use his blood in religious rituals. Then a mob began rampaging and 42 Jews were killed – all survivors of the camps."

Sam shook his head in disbelief.

"Just think," his brother continued bitterly. "The massacre started with that old blood libel. But it's not the Middle Ages any more, not even Nazi Germany. I tell you, Shmuli, Kielce has shattered the dream for many of us, that it is possible for us to make a future here again in Poland."

He sighed heavily. "It's not just the antisemitism and the economic hardships," he said. "It's seeing so many towns empty of Jews, where there used to be such vibrant communities; it's always being reminded of what it must have been like as they were removed from their houses, sent into ghettos, of the masses of Jews streaming into the unknown. And reminded of our own family in Zawiercie as well; always the tragedy is before one's eyes."

The brothers were silent.

"I'm not alone in this," said Yehuda. "So many of the Jewish survivors believe they have to leave Europe; it seems to them to have become a vast graveyard."

Sam shuddered involuntarily. "What are your plans, Yehuda?" he asked.

"I want to emigrate to Israel with my family, but the director of the orphanage is a communist and does everything in his power to prevent us from going there. But meanwhile, please stay with us as long as you like," he urged.

Sam knew that he was returning to Belgium, to his art studies. "But I promise I will come and see you in Israel," he said.

51

ANNIE

When Sam returned to Belgium, he found that so many new commissions had been coming in to their business that his associate had hired another employee. The new stitcher at the fur workshop was a skilled and attractive woman, whose name was Annie Lustig.

As Sam got to know Annie better, he learned that she had spent the war in Switzerland, that her family had perished in the camps, and she had only one brother left, who was living in the States. Just like Sam, she felt lost and lonely, and it was not long before the young man and woman became friends.

Sam's new companion was blonde with green eyes, had a full figure and was always impeccably dressed. Additionally, she was very cultivated, spoke several languages, and was as devoted to classical music as Sam. Annie had a strong sense of justice and was often in conflict with those who, according to her, dealt unfairly with others – invariably she was on the side of the weak and oppressed.

Soon the feelings of friendship which Sam and Annie shared turned into something more profound. Late in 1949, they were married in a religious ceremony before a rabbi. Sam had not yet received a death certificate for Hennie, and his union with Annie could not therefore be officially recognized by the Belgian government.

For a time they were happy together, but Annie soon began struggling with health problems and a feeling of weakness. One day she went to take a bath and fainted. When Sam wrote to Yehuda about his concern for his new wife, his brother wrote back recommending a health spa in Czechoslovakia. Sam went to Annie with the letter.

"Annie," he said. "Let's go to Carlsburg in Czechoslovakia. It's a health and holiday resort. You will be able to recover there."

Annie seemed relieved and happy about the plan. "What a good idea," she enthused, with a return of her former animation.

Together they made the long journey back to Eastern Europe, and as soon as they arrived in Carlsburg Sam took Annie to a doctor. He performed an extensive examination, but said he could find nothing wrong – yet Annie was steadily losing weight, became fatigued easily and often stumbled.

Discouraged, they returned to Belgium. Annie's health worsened, and they began a round of visits to different medical specialists. The situation was also costing them a small fortune because neither belonged to a health insurance fund.

The doctors prescribed various medicines for the nervous system, but they seemed to have no effect. Annie was no longer able to work, nor did she have the strength for any duties around the house. Her deterioration became very rapid. During his midday break Sam would go home from the fur workshop and prepare lunch for her, but soon discovered that traveling back and forth in this way was too hard. He decided to stay with Annie and work from home. At that point Annie could still walk alone, but soon she had to be supported at every step. By now, Sam was beside himself with anxiety.

A family doctor living nearby finally diagnosed the cause of her illness. "Annie has multiple sclerosis," he said. "It's a disease which develops slowly, until finally there is complete paralysis."

"What is the treatment?" asked Sam.

The doctor looked at Sam with compassion. "There are no drugs presently available to cure the disease. I'm very sorry," he added.

Annie's death warrant had been sealed, and she was barely 26 years old. But Sam and Annie were not ready to give up, and continued visiting various specialists. All their funds were disappearing, and Sam started to work in the evenings and sometimes through the night to make ends meet. There was no time left for art.

One day, a friend of Annie's paid her a visit. Her parents were farmers living next to Louvain, a town just to the east of Brussels, and she suggested that for a modest payment Sam and Annie might be able to stay with them for a while. Sam thought the country air and a quiet lifestyle would be good for his wife and agreed. Together the couple made the journey, and were charmed by the small farmhouse and the peaceful rural surroundings. The farmers were analphabets but were intelligent and kind. But after a few days there Sam was growing restless.

"Could I acquire some wood somehow?" he asked the farmer. "I would like to make a sculpture."

"Let me ask the forester," he replied.

As it happened, the forester had just cut down a linden tree which had reached ten meters in height. He sawed the trunk into sections, and gave some of them to Sam. He refused to take any money.

"It's a present," he said with a large smile.

Sam stripped off the bark, and from the wood he began creating his first large sculpture, more than a meter high. It represented the face of a young woman, with a countenance marked by sadness. After two weeks the couple rented a car and returned to Brussels, bringing the piece with them. Sam took it up to their attic and after his long working day began sculpting every evening. Soon he had completed the work and the experience gave him a passion for carving in wood that would remain with him the rest of his life.

Sam reveled in this new creativity, which for a time helped take his mind off their situation, but Annie's continuing decline meant that soon their friends stopped visiting. They were on their own, and both felt horribly lonely. As incredible as it may seem, Sam felt even more unhappy than he had been in the concentration camps; he and his wife even thought of a suicide pact. Two years went by in this way, as they both experienced an ever-growing sense of desolation.

Under this great strain, Sam eventually began to wonder if he was losing his mind. He tried to rally himself, and started to study again at the Academy, finishing the year with distinction. But then, once again, he felt the insidious onset of depression, and sensed that he was at the end of his tether. He decided that he and Annie should move into a rest home for a while, thinking that if medical personnel were available that would assist them in regaining health and strength.

He found a reasonably priced rest home in Dilbeek near Brussels, but the first night there didn't bring the hoped-for respite. Sam was lying next to Annie and was overcome by an agonizing pain in his lower back: he was suffering from a kidney impairment, and after a while it seemed as if sharp knives were piercing his flesh. He called a nurse. "Please, give me something against the pain," he asked.

She looked at him suspiciously and muttered, "Another drug addict."

No medication was forthcoming, and Sam remained several days in bed, hardly able to move. After a week a doctor came to see him and immediately gave him medicine. His condition improved somewhat and they returned home after another week.

He and Annie were worse off than before, physically, mentally, financially. Every day became a calvary. Annie lost the ability to speak, and after a while she stopped recognizing Sam and thought he was her father. Sam fed her like a child; she was no longer able to move her arms and hands.

Winter arrived and it was freezing.

One day, Sam went to his Academy class. When he returned home and walked into their little attic he noticed immediately that the bed was empty. Before leaving he always left the door opening on to the balcony a little ajar to bring some air into the room. The door was wide open.

Filled with dread Sam went out onto the small balcony. Annie was lying there; she was still breathing. He carried her back to her bed and called an ambulance. Shortly thereafter she died from pneumonia.

How had she succeeded in dragging herself to the balcony? Sam wondered. *Had there been a moment of lucidity in which she decided to kill herself?*

Only God knows, he finally concluded. *He alone was the witness of this drama.*

52

TRAVEL TO RIO

Even though Sam's life with Annie had been so sad, her death did not come as a deliverance; he was actually left with an even greater loneliness. Several months after his wife had passed away, however, a new door opened for him.

Sam had always kept in contact with Hennie's relatives by letter, and most frequently had corresponded with her cousin Mathilde Teichteil who was living in Brazil. Mathilde had put him in touch with a Brazilian painter named Roberto dos Santos, who wrote to Sam urging him to come to Rio de Janeiro. He promised to organize an exhibition there for Sam's artworks.

Sam decided that he would make the journey and worked hard to put money aside. Annie's illness had left him penniless, and before leaving Belgium he had to put a deposit of 15,000 francs in the bank. This was all he possessed.

Six months after Annie had passed away, in the spring of 1953, Sam drove to Genoa with a lady friend who was taking the same boat to Brazil. They decided to make the journey a leisurely one, and drive through the scenic regions of Luxembourg and France. It was the month of May, the weather was glorious, and for the first time after an indescribably long period Sam felt a sense of wellbeing.

As they made their way south toward the Mediterranean and arrived in Provence, Sam found himself thinking of the Dutch painter Vincent van Gogh, the brilliant and temperamental artist who had lived in the region for two years in 1888 and 1889. Coming from the north with its gray skies and flat lands, he had been enchanted by the warm bright colors of the landscape, and the countryside over which the golden sunlight poured. Making his home in Arles, living in the little Yellow House he made famous with his paintings, he ignored the spectacular Roman ruins in the city. Instead, he had set up his easel outdoors, painting gnarled and twisted olive groves, obelisk-like cypresses, and farmers sowing and reaping. It was one of his more prolific periods, and he completed hundreds of paintings.

Sam and his friend were not able to visit the Yellow House, which had been bombed during the war. It was here also that van Gogh had a tumultuous fight with his friend, Paul Gauguin, and sliced a blade through his ear; he had then entered the Saint-Paul-de-Mausole asylum in Saint-Rémy, close to Arles, where he spent more than a year. Once again he produced an astonishing number of works, some of them his most famous. In the asylum garden were beautiful irises and lilies which captured his imagination; other pictures were filled with a restless swirling energy. Gazing through the barred window in his room one night, as the dawn was sending forth its first rays of light, he saw the countryside illumined by enormous stars.

The travelers drove on until they arrived at the coastal road which wound its way between the south of France and Tuscany, a region called the Italian Riviera. Sam was ravished by the scenery. Each bend of the road disclosed another exquisitely curved bay, set like a jewel in its surrounding headlands. The pure white sands of the beaches were edged by waters ranging in shade from aquamarine to azure to cobalt, deepening as they reached the wide blue expanse of the sea, where white boats with sails like wings floated in the shimmering light. The colorful villages that clung to the hills behind each bay had their own picturesque charm, with houses painted in dusty pinks and ochres that seemed to capture the essence of the summer light. And each night the stars of the southern skies, large as daisies, spectacular as van Gogh's pinwheels, were blazing down.

As each turn of the road revealed another dream-like view, Sam felt he understood something of the ecstasy that had flamed in van Gogh's soul. The sun poured a benison of light and warmth over all and the wings of his spirit began to revive in the incredible natural beauty. Like the Dutch artist, he found it as a signpost to something larger, a connection to the cosmos, a glimpse of the larger verities that he sensed existed beyond the realms of time and space.

Eventually the travelers arrived at Genoa, where they had still a couple of days before the departure of the boat. The city was a fascinating one, with grand medieval houses set on tiny winding streets, but they soon discovered it was quite a dangerous place. By day, as they browsed in the markets, they were offered false gold by vendors with equally false and insinuating smiles. As they wandered and fell into casual conversations they met a number of Italian fascists who were still hankering after Mussolini. One evening as they walked they heard a cry from a distance, and learned that someone had been assassinated. All in all, they were relieved to finally board the *Sebastiano Cabotto*, named for the Venetian explorer. This was despite the fact that it was not a luxurious vessel.

There were two decks on the ship. The downstairs one was dirty and filled with poor Italian families emigrating to Brazil; the children were ill-clothed and many were sick. On the upper deck traveled the tourists, most of whom seemed to be wealthy Italian, Portuguese or Spanish families going to visit their relatives in South America. Large diamond rings flashed on the fingers of the women. Sam too was forced to travel on the upper deck, although it took an alarming part of his savings, because he had a tourist visa for Brazil. But he enjoyed plunging into the sun-warmed waters of the small swimming pool, and the food was also good. He had brought some art materials and made several drawings and paintings, and the days passed quickly, in dream-like succession.

The boat finished its long journey across the Atlantic and docked at Brazil's seaport of Recife. Sam went ashore with some of the other passengers, marveling as he felt the tropical heat enveloping him and the warm raindrops plashing down on his head. He had never seen people walking with bare feet and at the same time carrying umbrellas! Their clothes were bright and colorful, and the colonial buildings around the waterfront were painted in charming pastel shades. The atmosphere seemed both relaxed and yet vibrant, forming a stunning counterpoint to the mood of the cities in Europe he had just left. In the shops, he was immediately drawn to some beautiful sculptures made from cherry wood, but soon they were boarding again, and the ship resumed its voyage.

As they traveled southward, Sam spent most of the time on deck, gazing at the gorgeous tropical scenes as they slid past: the sprawling golden beaches with backdrops of lush vegetation, where birds with bright plumage fluttered their wings. It seemed to him a natural paradise, and when they finally sailed into Rio de Janeiro, he discovered a city of mesmerizing beauty. Lying in a narrow plain between the blue waters of Guanabara Bay and the Atlantic Ocean, it is surrounded by forested mountains and soaring peaks, including the distinctively shaped Sugarloaf. The complex intersecting of mountains and sea causes the whole city and its environment to resemble an immense natural amphitheater. High above all towers the colossal white statue of Christ the Redeemer, with arms outstretched as if to embrace the world.

Sam was dazzled by the scene and could sense the vitality of the city, but he was soon brought down to earth. He had some unforeseen challenges in taking his artworks out of the port.

"First," he was told, "you need an *agente* to help you with the paperwork."

Sam had thought that he would merely have to sign a few documents and this would take care of the red tape, but apparently he didn't understand how things worked in Brazil. A man named Luis approached him.

"Your signature must be confirmed first," he explained. "I'll take you to a notary."

The two men entered a dilapidated house next to the harbor. The notary looked like a tramp. A shabby couple who appeared to have been lounging all day in the dirty corridor were roped in as witnesses. But the all-important papers were acquired, and Sam proceeded with them to the depot, where he learned he was required to pay admission taxes in order to retrieve his work.

He began to protest, but the agent shrugged his shoulders. "That's the law. Pay him or you'll never see your stuff again."

After paying the notary, Luis, and the fees, Sam took a taxi to Copacabana where Mathilde Teichteil was living. He had only a little money left.

Sam received a warm welcome from Mathilde. She had no room for him in her apartment, but her friend who lived one floor above offered to let him stay there free of charge. Mathilde's friend was a kind and intelligent German lady who possessed an extensive library; she also allowed Sam to put his artworks on the balcony. But his immediate problem, because of all the unexpected expenses, was money.

Had he even thought about it, Sam would never have dreamed that he could find work in Brazil in his own line of trade as a furrier. But some kind influence was working on his behalf, for that is exactly what happened. Many of the Brazilian women wore fur stoles when they went to the theater or casino, which meant there was a thriving trade in the business, and he was soon engaged by the firm *Pelleteries Americaines*. He needed to take an overcrowded bus to his place of work, and it required an hour to get there, but at least it was solving his pecuniary problems. In the evenings he would return home tired and sweaty, for the temperature varied between 35 and 40 degrees.

Sam soon found other ways to save on money as well. He would dine in a cheap restaurant in the center of town where the food was quite good, although one had to queue to find a place to sit. Other times he would just go to one of the many kiosks which sold strong, sugar-laden coffee. He tried to avoid the cafes. The first time he sat down in one he suddenly he felt someone seizing his leg – it was a child who fell upon his shoes and began polishing them to an almost military sheen. It was a practice which he discovered to be almost a national institution.

Another source of patriotic pride was, of course, the famous Carnival. When it came around, Sam attended with his neighbors. He found the floats spectacular, but the noise was deafening, and he and his friends needed to hold hands for fear of losing one another. Many carnival-goers were drunk, and others danced 48 hours without stopping.

Sam needed only three hours before he was happy to return home.

53

THE FIRST EXHIBITION

After the Carnival, Sam contacted the painter who had encouraged him to come to Brazil, Roberto dos Santos. It was a connection that proved of enormous benefit to him. As well as having a large and generous heart, Roberto had numerous contacts and considerable influence in Rio's art world. He introduced Sam to many other artists and, most importantly, arranged a meeting with the French-speaking director of the Arts Museum. Sam brought some of his works with him and waited with a fast-beating heart as the director examined each piece. He was thrilled when the director finally looked up with a smile and spoke.

"Young man," he said, "you can have an exhibition here in August."

His first exhibition ... in a museum!

Meanwhile, Mathilde was ensuring that Sam's gifts were being brought to the attention of the Jewish community in Rio – a large group, well-integrated into Brazilian culture and society. Mathilde impressed upon Sam that the Jews in Brazil had a long and venerable history, dating as far back as the voyages of Columbus. On his famous first expedition in 1492, the captain had among his crew six practicing Jews, as well as six so-called *conversos*, Jews who had converted to

Christianity. That was the same year that Ferdinand and Isabella of Spain issued their Alhambra Decree, expelling all Jews, as did Portugal five years later. But the new realms opening up on the other side of the world were beckoning, and many Portuguese Jews followed across the "ocean blue" to settle in Brazil. The first synagogue of the New World was founded in Recife in 1636.

Many of the Jews residing in this new haven had already been forced to convert to Roman Catholicism, though a number still clung to their old traditions. Even as they were rising in economic and political prominence during the 17th century, however, the long arm of the Portuguese Inquisition began reaching the Americas. Many of the *conversos* were accused of secretly conducting Jewish rituals, and imprisoned or tortured. This persecution led a great number to flee to the West Indies, New Amsterdam (now New York), or Europe, but the emigration also greatly damaged the Brazilian economy. In 1773, a Portuguese royal decree finally abolished discrimination against Jews, and after the first Brazilian constitution in 1824 granted freedom of religion large numbers of European Jews began arriving. Their numbers swelled with Russian and Polish Jews escaping pogroms and revolution, then again with increased emigration after the world wars, giving Brazil one of the largest Jewish communities in the world.

Through Mathilde's good offices, Sam received a request from a Jewish organization to carve the bust of a well-known professor of chemistry named Fritz Feigl, who lived in Rio and was a candidate for the Nobel Prize. Sam discovered that the professor was a charming man, who had similar tastes in music and literature to his own. He posed for Sam in the garage of his villa. During their long sessions together, as the piece began to come to life under Sam's fingers, the two men talked and listened to classical music.

Sam learned more about the professor's background as well. He had been born into a Jewish family in 1891 in Vienna, which was then the capital of the Austro-Hungarian empire, and after exemplary service during the First World War joined the faculty at the University of

322

Vienna. Forced to retire after the Anschluss in 1938, he was able to travel from Austria to Belgium, but when the Nazis invaded the country in 1940 he was sent to a concentration camp.

Sam listened intently as the professor recounted his story, and at that point laid down his tools and sat looking at him with wide eyes.

"Where did they send you?" he asked.

"It wasn't one of the better-known camps," responded the older man. "It was in the south of France, near Gurs."

"I was there too," Sam blurted out. "In 1940!"

The men looked at one another in surprise.

"How did you get out?" asked Sam.

"My wife had been away when I was transferred to the camp. She contacted the Brazilian Ambassador in Vichy who helped us gain visas for Brazil, and we came here in November 1940 as refugees," explained the professor. "And what about you, Sam?"

It was Sam's turn to describe some of his experiences in the camp. He discovered that the professor also remembered and had suffered at the hands of the infamous Chief. As Sam told the professor the story of his escape the older man listened enthralled. Sam concluded his story by telling him of the postcard of the Eiffel Tower he had sent to the Alsatian bully, after he had reached Paris.

The professor dissolved in laughter. "Young man," he said wiping tears of mirth from his eyes with a large handkerchief, "I wish I could have seen his face when he read it!"

After the end of the First World War, the professor had received many invitations to work in other parts of the world, but, out of gratitude for his family's reception in Brazil, he and his wife settled permanently in Rio, and his distinguished academic career had continued there.

Sam enjoyed the professor's company, and was almost sorry when the bust was completed. After he had put the finishing touches on the piece, he displayed it to the professor and his wife. Mme Feigl felt the sculpture needed to be changed a little – her husband's head was slightly inclined and she wanted it to be upright. But Sam didn't change anything. The resemblance was startling and he was proud of his accomplishment: it was his first commissioned portrait, and although he didn't receive a lot of money he felt a quiet satisfaction.

The inspiration to create another portrait was burning within him. He obtained a piece of teak wood and worked with it on the balcony; it was a tight squeeze because his other artworks were also kept there, and he was forced to hold the sculpture between his feet while he was carving. The face of a woman emerged from the wood. Her eyes were half closed, and her countenance was filled with sadness. Was it the memory of Hennie, or of Annie?

He created a series of naked women. A young woman would pose for him from 10 am to noon each day. She had her prayer book with her and afterwards she always went to church. Meanwhile, the date of the exhibition was approaching. Sam had invitations and posters printed, but suddenly, after they had been sent out, the museum director told him that the exhibition hall was unavailable on the dates which had been decided.

"In that case, I'm putting all my works in front of the door!" Sam expostulated furiously.

His threat had the intended effect, and a hall was found to hold the exhibition. Sam had no money to frame his pictures properly, so he glued them onto larger canvases. The big day finally arrived, the moment of fulfilment of a long-held dream: the desire accomplished which is "sweet to the soul."[1] He was gratified that many of the well-known figures of Rio society attended the exhibition – but a little taken aback when the director himself never showed up. Three days later he sent Sam his excuses. Sam understood that things were a little more casual in Brazil.

The reviews of his exhibition in the media were highly complimentary, but Sam was to discover that this did not necessarily convert to monetary compensation. He sold only one small wooden sculpture, and in addition the effort he had put into organizing the exhibition began to cause him health problems. The work had been too strenuous for him; he developed an ulcer and suffered so much pain in his stomach that he was unable to eat.

One day at the exhibition he approached one of the visitors and spoke to him.

"Sorry," he said, "but are you by any chance a doctor?"

The man was astonished. "Yes I am, but how did you know?"

It had been Sam's intuition. As it happened, the doctor was one of the most famous physicians in Rio, and he gave Sam an appointment for the following day. He put Sam on a strict diet: almost nothing to eat but plain boiled potatoes. The doctor refused to be paid but accepted a small painting for his services. And Sam gradually recovered his strength.

By now he had spent a year in Brazil and began to feel restless again. He had some amorous encounters, but they had led nowhere. It was time, he decided, to return to Belgium.

---

1. Proverbs 13:19.

54

THE FLOODGATES OPEN

Sam worked in Rio for another six months, saving money for his return to Europe. Eventually he embarked on a not very comfortable Argentinian ship. It was hot and steamy as they crossed the Atlantic – 40 degrees in the shade. Sam discovered there were two other artists on board; the three spent their time painting one another and this made time pass swiftly. It was an idyllic voyage, and soon they were sailing past Gibraltar into the Mediterranean and docking at Genoa.

The weather in the south of Europe was a shock to Sam after coming from the balmy tropics. It was freezing, but he was determined while he was in Italy to see the works of some of the great Renaissance artists and sculptors, especially Michelangelo and Leonardo. He arrived at the House of Students in Florence, a patrician 18th-century residence filled with sculptures and surrounded by a beautiful garden, but bitterly cold. The city had an embarrassment of riches in the way of famous artworks, and he went to visit the most renowned museums: the Uffizi Gallery and Pitti Palace, with works by Raphael, Titian and other masters, and of course the Accademia Galleria, with Michelangelo's famous *David*. But it was mid-winter, the museums were not heated, and as Sam made his way through them he was shivering. After eight days he took the train to Brussels.

Here also it was ten degrees below zero; the cold seemed to pierce through his body, and he thought with regret of sunny Brazil. He had just enough money to get a taxi to the home of his friend Camille, who together with his wife Rosa received him with great kindness, assuring him he was welcome to visit with them as long as he wished. He stayed with them for a week until he found work as a furrier with someone for whom he had worked before the war, then took his deposit of 15,000 francs from the bank and rented a small apartment. The coal stove didn't give enough heat, and the cold and loneliness made him wonder again if he should have left South America.

When spring arrived, Sam's spirits lifted a little, but the nights remained difficult to endure. He wasn't able to sleep and made one drawing after another. For the first time he made a bust out of plasticine of an inmate of the concentration camp. He made it on the kitchen table. The face was thin – the bones protruding from the skeletal countenance. It was the face of living death, a man who carried a look from another world.

It was as if the floodgates opened, a new spring of creativity that had been biding its time within the depths of his being, waiting to gush forth. All the agonies and extremities of the years of war, the horror of the concentration camps, the images that had imprinted themselves in fire on his soul, began to come forth and be born into the light of day. How does one portray the impact of the worst crime ever committed? How delineate the depths of woe no human mind could conceive? How does one illustrate the unthinkable, and incarnate the unimaginable?

In sculptures of wood, bronze and marble, in black and white graphics, in portraits of living men and women, that was Sam's task; it came unbidden but was laid upon him, and he could do naught else – for none but he who had lived through those years might undertake such a venture. The anguish of that time of intense suffering seemed to burst forth from the pictures and images as if restrained for too long: a misery that could not captured in words, but was present in the starkness of the elongated figures, in the sadness that marked each countenance, in the skeletal bodies bundled together in death, all the savagery and sorrow of camp life.

But there were also other images being birthed, and they had to do, fundamentally, with LIFE – life lived in the very teeth of death – defiant, assertive, with a deliberate asseveration of joy. It was the Jewish theme of the ages.

Although Sam was not conventionally religious he began to take up ideas from the world of Judaism – memories of his childhood, the celebration of the Jewish feasts, the Passover meals, Hasidic dances and weddings. These creations, in which he drew upon the rich faith of his people, often conveyed a dreamlike intensity. Strong vertical lines were used to draw the eye upward, as if to suggest that through the earthly rituals the participants were lifting their souls heavenward. And in all these works, both those emerging from his Auschwitz experiences as well as those springing from his spiritual heritage, there was a frequent juxtaposition of light and darkness. This meant that, in the Holocaust pictures, intense suffering became bathed with a light of transcendence, while the more religious images were charged with an aura of sacredness.

Sam's portraits, too, stamped themselves with power upon the mind of the viewer. The faces he chose to delineate were those of rabbis and prophets, saints and mystics, men and women emerging from some profound affliction. Each countenance seemed to display the lineaments of suffering love, as if the hardly won qualities of humility and devotion had been carved into their very features. In the intimation of the burdens they carried, in their patient submission to their ordeals, breathed an echo of the divine compassion for the world and its hidden sufferers. A deep spirituality was also evinced in his representation of biblical characters: great Old Testament figures such as King David, whom he depicted worshiping with his lyre, his face turned to the sky in ecstasy, ablaze with love:

When I consider Your heavens,

the work of Your fingers,

328

The moon and the stars,

which You have ordained,

What is man that You are mindful of him?

... O Lord our Lord,

how excellent is Your name in all the earth.[1]

Sam even portrayed a crucified Jesus, wrapped in a tallit. In this he followed Chagall, who had painted a series of crucifixions during the Shoah featuring the image of Christ as a Jewish martyr, identified completely with his brethren; it was this figure alone, Chagall believed, that could serve to represent the extremity of the suffering of European Jewry.

The distinctive features which would mark Sam's art were taking shape, first in his soul and then in his material, as he wrestled with wood and bronze, with outline and color, with the representation of facial expressions. As this new creativity was taking place, Sam's physical strength was also improving and his love of music reviving. One evening, he went to the Palace of Fine Arts to attend a concert of classical music. During the intermission, to his delight, he bumped into an acquaintance from Antwerp named Frida Bucher. This encounter would change his life.

Their joy was great in seeing one another again after all the sad years that had intervened, and they hugged each other. Frida introduced Sam to her husband, Haim Zajdman, and the men looked at each other with astonishment. They had been friends when they were growing up in Zawiercie; sometimes as children they had fought together because they came from different schools. Frida and Haim insisted that Sam must come to stay with them in Antwerp, and he took up their invitation.

There in Antwerp Sam met a woman named Mania Weisberg, who was married to a wealthy diamond merchant named Schongut. Mania asked Sam to paint her portrait, and thereafter he came to

Antwerp three times a week to complete the work; she and her husband received him with great warmth and hospitality. After two months the portrait was finished, and Mania was ecstatic. Her mouth displayed a slight smile, and she felt it was reminiscent of the *Mona Lisa*. Mania gave Sam a nice sum of money which also lifted his spirits. Soon more commissions were arriving, and he began to receive many accolades as his work generated a frisson of excitement in the art world. Frida had put Sam in contact with the director of the Jewish Cultural Center of Antwerp who was organizing an exhibition for Jewish artists, and Sam was invited as guest of honor.

The art critic Jos Peeters came to the exhibition and showed a great deal of interest in Sam's work. "You'll become a world-famous artist one day ... but it will happen after your death," he said.

"In that case I do hope it will take a lot of time before I'll become famous," Sam said, smiling.

Peeters wrote an enthusiastic article about Sam in the *Israelitisch Weekblad*. He had also predicted fame for the writer Leon Blois and the painter Alfred Ost, and both had indeed become celebrated in their fields. *Was the prediction of the art critic some kind of prophecy?* Sam wondered.

Sam was a professional artist and most of the others who had works on display in the exhibition were amateurs. One of these was a young woman named Edith Beck, who was profoundly impressed by Sam's creative gifts. She liked to linger in front of one of his wooden sculptures, entitled *Maria Dolorosa* – the carved face seemed to her to express infinite pain and sadness. As she stood there one day admiring it, Sam himself entered the room. Someone whispered to her, "That is Sam Herciger."

Edith approached him. "Your work is beautiful," she said. "Congratulations!"

"Thank you," said Sam, turning to look at her. She was attractive and her face was alive with intelligence and vivacity; she was also much younger than he. At that moment, Mania came to speak to him and took him by the arm, drawing him aside.

Sam paid no further attention to the young artist who had looked at him with such adoration in her eyes.

---

1. From Psalm 8:1,3–5.

55

ISRAEL, AND A MEETING

Spring of 1955. The thought of a trip to Israel began to beckon Sam. Yehuda, his brother, had by now established himself there, and wrote regularly. Sam decided to pay him a visit and was excited: his first journey to the Promised Land!

After again working hard to save money for the voyage, he traveled to Marseille in the south of France, and from there took a boat to Israel. The shabby old vessel was called *Artsa* (to our land), and packed with Jews coming from Morocco to make aliyah. On board there was a joyous atmosphere, a sense of excitement and anticipation. A little dance orchestra played each evening, and falafel and drinks were sold on the deck. Sam had brought some of his drawings on board, and on the first day of sailing exhibited them to his fellow travelers, to much interest and applause. He had them all laughing as he told them jokes from his endless repertoire, and enjoyed the journey very much.

As the boat drew near the shores of Israel, Sam joined the other passengers as they gathered on the deck to catch their first glimpse of the fabled Holy Land. They sailed over shimmering waters that were darkening with the purple haze of sunset, and came into the beautiful blue bay of the port of Haifa, nestled into the verdant embrace of Mount Carmel. And there, as he disembarked, Yehuda was waiting for him, to hug him tightly. They drove to the apartment in Tel Aviv that Yehuda shared with his wife and two daughters, and Sam delighted in the warmth of their welcome. At night the two brothers slept in the corridor of the apartment, so as not to disturb the rest of the family. They had so much to catch up on and were telling each other jokes into the wee hours.

Their cousin Anda, who had hosted Sam in Krakow in the home of the redoubtable Uncle Jonas, also lived in Tel Aviv. She organized a party for Sam and invited their many relatives; they came from all over Israel to meet him, and Sam was overjoyed. He received warm invitations to stay with each one – but first, he knew, he had to see Jerusalem, the ancient capital of his people.

He took the rickety bus that rumbled its way across the coastal plain, past groves of oranges, then through the Valley of Ayalon, where the sun reputedly stood still for Joshua. The first gentle slopes of the central highland ranges appeared, and the bus seemed to give itself a metaphorical shake as it prepared for the ascent. They lumbered their way through the narrow defile that led them upwards into the heart of Judea, and Sam noted silently the number of burned-out tanks that remained on either side of the road. They were a vivid reminder of the battle for Jerusalem that had cost so many lives as the Jewish people returned to their land.

Finally, the Holy City appeared in its majestic location, floating like a vision on its mountain heights. Sam took a room at a small hotel close to Ben Yehuda Street, in the heart of the new city, and strolled from there to the recently opened Café Rimon. Over a plate of *hummus b' techina*, while he marveled at hearing the conversations in animated Hebrew which were taking place about him, he spread open a map and planned his explorations.

Soon he set out along Jaffa Road, walking until the ramparts of the Old City, massive yet still graceful, came into view. He had known that he would not be able to enter any of the ancient gates or visit the *Kotel* (Western Wall), for the Old City was occupied by the Jordanians.

But he wandered through the narrow streets outside the ramparts, through King David Street and *Rehov HaNeviim* (Street of the Prophets), where the stone walls and buildings reflected the golden sunlight under the arching blue dome of the sky. As he did so, he began to comprehend why the rabbis believed that it is here in Jerusalem that God is closest. He became aware of longings like prayers deep within his heart, like birds with folded wings, waiting to take flight.

Sam traveled next to the kibbutz of Yad Mordechai, located close to the beach town of Ashkelon on the southern coastline of Israel, where his cousins Eva and Shoshana were living. The kibbutz was named after Mordechai Anielewicz, the commander of the Warsaw Ghetto Uprising, who had been killed just a few months before the kibbutz was established. It was also the location of the Battle of Yad Mordechai, during which 130 kibbutz members, with only light weapons, fought against the Egyptians during the War of Independence in 1948. With great bravery they withstood the attack for six days in a crucial battle which enabled the new Israel Defense Force (IDF) to establish its southern defense line. The kibbutz had been built on socialist and Zionist principles, and Eva was married to Samek, a hardcore idealist who adored the kibbutz life. Shoshana had lost her husband during the '48 war.

Pesach was approaching and the holiday was solemnly celebrated in the kibbutz, with the religious meaning of the Exodus narrative giving way to a more modern interpretation linked to the agricultural cycle of the land. Sam was asked if he would make drawings to decorate the dining room for the occasion, and threw himself into the project. He made large sketches, gleaning from the impressions of the land he had gathered in his brief stay, and its wonderfully varied landscape: the fertile coastal plain, the gentle foothills and rocky mountain heights, the towers of Jerusalem, glimpses of the ethereal blue waters of the *Yam HaMelekh* (Salt or Dead Sea), and the spectacular desert scenery in the Negev, adorned with a myriad of wildflowers.

One night, cannon fire shook the kibbutz: the Egyptians did not respect the current ceasefire and were shooting at the region from the Gaza Strip. The drawings disappeared. Sam presumed they had been destroyed by the shooting.

From the south, Sam then traveled to the far north of Israel to visit his friend Michael, who during the war had fought in the Jewish Brigade with the Allies. He lived in Kibbutz Dan, situated close to the Syrian border, and overlooked by towering, snowcapped Mount Hermon. Here the famous Jordan River finds its source, fed by the rains and snowmelt that pass through the rock of Hermon and emerge at its foot to form hundreds of springs. This makes it a place of natural beauty, a region of streams and lush vegetation, with woods of oak, oleander, and plane trees, and abounding with wildlife.

Sam immediately fell in love with the scenery. He wandered through the orchards surrounding the kibbutz, plucked fruit from the heavily laden branches, and watched the flocks of songbirds soaring overhead. Michael took him to the source of the Jordan, where the streams sprang out of the living rock, and he waded barefoot through the cool gushing water. But Michael had also taken his gun with him. There were frequent Syrian infiltrations and it required immense courage to stay there, build up the land, and make it fruitful.

Sam also went to visit another cousin, Yitzhak Herciger, who was a fisherman living in the village of Michmoret, beautifully situated on the shores of the Mediterranean exactly halfway between Tel Aviv and Haifa. Yitzhak had been deported to the camps at the age of 13 but had survived thanks to his strong appearance – he looked much older than his age, and during the selections was sent to a labor detail. Now he shared with his wife and daughter a house with a huge garden right on the beach. It was a small paradise, and Sam stayed with them for a week. Each day Yitzhak went out to sea on his boat, and each night they enjoyed delicious grilled fish from his catch. The last day of Sam's stay there was a terrible storm. Huge waves dashed violently against the shore and the house shook. Sam even thought it might collapse, but the next morning the sun was shining.

The six weeks of Sam's holiday had passed. He was impressed by the way in which the native-born "sabras" and new immigrants were building up the land, coaxing the formerly barren landscape into fruitfulness. There was a sense of wonder and a vitality among the people, even though war still threatened on every side. More than that, Sam sensed that during the time he had been in Israel his artist's soul had expanded under the influence of the places he had visited. Beneath the strong clear light, in the radiant air, they were redolent with the memories of his people, evoking biblical and historical associations at every turn. Gazing over the sundrenched beauty of the landscape where patriarchs had walked, prophets declaimed, kings and armies clashed, where the stories destined to reach and impact the whole world were set down, he was indescribably moved.

Perhaps it was the trip to Israel that turned the key and opened the door to his future life. After his return to Belgium Sam was penniless again. He worked hard, not only to make as much money as possible, but also in order not to feel so lonely. He thought of emigrating to Canada. A friend of Annie's lived there; she was a single woman and they corresponded on a regular basis. He went to the Canadian Embassy to apply for a visa.

But destiny changed his plans – destiny in the shape of a woman!

Before the date of his departure Sam went to a party organized by a Jewish philanthropic organization. He danced with several partners, and when the music stopped he placed a cigarette on his lips. A young woman approached him.

"Do you need a match?" she asked.

Sam was surprised. "Ah, yes ..."

"Don't you recognize me?" she said.

There was silence.

"We exhibited together in Antwerp. My name is Edith."

"Ah, yes."

Oh, God, she thought, crestfallen. *He doesn't remember me.*

But Sam was searching his memory and it came back to him – the girl who had looked at him with the adoring eyes.

"Yes, I do remember," he said suddenly, emphatically, and invited her to dance. At one point there was a break in the music and they paused, close together. Edith's face was upturned to his, and the light fell on it. He was arrested by her luminous countenance, its heart-shaped lines, and the delicacy of her features. She appeared spellbound by what he was saying.

He danced only with Edith for the rest of the evening, and accompanied her to the train. It was November and raining, the sky was black, with dense, lowering clouds.

Edith shivered and Sam put his arm around her. "Can we meet next week?" he asked.

"Yes."

"I'll wait for you at the café in the station." He kissed her lightly.

After the week had passed, Edith found him sitting at the end of the café in the central train station. There was no cloth on the tables, and the naked walls were depressing. They drank tea together, and Sam leaned forward.

"Would you like to come to my place, Edith?" he asked. "I would like to show you my drawings."

A little uncertain, she went with Sam to his small apartment in Schaarbeek, comprising one room with a couch that doubled as a bed, two chairs, a table and a coal stove. But he had bought a bouquet of red roses, which lent some vivid color to the sparse surroundings. Paintings were stacked against the wall, and as he showed them to her his eyes began to glow. Edith's doubts fled away.

Sam did not know it yet, but she would love him more than she loved herself, and would be willing to suffer and die in his place. She had looked past his outward insouciance and the brittle confidence that

337

had come with artistic success, and had read the questions and longings in his heart. She would be a true helper to him, an *ezer kanegdo,*[1] offering hope and assurance, providing joy in the journey, sharing his artistic dreams, helping to push open the doors to the future and assuage the memories of the past.

"Journeys end in lovers meeting ..."

---

1. A "helpmeet" is from Genesis 2:18. The final quote, on lovers meeting at journey's end, is taken from Shakespeare's *Twelfth Night,* Act II, Scene 3.

EPILOGUE

Sam and Edith married and had two children; they both continued to study art while living in Antwerp. Sam concentrated on engraving, drawing and watercolor, and his wife on painting and charcoal. They had a workshop at Lange Leemstraat, 184.

Eventually Sam exhibited his art in a number of international museums and galleries. He has works at the Museum of Eilat, Israel, the Jewish Museum of Belgium, Hatima Tova, *Beit Lohamei Haghetaot* (Ghetto Fighters House Museum) and the Vancouver Holocaust Education Center.

Sam and Edith emigrated to Israel in 1969 and settled in Arad in the Negev, where they established an artists' colony which drew many thousands of visitors. They lived and worked there until Sam's death in 1981.

ABOUT THE AUTHOR

Lesley Ann Richardson is originally from Queensland, Australia, where she grew up and eventually studied English Literature and Theology. In the 1980s she moved to Israel, and spent a number of years working for different Christian organizations in the land. While there, she met and married her husband, David Richardson, in Christ Church in the Old City of Jerusalem. David was a Canadian, who himself had a remarkable life story, which she also set down in a book. Later she went on to publish *Bible Gems from Jerusalem,* an award-winning work on history and theology in the feasts of Israel. Lesley is presently living on Vancouver Island, Canada, the home of her late husband, and devoting herself to writing and teaching.

Dear Reader,

If you have enjoyed reading my book,
please do leave a review on Amazon or Goodreads. A few kind words
would be enough. This would be greatly appreciated.

Alternatively, if you have read my book as Kindle eBook you could
leave a rating.
That is just one simple click, indicating how many stars of five you
think this book deserves.
This will only cost you a split second.
Thank you very much in advance!

Lesley

PHOTOS

This is a selection of the works of art by Sam Herciger. The majority of works are undated.

Selfportrait, oilpainting (date unknown)

De Profundis, *the linocut which began the series* Planet
Auschwitz

The Muselman, linocut from Planet Auschwitz

The Treasure: a Bowl of Soup, linocut from Planet Auschwitz

The Dead and the Dying, linocut from Planet Auschwitz

Arbeit Macht Frei, linocut from Planet Auschwitz

The Tree-Hanged Man, linocut from Planet Auschwitz

Between Life and Death, linocut from Planet Auschwitz

*Eli, Eli, Lama Azavtani [My God, My God, Why Hast Thou
Forsaken Me], linocut from Planet Auschwitz*

Diminuendo (Death March), linocut from Planet Auschwitz

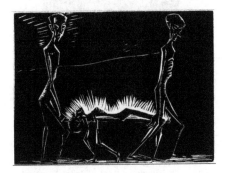

The Burial, linocut from Planet Auschwitz

On The Electric Wires, linocut from Planet Auschwitz

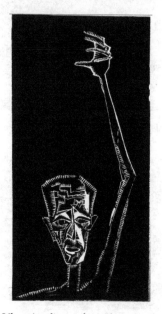

The Liberation, linocut from Planet Auschwitz

Adam and Eve, linocut (Arad, Israel, between 1978-1980)

Love, linocut (Arad, Israel, between 1978-1980)

Jewish Wedding, linocut

The World of Kabbalah, linocut (Arad, Israel, between 1978-1980)

Yom Kippur, linocut

Guarding the Torah, linocut (Arad, Israel, between 1978-1980)

Time, linocut (Arad, Israel, between 1978-1980)

Succot, linocut

Jesus with Tallit, linocut

Shabbat, linocut

Hasidic Jew, plaster sculpture (date unknown)

The Mermaid, wooden sculpture (Belgium, date unknown)

The Prophet, wooden sculpture (date unknown)

Mother and Child, wooden sculpture (Arad 1980). Sam's last sculpture

Learning Kabbalah [Jewish Mysticism] oilpainting (date unknown)

Working Woman, oilpainting (date unknown)

Simchat Torah [Joy of Torah festival], oilpainting (date unknown)

Sunflowers, oilpainting (date unknown)

The Cosmos - Beginning and End, linocut (Arad, Israel, 1980 Sam's last engraving 2 days before his death)

ACKNOWLEDGMENTS

First of all, my deepest thanks must go to my dear friend Annabelle Herciger-Tenzer, for entrusting me with the notes containing Sam's memoirs, and giving me the priceless opportunity of turning these into a book. It has been an exciting and emotional journey for us both, and it is my wish that Sam's story will be treasured by her family for generations. And I hope it's not too long before we can meet again at the Café Rimon in Jerusalem over a decadent Viennese coffee.

I would also like to extend my sincere thanks and appreciation to friends and family in widely separated parts of the world: Australia, North America and Israel, all of whom have contributed in some way to the making of this book.

First, of course, Israel. A special mention must be made of David and Carol Pileggi and the congregation of Christ Church in the Old City of Jerusalem. (David, I hope to come on one of your legendary tours of Poland in the near future.) And my other Israeli friends – Katherine Snyder, David Decker, Deborah and Noam Cohen and Irene Bredlow (Queen Irene, we always loved staying at your home in Poriyya Illit, with its views of the rolling hills of Galilee).

I'm grateful for the ministries of Bob O'Dell and Gidon Ariel at Root Source, and Christine and Peter Darg at the Jerusalem Channel, as well as Jay and Meridel Rawlings and their talented sons at Jerusalem Vistas. Rosalind Hershkovitz, it has been wonderful to share in and contribute to your concerts at Christ Church during the feasts, as we are all uplifted by your beautiful songs.

So many of you have helped shape my knowledge of Israeli history and culture, and enriched my understanding of the significance of this tiny land set in the midst of the nations. Then, of course, were all those who passed through the doors of our home in Rehavia in Jerusalem, enhancing our lives with their company.

Here I would particularly remember our "Georgia Rose" friend Carrie Burns, with whom we shared so many memorable times, and who would always shed a tear when she left us. Her experience as a volunteer at Auschwitz for six months has given rise to the moving and powerful reflections set down in her weekly blog, which have provided me with much inspiration. Jessie Zacharias was another who brought light and shalom into our house when she stayed with us, as did Trevor and Natalie Haug, Myriam Malga, Flavia Giacarini, Bill Mills and Maria Tilroe, and Gord and Lynn Winder.

During our time in Jerusalem, we were grateful to live in the lovely apartment owned by Shari and Alex Mandel of Connecticut, whose kindness and warmth contributed so much to making our sojourn in Israel so rewarding and enjoyable.

To Canada. Here on Vancouver Island, I want to especially acknowledge Bill and Edie Southward and the congregation at Temple Yeshua. I would like to honor them for the welcome they showed me when first I arrived in Victoria with my Canadian husband Dave, and for all the warm fellowship with which they have provided me since then. Here I would make special note of Mike Cruikshank, who was always there when I needed some technical help, and Wendy Frandle, for her conviction that this was a story that must be told. I'm also appreciative of the work Sharon Hayton has accomplished in her long leadership of CMJ Canada, and thankful for the opportunity to participate in Canada-wide teaching sessions on the feasts of Israel.

A big thank you also to Garry and Melanie Lech, on whose beautiful property I have been living while working on completing the book, and who have surrounded me with unstinting warmth, security and love during that time. John and Lynne Schaper, I'm grateful for your ongoing friendship; you have been examples to me of commitment and compassion. And of course, a huge "shout out" to my beloved friends Maggie Simpson and Bernadette Harding, with whom I have met each week, to share together our ongoing stories, our dreams and our challenges, as well as much laughter.

I must especially also thank Doug and Marlene Richardson, my brother and sister-in-law, and their families: Leanne and Ron, Marcie and Michael, and Scott and Margaret Rose, who have shown such steadfast kindness since Dave first brought me in tow with him to Canada. Such an amazing family; I am so glad to be a part of it!

So many others here have opened up their generous Canadian hearts and poured the blessing of their friendship into my life. Here I must especially mention Valley Hennell, Mary Edwards, and Jim and Lorill Vining. Jim has set to music my husband Dave's poem, quoted at the beginning of the book, and it can be found on his website. I also want to acknowledge Pete and Yalile Schibli, John and Ann Wenman, Barb and Val Izbicki and the group in their house, Aneil Perwal, Lisa Warden, Laine Warden, Ralph and Pam Gerrard, Junine Houlden, Marnie Spencelayh, Irene and Rob Knechtle, and Stewart and Jan Wilson. Stewart's weekly post "stewznews" has provided invaluable material on political and other developments in Israel. I'm grateful, as well, for my long friendship with Nicki Jeffery in Ontario, who I first met when working with Middle East TV in Jerusalem.

Moving on to the US, I would like to make a particular mention of George Jones and his wife Jacquie, for their warm friendship and gracious generosity. I share Jerusalem memories with them, as with Don and Marta Patten, Irma (Sarah) Mendoza, Kay Harris, Tammy Watt, Diane Herndon, Julia and Rhett Brown, Stan and Marlene Sholar and Amy Amar. Agnes Natukunda from Uganda is another whom I have met through our Israel connection, and she has been a strong and inspiring confidante for me while I have been in the throes of the creative process.

Turning to Australia, I am always conscious of the bond I share with my lovely sisters, Janet, Sarah and Katie, who have been a constant source of love and support throughout my travels. And there is my other "sister" Joanna Tait, as well as my nephews and nieces, who are all so delightful and personable, and whose careers are a joy to follow.

David Badgery, who has been a friend since university days, has given much generous support to the land and people of Israel. Colin Barnes, historian of the Holocaust, and Heather his wife: we go way back also, to Anglican School days in Jerusalem. Thanks to Jenny and Doug Brecknell and the good folks at Chapel Hill Uniting Church in Brisbane for letting me hone my thespian and writing talents in their midst. And to Cheryl Beningfield for her continuing friendship and love.

Turning now to the publishing process: I'm particularly fortunate to have found the remarkable Liesbeth Heenk at Amsterdam Publishers in Holland, and can rejoice in the knowledge that Sam's book is in the best and most professional of hands. I'm so impressed by her vision, hard work and dedication, as well as that of her gifted team, who work together ensure that so many of these incredible stories reach the world, impacting the nations with the memory of what once took place, and must never take place again.

May Sam's memory continue to be a blessing to all of us and to all who read his amazing story.

AMSTERDAM PUBLISHERS FURTHER READING

The series **Holocaust Survivor True Stories WWII** by Amsterdam Publishers consists of the following biographies that are all standalones:

Among the Reeds. The true story of how a family survived the Holocaust, by Tammy Bottner

A Holocaust Memoir of Love & Resilience. Mama's Survival from Lithuania to America, by Ettie Zilber

Living among the Dead. My Grandmother's Holocaust Survival Story of Love and Strength, by Adena Bernstein Astrowsky

Heart Songs - A Holocaust Memoir, by Barbara Gilford

Shoes of the Shoah. The Tomorrow of Yesterday, by Dorothy Pierce

Hidden in Berlin - A Holocaust Memoir, by Evelyn Joseph Grossman

Separated Together. The Incredible True WWII Story of Soulmates Stranded an Ocean Apart, by Kenneth P. Price, Ph.D.

The Man Across the River. The incredible story of one man's will to survive the Holocaust, by Zvi Wiesenfeld

If Anyone Calls, Tell Them I Died - A Memoir, by Emanuel (Manu) Rosen

The House on Thrömerstrasse. A Story of Rebirth and Renewal in the Wake of the Holocaust, by Ron Vincent

Dancing with my Father. His hidden past. Her quest for truth. How Nazi Vienna shaped a family's identity, by Jo Sorochinsky

The Story Keeper. Weaving the Threads of Time and Memory - A Memoir, by Fred Feldman

Krisia's Silence. The Girl who was not on Schindler's List, by Ronny Hein

Defying Death on the Danube. A Holocaust Survival Story, by Debbie J. Callahan with Henry Stern

A Doorway to Heroism. A decorated German-Jewish Soldier who became an American Hero, by Rabbi W. Jack Romberg

The Shoemaker's Son. The Life of a Holocaust Resister, by Laura Beth Bakst

The Redhead of Auschwitz. A True Story, by Nechama Birnbaum

Land of Many Bridges. My Father's Story, by Bela Ruth Samuel Tenenholtz

On Sunny Days We Sang, by Jeannette Grunhaus de Gelman,

Creating Beauty from the Abyss. The Amazing Story of Sam Herciger, Auschwitz Survivor and Artist, by Lesley Ann Richardson

Painful Joy. A Holocaust Family Memoir, by Max J. Friedman

I Give You My Heart. A True Story of Courage and Survival, by Wendy Holden

Flower of Vlora. Growing up Jewish in Communist Albania, by Anna Kohen

A Life in Shelter, by Suzette Sheft

The Boy behind the Door. How Salomon Kool Escaped the Nazis, by David Tabatsky

Zaire's War, by Martin Bodek

In the Time of Madmen, by Mark A. Prelas

The Series **Holocaust Survivor Memoirs World War II** by Amsterdam Publishers consists of the following autobiographies of survivors that are all standalones:

Outcry - Holocaust Memoirs, by Manny Steinberg

Hank Brodt Holocaust Memoirs. A Candle and a Promise, by Deborah Donnelly

The Dead Years. Holocaust Memoirs, by Joseph Schupack

Rescued from the Ashes. The Diary of Leokadia Schmidt, Survivor of the Warsaw Ghetto, by Leokadia Schmidt

My Lvov. Holocaust Memoir of a twelve-year-old Girl, by Janina Hescheles

Remembering Ravensbrück. From Holocaust to Healing, by Natalie Hess

Wolf. A Story of Hate, by Zeev Scheinwald with Ella Scheinwald

Save my Children. An Astonishing Tale of Survival and its Unlikely Hero, by Leon Kleiner with Edwin Stepp

Holocaust Memoirs of a Bergen-Belsen Survivor & Classmate of Anne Frank, by Nanette Blitz Konig

Defiant German - Defiant Jew. A Holocaust Memoir from inside the Third Reich, by Walter Leopold with Les Leopold

In a Land of Forest and Darkness. The Holocaust Story of two Jewish Partisans, by Sara Lustigman Omelinski

Holocaust Memories. Annihilation and Survival in Slovakia, by Paul Davidovits

From Auschwitz with Love. The Inspiring Memoir of Two Sisters' Survival, Devotion and Triumph Told by Manci Grunberger Beran & Ruth Grunberger Mermelstein, by Daniel Seymour

Remetz. Resistance Fighter and Survivor of the Warsaw Ghetto, by Jan Yohay Remetz

The Series **Jewish Children in the Holocaust** by Amsterdam Publishers consists of the following autobiographies of Jewish children hidden during WWII in the Netherlands. They are all standalones.

Searching for Home. The Impact of WWII on a Hidden Child, by Joseph Gosler

See You Tonight and Promise to be a Good Boy! War memories, by Salo Muller

Sounds from Silence. Reflections of a Child Holocaust Survivor, Psychiatrist and Teacher, by Robert Krell

Sabine's Odyssey. A Hidden Child and her Dutch Rescuers, by Agnes Schipper

---

The Series **New Jewish Fiction** by Amsterdam Publishers consists of the following novels, written by Jewish authors. All novels are set in the time during or after the Holocaust. They are all standalones.

Escaping the Whale. The Holocaust is over. But is it ever over for the next generation? by Ruth Rotkowitz

When the Music Stopped. Willy Rosen's Holocaust, by Casey Hayes

Hands of Gold. One Man's Quest to Find the Silver Lining in Misfortune, by Roni Robbins

The Corset Maker. A Novel, by Annette Libeskind Berkovits

There was a garden in Nuremberg. A Novel, by Navina Michal Clemerson

Aftermath. Coming-of-Age on Three Continents, by Annette Libeskind Berkovits

The Girl Who Counted Numbers, by Roslyn Bernstein

The Butterfly and the Axe, by Omer Bartov

CPSIA information can be obtained
at www.ICGtesting.com
Printed in the USA
LVHW081628230422
717054LV00015B/328/J